More Advance Praise for *American Apartheid*

"*American Apartheid* should be required reading for anyone concerned with equality and justice in America. The book is a comprehensive, understandable and shocking insight into the oppression that we Native Americans are still dealing with in the twenty-first century."
—Michaelynn Hawk, Crow Tribe; Director/organizer of Indian People's Action and Jeannette Rankin Award recipient

"I am so happy to see tribal youth—and the cultural continuity they represent—included in *American Apartheid's* beautiful photographs and thoughtful, informative text. In addition to the difficult issues we face, which are detailed conclusively here, readers will see what is good and true and eternally meaningful about our communities."
—Julie Garreau, Cheyenne River Sioux Tribe; Executive Director of the Cheyenne River Youth Project

"*American Apartheid* paints a picture of the daily life of Native people that is full of hope. It reminds us, as American Indians, that understanding how to walk in the present requires knowing how and why our ancestors created the path we are on—and that we have a collective responsibility for the wellbeing of our descendants. The stories in this book reflect the relationality, continuity and reciprocity that have always been at the center of social change in Indian country. We will always find a path to revive and survive as nations and cultures."
—Judith LeBlanc, Caddo; Director, Native Organizers Alliance

"Two topics foreign to the mainstream media are immediately noticeable in Stephanie Woodard's book, *American Apartheid*: voter suppression and gerrymandering of Indian reservations—two issues that must be addressed in order to have self-determination and inclusion in Indian country."
—Tim Giago, Oglala Lakota, Harvard Neiman fellow. editor of *Native Sun News Today*,

"In this book, Stephanie Woodard continues her commitment to amplifying Native American voices, highlighting stories of struggle but also of hard-earned progress toward self-determination. Throughout my life in Alaska, I have learned that when people are free to control their own lands and resources, they control their futures."

—US Senator Mark Begich

"I spent my career in political life, which included nearly two decades as a Senator from South Dakota, in service to my state's citizens, including its Native people. This important book shows us how resilient Native Americans have been and how much adversity they have faced, and are still facing, in working on behalf of their land and people."

—US Senator Tim Johnson

"This book is a magnificent culmination of Stephanie Woodard's work reporting on people who know what really matters."

—Christopher Napolitano, Creative Director, *Indian Country Media Network*, 2011–2017

"In *American Apartheid*, Stephanie Woodard captures the true spirit and determination of Native Americans who rise above discrimination and take actions that improve the conditions of their people. Reading it gives me hope that the continued efforts of Native Americans will one day mean an end to the 'American apartheid.'"

—Bruce A. Finzen, attorney, Robins Kaplan LLP

"Stephanie Woodard's deep respect, keen observations and analysis in *American Apartheid* represent a fresh approach to urgent contemporary issues confronting tribal governments and American Indian people. The American Indian voices resonate with resilience, outrage and optimism for their children's lives. Listening could improve all of our lives."

—Marti L. Chaatsmith, Comanche/Choctaw; interim director, Newark Earthworks Center

American Apartheid:

The Native American Struggle for Self-Determination and Inclusion

Stephanie Woodard

PUBLISHING

New York, NY

Printed in the United States of America.
10 9 8 7 6 5 4 3 2 1

No part of this book may be used or reproduced in any manner without written permission of the publisher. Please direct inquiries to:

Ig Publishing
Box 2547
New York, NY 10163

www.igpub.com

ISBN: 978-1-632460-68-4 (paperback)

Cover photographs, left to right, top to bottom: Navajo permaculture teacher Justin Willie; dreamcatcher by Izzie Zephier, Ihanktonwan Dakota; Crow Creek Sioux reservation (Stephanie Woodard). Puyallup tribal members; Zuni Pueblo dance group Anshe:kwe; Joseph Holley and his grandson (both Western Shoshone) collecting sweat-lodge rocks (Joseph Zummo).

CONTENTS

In northern Nevada, a community map welcomes visitors to the Battle Mountain Band of the Te-Moak Tribe of Western Shoshone Indians and guides them to its library, its environmental department, and other tribal offices. (Joseph Zummo)

Introduction

A DERELICT SALOON WITH AN ATTACHED JAIL sits just north of Pine Ridge Indian Reservation, on the deserted main drag of a blink-and-you'll-miss-it South Dakota town. The wooden exterior is weathered in streaks of black and gray, and the front door is boarded up. Crumbling longhorn skulls hang from a faded sign proclaiming that the bar was built in 1906. It also read "No Indians Allowed" until, at some point, the word "No" was mostly painted over. The lockup is a rusted open-air cage with doors that creak when pulled open. No one drinks here anymore, but it is easy to find booze nearby. Road signs along area highways direct travelers, including those from Pine Ridge, which has long banned alcohol, to bars and stores selling liquor. A field is planted with signs that tilt this way and that as they compete for customers: "Horseshoe Bar," "3 Blocks Wagon Wheel Bar," "2 Blocks Bud Light," and more. In the midst of them, another tilted sign touts a church, seemingly as an antidote for the alcohol.

The tumbledown saloon and sagging signs deliver a message that applies far beyond this remote corner of the plains.

Native people are not welcome—or maybe they are, to one kind of establishment that offers oblivion and another that extends an alien religion as a way to fend it off. Both institutions are predators of a sort, pushing and pulling at Native communities in a pattern I have seen in various guises during nearly twenty years of involvement with Indian-country stories, first as an editor and then, since 2000, as a reporter. In one story after another, I observed that tribal communities are set apart from the rest of us geographically, socially, politically, and economically. These include both Indian reservations and the urban Indian neighborhoods to which tribal members moved or were relocated in past decades by the federal government. Indigenous people are isolated in an archipelago of deeply impoverished islands in the vast sea of American wealth. At the same time, tribal members seek to participate—among many ways, they serve in the US armed forces in a greater proportion than any other group, they have been fighting for equal voting rights and the chance to participate fully in our democracy for almost a century, and they have a sense of responsibility to the earth and all its inhabitants that informs their lives.[1,2]

The word "apartheid" was first used to describe South African policies that segregated and discriminated against that country's original inhabitants. It has come to mean more generally any system that works that way. As time went on and I reported stories in various subject areas—child welfare, sacred sites, health, and others—I acquired ever more detail about the ways in which the word is an apt description of the relationship between the United States and its first peoples. In 2016, the economic strictures placed on Indian country came into sharp focus for me while I was covering a Navajo family's struggle to obtain a reasonable payment in return for renewing the right of way for an oil pipeline crossing its homesite. In looking at how the federal government had arranged for an oil company to offer a pittance for access to the family's land, I learned about the systemic nature of tribal members' economic isolation. It is no mistake that many reservations are poverty-stricken, while money pours through them to a surrounding ring of dusty, angry border towns that are resentful of their dependence on a reservation. Paternalistic federal policies target Native people with heavy-handed precision. The United States controls a remarkable range of contemporary Native life, but not necessarily for Natives' benefit. If a tribe wants to build a housing development or protect a sacred site, if a tribal member wants to start a business or plant a field, a federal agency can modify or scuttle the plans. Conversely, if a corporation or other outside interest covets reservation land or resources, the federal government becomes an obsequious bondservant, helping the non-Native entity get what it wants at bargain-basement prices.[3]

In the chapters that follow, you will see how Washington clamps down on Native people and their governments, exacerbates economic distress and keeps tribal people separate, unequal and exposed to predatory interests. Despite the energy, creativity and hard work I have observed repeatedly in Native communities, their people are walled off from the prosperity that should be the reward for their efforts. Segregating them so thoroughly leads to terrible consequences, including difficulty protecting their sacred places and starkly high rates of police killings, incarceration, taking of Native children into foster care and child suicide. Many may have heard of broken treaties, massacres and the abusive boarding schools to which Native children were sent for about a century. These are among the experiences that are often described as historical trauma, with a legacy of effects that endure for the children and grandchildren of those who went through them firsthand.[4] However, new traumas keep piling on, as Native families and communities are cheated of the worth of their land and resources, see relatives shot dead by officers of the law, are shipped off to prison, and find that their children have shot or hung themselves. The re-traumatizing is continual.

Journalists are witnesses. We go to places, try to figure out what is happening—particularly when the powerful would like the situation kept quiet—and report it to the world. Over the years, I have had the opportunity to cover stories that few other mainstream journalists were writing about. In doing this kind of reporting, rather than chiming in on the people and events that many were covering, I felt that I was doing my job properly. I remember watching a September 2010 meeting of the Fall River County Commission, in Hot Springs, South Dakota. At stake were the voting rights of Oglala Sioux Tribe members: Would the county provide ballot-box access for the upcoming federal election, or would it not? A few times, I looked up from the pad in which I was taking notes to glance over my shoulder, expecting additional national reporters to file into the room. More journalists must want to write about a dramatic face-off between county officials and tribal members, I thought. This was Little Bighorn—for today! You have already figured out that there were no other national journalists there.

In 2016, this changed for a while, as mainstream reporters from around the nation and the world covered the anti-oil-pipeline demonstrations just north of the Standing Rock Sioux Indian Reservation, in North Dakota. The work of the excellent Native journalists who were there became more widely known. Once the Standing Rock Sioux Tribe's effort to keep the pipeline from crossing its water supply moved from the camps to the courts, mainstream coverage abated. Still, more non-Native journalists and their audiences became familiar with Indian country. They now

Chief Arvol Looking Horse, Sioux spiritual leader, left, spoke to the press during 2016 anti-oil-pipeline demonstrations on the Standing Rock Sioux Indian Reservation, in North Dakota. (Joseph Zummo)

have a better understanding of treaties, sacred sites, environmental justice, and other American Indian concerns. Native America is a part of the national conversation.

At that time, tribal nations were emerging from a period during which the Obama administration supported tribal self-determination and, among many positive acts, settled numerous tribes' long-running lawsuits against the federal government for mishandling their resources. As the succeeding administration got underway, ideas for turning back these gains were floated, although these were for rights that all Americans had taken for granted, from secure elections to freedom of speech.[5] The most vulnerable among us became more so.

On the Standing Rock Sioux Indian Reservation during 2016, the mainstream press, alternative press, and social media closely followed the suffering of tribal members and their allies demonstrating against the building of an oil pipeline. The coverage occurred as the North Dakota police, police from other states, and private contractors subjected demonstrators to near-lethal shootings, gassing, hosing with cold water in below-freezing temperatures, arrest, and other aggressive tactics. In 2017, as the new administration withdrew federal protections from vast acreage, coalitions of tribes, environmental groups, and more took action together.

Several tribes sued over the diminishment of Bears Ears, an ancient and revered southwestern landscape; Sioux tribes promised "war" over a foreign company's renewed mining claim in sacred land in the Black Hills; and northwestern tribes took a leadership role in a multicultural coalition that submitted to the Washington State legislature a bill designed to reduce police shootings of civilians.[6,7] Members of the Puyallup Tribe, which was part of the coalition, also protested construction of a liquid natural gas plant on traditional fishing lands guaranteed the tribe within the Port of Tacoma, Washington, under the Medicine Creek Treaty of 1854. Nationwide, government actions that tribes once bore as local, if unfortunate, issues now faced collaborative actions.

Many of the groups were formed, or encouraged, by experiences and interactions at Standing Rock. Indigenous response did not start there though, Chester Earl pointed out. A Puyallup tribal member whose cousin Jacqueline Salyers was shot dead by a Tacoma police officer in 2016, Earl is a leader of the multi-racial group that developed and collected signatures for the police-oriented legislative bill;[8] he also spent a short time in jail for protesting the construction of the gas plant.

"The need to raise our voices has been going on for a long time for Native people," Earl said. His tribe and additional indigenous people have coped for generations with warfare, massacres, and, more recently, modern conflicts. "We Puyallups and others were shot at and beaten for proclaiming our fishing rights during the 1960s and 1970s. I know of Native people who went on to participate in multi-tribal actions at Alcatraz, at the Bureau of Indian Affairs [BIA] building in Washington, DC, during the occupation of Wounded Knee, and in other events." The world saw Native needs each time, then forgot them, it seems, according to Earl. "Standing Rock helped us grab the world's attention once again. Non-Native people recognized that indigenous people feel they must lead the way and protect the earth and all who dwell here. It is our duty."

Earl recalled that the African American mother of another leader of the police-bill coalition called that fight a success—even though the state's legislature had not yet acted on it when I spoke to Earl in early 2018. "She pointed out that the three hundred and sixty thousand people who had signed the legislative proposal represented multiple races, ages, and genders," Earl said. "We've won the hearts and minds of Washington State's citizens already."

During 2016, "We are unarmed" was the cry of demonstrators on the Standing Rock Sioux Indian Reservation, along with *"mni wiconi,"* or "water is life." (Joseph Zummo)

The situation in Indian country is not, and has never been, hopeless. During visits to Native communities around the country, I have seen that culture is a shield[9] that has persisted, indeed thrived, despite all efforts to stamp, starve, and regulate it out of existence. Throughout this book, you will see examples of robust heritage lifeways. The ongoing hum of tradition underlies the cacophony of problems that tribal members are constantly fighting to resolve.

MY FOCUS ON NATIVE SUBJECT matter started in the late 1990s, when I was deputy editor of *Garden Design* magazine. As part of an effort to offer readers more environmental coverage, I assigned a writer to report the story of a guitar owned by music star Rosanne Cash. The Gibson guitar company had made the instrument from sustainably logged wood provided by the Menominee Tribe's timber-products firm. Before asking the writer to trace the guitar back to its origins in the Wisconsin forest, I did the due diligence any editor engages in when assigning a story. I visited Cash at her New York City house and talked to representatives of Gibson and the tribal enterprise. I interviewed forest-products engineers who had visited the forest as part of a Rainforest Alliance program that certified timber as sustainably logged for buyers that wanted such products.

I learned unexpected things, which would set a pattern for my reporting in years to come. In Indian country, you can expect to be frequently surprised by facts or ideas that lie around the next corner. Officials of Menominee Tribal Enterprises told me that the tribe had logged its 235,000-acre forest intensively for 150 years, extracting 2.5 billion board feet of lumber according to principles laid down by nineteenth century chiefs. The tribe had, in essence, removed the forest three times over during that period. Yet the tract looked untouched, said the engineers who had toured it. They raved about its biodiversity and beauty. I saw striking satellite photographs, in which the tribe's forest was a darker green than the surrounding areas. The Menominees had managed this by making harvesting decisions with all the forest's inhabitants in mind. If felling a tree in a certain direction would destroy a butterfly habitat or food for ruffed grouse, the forester looked for another option. Essentially, the forest was treated like a garden. As a result, it was in radiant health. According to one engineer, the timber cut from it was so good, new grades had been created just for the Menominees. To top it all off, the forest-products company supported job creation that easily outstripped that of most small businesses its size.[10]

The tribe had improved its forest by using it aggressively: to me, sitting in an office building in New York City, this sounded like alchemy. At the time, *not* interacting with nature was more typically understood as the way to protect it—a concept that has fallen by the wayside to a large degree because of the influence of indigenous people and their ideas. I thought, if Native timber-products companies were so interesting, their gardens must be amazing. I called Native Seeds/SEARCH, a Tucson seed bank for heirloom indigenous crops, and talked to Angelo Joaquin, a Tohono O'odham tribal member who was then its director. He suggested I talk to Clayton Brascoupé, a Mohawk/Algonquin farmer who lives at Tesuque Pueblo and runs the Traditional Native American Farmers Association, in Santa Fe. Brascoupé showed me around the remains of ancient Puebloan plots north of the city, then put me in touch with farmers at Cochiti Pueblo, which is south of Santa Fe. I ended up in a field there, face-to-face with corn, beans, squash, and an indigenous culture's time-honored yet contemporary way of doing and being.

My first inchoate thought was that I had no idea how to use the English language to describe what I was seeing. A culture's concepts are most accurately conveyed in its own language, so even the basics confused me. To begin with, was I looking at a garden, which implies guardianship by a caretaker who cultivates each plant as an individual, as the Menominees did the trees in their forest? Or was this large prolific plot better called a farm, which connotes large-scale (and nowadays often industrial) production of food? If there were no exact equivalents, which words came closest? I started to worry about the ancestry of the English synonyms from among which I would choose as I wrote about this place. Anglo-Saxon contributions to our vocabulary have a sense of simplicity and candor that made sense for these unpretentious plots. The Latin contribution came into English as the language of scholars; using this part of our vocabulary might convey the contemplative aspects of Native life, including the thinking and activities surrounding the growing of food crops.

I was dumbstruck—no other way to describe it. I posed the language question to two older Pueblo gentlemen who were showing me around Cochiti: Gabe Trujillo and Joseph Benado. "Those aren't the distinctions we make," Benado said. He went on to describe a vocabulary that tracked the English words in some ways but diverged in others. Shifting from English to Keres, the language of the southern Pueblos, Benado explained, as the governor of the Pueblos translated, that plant-rearing is akin to child-rearing for his people. The two activities share terms and concepts. Both involve spiritual and practical considerations.

Benado expanded on the linguistic characteristics of Keres by describing the life cycle of corn: "You plant the corn, and the seed has one name. When it sprouts, it has another. As it grows, it has another name. As the ear comes to life, it is called another thing. When it is ripe, it is called another, and when it's harvested, another. As it dries, it has another name. When the stalk has dried in the field, it has another; and what's left goes back into the earth." Returning to English, Benado added, "I enjoy what I do so much. When I look at my family's table, filled with what I have grown, I feel such joy at having provided for them. Farming makes you a better person, because you are always looking forward to next year."

When Benado made that first language shift, from English to Keres, the timbre of his voice changed. When he spoke in

English, it was low-pitched, or what we might call bass. In Keres, he was a baritone, with the words accompanied by a resonant breathiness and overtones, or higher related notes, that proceeded in harmony with the basic pitch. Had I not been there in person, I would have thought two different people had spoken in turn. Embedded in each language was an identity so powerful that it transformed the speaker physiologically and further emphasized the cultural divide.

Over the years, I have become used to writing across the divide and describing, however imperfectly, what I saw in one Native community after another. Though I started out writing about agriculture and culture, I quickly realized that you cannot talk about crops without talking about the land, and you cannot talk about the land without talking about why the original people of this country have so little of what they once held. And you cannot consider that without looking at the human-rights crisis this has wrought in communities whose interaction with the natural world is the basis of every aspect of life, from the most mundane to the most rarified.

Early on, I began receiving weekly and sometimes daily calls—and later emails and texts as well—from all over Indian country alerting me to events and people I might want to look into and write about. A lot of the leads ended up as articles; some became yearlong, or even multiyear, series. Eventually, they led to this book. Along the way, I have never lost the feeling that with each reporting assignment I am a visitor to a world whose outlines I can only begin to sense.

American Apartheid

1.

Destitute by Design

T HEY ATTACKED MY AUNT LIKE COYOTES attacking sheep in a corral," recalled Navajo tribal member Roberta Tovar. "They were going, 'Mary, Mary, just go ahead and

From left, Navajo tribal members Charles Irving, his granddaughter Serfina Garcia, and his daughter Roberta Tovar describe their fight to obtain a fair price for an oil pipeline crossing their reservation property. (Joseph Zummo)

sign it.'" We were sitting in the breakfast room of the Gallup, New Mexico, chain hotel where Tovar works as a night clerk. The meal had been cleared, and the shades had been pulled against the southwestern sun, which was becoming piercingly bright as the morning progressed. Outside, cars and trucks rolled by on old Route 66, with its hodgepodge of billboards and neon signs beckoning tourists to motels, cafés, and shops touting Native-made crafts.

Tovar folded her hands over the documents she had brought to help illustrate her story. She recounted her family's struggle with the federal government and an oil company over the agreement that both entities wished her relatives to endorse. What Tovar and her relatives wanted was a fair price for renewing the right-of-way for an oil pipeline that crossed their reservation home-site north of Gallup. On the other side, the government and the company wanted the family members to accept $6,656 for twenty additional years of access to their land, or about $333 per year. The amount was to be split among nearly fifty people, for an average of a little more than six dollars per year each.[1]

The deal was not unusual for Indian country. In 2015, the Department of the Interior reported that 60 percent of Native land-owners earned less than twenty-five dollars annually from leasing and other land-related income agreements that year. Some received as little as a few cents.[2] Such arrangements are negotiated on land-owners' behalf by the federal government as part of its legal func-tion as the trustee for tribes and tribal members. The pipeline was on Tovar's family land to begin with because her mother had agreed to it decades before. At the time, she was a non-English-speaking seventeen-year-old, and her husband, with whom she might have consulted, was working at a job in another state. Tovar believed her mother did not understand what she was signing.

As we look at how tribes were transformed from flourishing precontact societies to today's marginalized and often poverty-stricken communities, we find that federal policies, bureaucratic incompetence, official corruption, and racism eat away at reservations, delivering their resources to others and walling them off from surrounding prosperity. It is a pattern we will see repeatedly in this chapter and the ones to follow. For many tribes and tribal members, the forces that keep financial independence out of reach are the same ones that ensure prosperity for others.

Many of us are now familiar with the fight against new pipelines, epitomized by the Standing Rock Sioux battle against the Dakota Access Pipeline, or DAPL, in North Dakota. However, DAPL, like the pipeline on Tovar's family property, is just one of many oil, gas, and electrical-transmission lines, roads, railroads, and other infrastructure projects that cross Native lands nationwide. These generally deliver big benefits to outsiders while skipping past Native economies and damaging, or threatening to damage, tribal land, water, and sacred sites.

The easements started appearing in the 1880s, when Congress began passing laws that authorized particular companies to build specific projects across reservations. These were mostly railroads and telegraph and telephone lines, with the list of possible types of projects lengthening as the years went by. At first, any given law might or might not have required tribal consent to the easement and the related payment. In the Act of March 2, 1899, Congress extended its power—and that of corporate interests—even further by eliminating the need for tribal consent; the act also allowed companies to bypass Congress and go straight to the Department of the Interior for permission to cross reservations, according to a history of the statutes governing this process from the Departments of Energy and the Interior.[3]

Though Congress restored tribal consent to the easement procedures in the Act of 1948,[4] federal hegemony endures in the matter of permission to cross Native land. Today, the federal government awards corporations and individuals leases that allow them to drill, frack, mine, farm, ranch, and fell timber in Indian country at fire-sale prices. Those benefiting from federal largesse have included Koch Industries, ConocoPhillips, Halliburton, Peabody Energy, Cabela's, Home Depot, Walmart, PetSmart, Office Depot, Dollar General, and other familiar names, as well as local farmers and ranchers, Terry Beckwith told me. He is a realty expert with ICC Indian Enterprises and a Quinault Indian Nation member who travels widely, giving seminars to tribal members on land ownership and on navigating leasing and right-of-way agreements.

Little of this business activity creates wealth for Native land-owners. Instead, the slow drip of income from external sources helps tribal nations and their members survive while keeping them vulnerable—as isolated economically and politically as they are geographically from the nation's population centers large and small. Brett Lee Shelton, an Oglala Sioux attorney with the Native American Rights Fund, told me that current leasing and right-of-way procedures are "a huge drain on Indian economies and essentially a taking of resources that hadn't yet been taken in the treaty-making process. If you wanted to design a system to keep Indian landowners poor, you would use exactly this sort of trick."

Beckwith pointed to an anomaly that is typical of many

reservations. With more than seventeen million acres, the Navajo homeland, which they call Dinétah, is bigger than West Virginia. If you added up the value of the land, the grazing rights, the mineral rights, the homes, and other structures, the total would be comparable to that of a Fortune 500 company, Beckwith said. Yet this valuable homeland and plenty of hardworking tribal members add up to persistent destitution, not prosperity.[5] Navajo Nation[6] and Arizona State[7] figures show that just over 40 percent of the population on the Navajo reservation lives below the poverty line.

The situation at Pine Ridge Indian Reservation is similar, despite a buzz of enterprise that is almost audible throughout the Oglala Sioux's South Dakota homeland. The county that overlaps most of the reservation is one of several majority-Native counties—five of them in South Dakota—that are among the very poorest in America.[8] There are plenty of reservations with little economic activity beyond a tribally owned travel plaza and/or a small casino, or even none whatsoever—no shops or service businesses, no places to buy a cup of coffee or have a tire changed. Pine Ridge is different.

On a visit a few years ago, I found plenty of enthusiastic entrepreneurs as I drove around, past bluffs, rolling prairie, and the eponymous pines sprouting at rakish angles out of long white cliffs. Tribal members ran bed-and-breakfasts, cafés, grocery stores, gift shops, guide services, a woodworking shop and crafts businesses. I heard about a van that plied reservation roads delivering beads and other items to craftspeople. I bought a bracelet from a seller at a convenience store, a quilt with a star pattern at a museum gift shop, and a pen with a colorful beaded covering from construction workers taking a break by the Wounded Knee memorial. I considered purchasing the handsome war club hanging behind the cash register at the hardware store. I stayed at a family-owned motel. I could have ordered a specially decorated cake. However, all of this creativity and industriousness, along with a large, valuable homeland, had not prevented dire privation for most people there.

In 2015, Narayana Kocherlakota, then president of the Federal Reserve Bank of Minneapolis, reported that tribal members' average income nationwide barely topped $10,000. "Poverty rates on reservations are nearly triple the national rate," he told a conference on community development, "and over forty percent of children on reservations live in poverty."[9]

Some tribes, notably the small number in or around urban areas, have done well with gaming businesses; they typically donate generously to surrounding communities and fellow tribes. However, they are still few and far between. Tribal members, like Tovar and her relatives, may be employed in tribal or off-reservation businesses. Or they may own small and micro-businesses. Even in the context of all of this effort, indigenous people have the nation's lowest incomes and lowest personal wealth as indicated by measures such as homeownership; these are accompanied by the highest death rates from certain chronic diseases, some of the highest infant-mortality rates in the United States, and a rate of exposure to violent crime that is twice the national average.[10] "We are the poorest of the poor and the sickest of the sick," said Sally Willett, who is Cherokee and a retired Interior Department administrative law judge.

THE DAY AFTER OUR MEETING in Gallup, photographer Joseph Zummo and I followed Tovar and her husband as they drove to her family's homesite about a half hour north of town. A dozen modest houses were clustered together in a dry, juniper-dotted valley. Sheep grazed on the sparse grass, and a small herd of goats trotted smartly down a lane in the company of two dogs. As we arrived, we heard the high, pure tones of an eagle-bone whistle calling the family to prayer. We met Tovar's relatives in a tipi, stepping through its low oval opening into the conical interior. Canvas walls softened the brilliant midday light. Tovar's cousin, Anselm Morgan, a roadman or pastor in the Native American Church, stood on the far side of a low fire. Additional relatives sat around the edges, and children came and went. (Tipis are not typical Navajo structures; however, Tovar told me, the Native American Church's multi-tribal adherents, including her family, use them for services and, as in this case, for meetings.)

Navajo family homestead north of Gallup, New Mexico. (Joseph Zummo)

Morgan began with a blessing for the day. An eagle feather in hand, he gestured to the four cardinal directions, the sky, and the earth. He poured a small amount of water on the ground. As the sharp herbal scent of burning cedar wafted from the fire, family members described their frustrations with the Bureau of Indian Affairs and the oil company. They spoke in Navajo, stopping periodically to translate into English for me.

The "coyotes" Roberta Tovar referred to when we met in Gallup were staff members from a BIA office on the Navajo reservation and employees of Western Refining, a Texas-based oil company. Together, they were urging her family to agree to the renewal of a right-of-way for a pipeline that carried some fifteen thousand barrels of crude a day from oil fields in the Four Corners region to a refinery near Gallup. On the way, it crossed a 160-acre plot owned by Tovar, her octogenarian aunt Mary Tom, and additional family members. Their land was in the New Mexico portion of the Navajo reservation, which also spans Arizona and Utah.[11]

The right-of-way grant had expired in 2010. BIA documents obtained through a Freedom of Information Act, or FOIA, request showed that initial negotiations with family members were fruitless. So Western Refining invited just a handful of them, including Mary Tom, to an October 2013 luncheon at the El Rancho Hotel in Gallup. Once a watering hole for the elite, the inn boasts over-the-top cattle-baron décor—trophy animal heads, massive branching chandeliers, sweeping red-carpeted staircases, and autographed photos of John Wayne, President George H. W. Bush, and other A-listers through the years. The purpose of the gathering: get the signatures needed to renew the right-of-way.

BIA employees were present because this division of the

Department of the Interior manages the fifty-five million acres of land the federal government holds in trust for Native owners. Tribes own about forty-four million of those acres; individuals like Roberta Tovar and Mary Tom own the rest. The BIA arranges business deals on Native land and is obligated by law to negotiate the best possible terms for the landowners. Instead—as we learned above from the level of payments it approves—the agency makes it cheap and easy for outsiders to exploit Native resources.

In a *Nebraska Law Review* article, legal scholar Brian Sawers provides decades' worth of figures showing that outside enterprises have exploited tribal land and products in exchange for tiny percentages of market value. That is no surprise, given the bureau's understanding of its assignment, according to Sawers: "The BIA's perceived mission for many years was to develop Indian-owned resources for the public benefit." Despite recent reforms, the federal agency "has little incentive to bargain hard with potential lessees."[12]

The family members gathered in the tipi said that those who were invited to the El Rancho Hotel were among the least able to understand or defend themselves—elderly, non-English-speaking, and with health issues. Those who were known to be advocating for a better deal, including Tovar, were not invited. She attended anyway at her aunt's request. When Tovar got to the luncheon, she was initially distracted by the food and drink on display. "All those desserts, all that water," she marveled. Soon a dismaying scene unfolded, Tovar said, with a BIA staff member sitting by Mary Tom and stroking her arm while an oil-company executive warned the elderly woman that she would "lose out" if she didn't consent to the offer. Tovar began crying and protesting and was soon escorted from the room.

Speaking through a translator, Mary Tom recounted that she had asked the officials at the luncheon for the whereabouts of additional family members. She learned that, like Tovar, they had not been invited. She remembered being distressed and confused: "Even when we have a meeting in our own language, it's hard for me to comprehend the issue. Someone has to explain," she said. She said that she had gotten out of the hospital shortly before the luncheon and was feeling weak.

Family members were near tears, as they took turns translating the octogenarian's account. Eventually, Tom said, she gave in and signed in return for what was termed a "bonus" of $2,000, a huge sum on a destitute Indian reservation. In a separate interview,

Navajo octogenarian Mary Tom, foreground, describes her difficulty understanding lease negotiations with the Bureau of Indian Affairs and an oil company, as her niece Louise Morgan translates. (Joseph Zummo)

her nephew Patrick Adakai said that the long-running controversy caused everyone in the family anguish, an unavoidable outcome no matter what route they took—to sign or to work for a better deal.

Personal accounts, court materials, and BIA documents received from the agency through the FOIA request show how closely the Bureau of Indian Affairs works with industry to make deals on tribal land. It may not be 1899, when Congress did away with the need for Native consent, but it felt like it was when I was reading the FOIA records. During the planning for the October luncheon, the BIA material reveals, more than a dozen emails flew back and forth between agency employees and company staffers to plan "pre-meetings"—so many that the area's BIA superintendent eventually emailed the others to ask, "Can you remind us all when the meetings are?" One corporate goal appears to have been keeping out family troublemakers: The company told the BIA it would like "as much as possible" to limit the gathering to the few whose signatures it sought.

When I contacted a BIA spokesperson to ask about the behind-the-scenes machinations apparent in the FOIA documents, she responded by email that the bureau did not coordinate with the oil company ahead of the luncheon and did not help it bar troublemakers. Were non-English-speaking elders pushed into signing? Not at all, according to the spokesperson, who claimed that BIA staffers, most of whom were tribal members, were present on the landowners' behalf, "providing technical guidance" and reassuring them in the Navajo language.[13] The oil company's corporate communications department declined to comment on the meeting or other interactions with landowners, citing pending litigation.[14]

Roberta Tovar was equally adamant: her aunt was pressured. I asked Tovar and her father, Charles Irving, if the officials' behavior at the luncheon—surrounding, stroking, and verbally cajoling Mary Tom—was considered socially acceptable among Navajos. They both recoiled, shaking their heads. "No," said Tovar. "That's why I said they were like coyotes on a sheep."

NATIVE LANDOWNERS MAY STRUGGLE with an information blackout as they try to decode the terms of the deals they are offered via the Bureau of Indian Affairs. Realty expert Terry Beckwith said the BIA frequently fails to provide owners with sufficient data to make decisions, or even to know what exactly will happen on their land. At an ICC Indian Enterprises seminar in the Bakken oil- and gas-producing region of North Dakota, an attendee showed his oil lease to Beckwith. "It had a line, his name written under it and the figure forty-seven dollars. So much was missing—terms and conditions, the exact location of the property, and more," Beckwith said. He advised the landowner and other attendees with similar documents to go immediately to the local BIA office to rescind their consent and obtain proper agreements.

On the Blackfeet Indian Reservation, in Montana, tribal member Leona Gopher waged a five-year battle to get the information she and her relatives needed to assess an oil company's offer of $1,850 for allowing a pipeline to cross their land for forty-five years. The fifteen co-owners would get $41.11 per year, with Gopher's cut coming in at less than three dollars per year for nearly a half century's worth of access to her property. This did not seem right to her. However, in order to object, she needed to know how the company had come up with the figure.

Her local BIA office told her to file a FOIA request. The office then estimated Gopher's tab for staff time and copying to complete the request at amounts that vacillated, but at one point topped $3,000. It was a sum that she did not have and that well exceeded the oil company's entire offer, let alone her portion of it. She took the matter to the Interior Board of Indian Appeals, or IBIA, an Interior Department administrative court that handles Native claims. Court records show that the IBIA ordered the Bureau of Indian Affairs to "complete the record."

Gopher's attorney used the completed record to allege that the oil company had not complied with federal regulations for pipeline deals. The errors cited ranged from an insufficient number of consenting signatures to a lowball appraisal based on use of the land for agriculture rather than for transmission of oil products, which is an industrial activity. "Out of 15 rules that are applicable to oil and gas pipelines, only two are partially in compliance," the brief claimed. Too late, said the IBIA: Gopher should have raised the objections earlier. The agreement went forward over her objections.[15]

When queried about this, the BIA spokesperson emailed me to say that Native landowners need not use FOIA requests to obtain their own "trust data or information." Yet IBIA court decisions and the BIA's own documents, including communications with Roberta Tovar's family and Leona Gopher, offer ample evidence that owners must use the Freedom of Information Act to pry records out of the agency.

Those familiar with Bureau of Indian Affairs operations say the difficulties tribal members have when dealing with the agency are common, though decidedly unusual anywhere else. "On what planet is a trustee allowed to withhold information from a beneficiary and then charge an exorbitant price to find out what the trustee is doing?" demanded Judge Willett. "Planet Indian country, that's where." Willett said the BIA uses "the mushroom approach" for its beneficiaries, which she defined as "cover the principals with manure and keep them in the dark."

Remarkably, the bureau allows lease applicants to determine the value of the Native property they want to use. The regulations define the result they produce as "fair market value." This has little to do with fairness or value when Indian land is concerned, claims one of Roberta Tovar's co-owners, retired Navajo Nation police captain Frank Adakai. "It is the lowest possible payment, peanuts compared to what a non-Indian landowner would get," Frank Adakai said in an interview. His brother Patrick, the retired government official, called the payments "chump change."

Having the lease applicant do the appraisal makes it easy to lowball landowners. "It is a conflict of interest built into the system," said Terry Beckwith. If you find this hard to comprehend, imagine that you have a piece of land or a spare room that you want to rent out, and the law allows prospective tenants to set the price. You are right: it is incomprehensible. Yet this is business as usual in Indian country. "In Indian affairs, there is a culture of believing that users have more rights than owners," said Judge Willett. "It is systemic disrespect."

Certain aspects of the leasing process could be readily fixed, according to Beckwith. Abbreviated leasing forms, some of them drawn up in the 1940s and 1950s and still used today, could be updated to include the purpose and time span of the agreement and remedies in case of an oil spill or other damage to the land. There could be better BIA record-keeping and more landowner control

Mary Tom's nephew Anselm Morgan, with a marker
showing the route of an oil pipeline across his Navajo
family's property. (Joseph Zummo)

of the valuation process. If leasing practices were improved, with
payments more clearly reflecting the value of the land and other
resources, Native landowners would earn more money. Their deals
would contribute to prosperity rather than prevent it. Beckwith
said that what he and other tribal members want is simple: "We
want to protect ourselves and our land and maximize the money
we can make on it."

These events are taking place today, but they sound like something out of decades or even centuries past, when tribal people

were cheated out of land and resources under color of law. The federal government has not changed its ways, commented Cris Stainbrook, the Oglala Lakota head of the Indian Land Tenure Foundation, which works to develop Native economies and recover alienated reservation land to American Indian ownership. "It has maybe gotten a little smoother," he said, at least compared to the days when the US cavalry would attack Indian camps and slaughtered their occupants.

BETWEEN THE EARLIEST DAYS of the American republic and the end of the nineteenth century, millions of acres of Native land were traded through treaties and other actions for a range of protections and benefits, including health care and education. In 1887, Congress passed the General Allotment Act, or Dawes Act, which would hobble Native communities, rendering them vulnerable to outside interests.[16]

The act divided many of the communally held reservations into individually owned allotments that were usually small multiples of 40 acres. (The 160 acres Tovar's family owns is a typical size.) Like much of federal Indian policy, then and now, the process had a slapdash quality. A few reservations had already been allotted when the act was passed. After passage, additional reservations were divvied up—some entirely, others partially, and yet others not at all. Tribal members received some of the tracts, while the rest were declared excess and sold to settlers. The Native-owned allotments were supposed to assimilate tribal members by turning them into property owners and farmers after the European pattern. However, Native allotments had none of the advantages of non-Native-owned real estate. The plots tended to be in arid areas that were not suitable for agriculture. Nor could Natives who wanted to farm necessarily afford the needed equipment. Farming in Indian country decreased after allotment, instead of increasing, according to Stainbrook, of the Indian Land Tenure Foundation.

In the face of this trend, Congress eventually authorized leasing of Native allotments to non-Natives. This, in turn, allowed outsiders to extract profit from Native land by means of exploitative leasing and right-of-way grants, with federal agencies controlling the process. "All roads lead to the General Allotment Act," said Judge Willett of the economic problems plaguing today's reservations. However chaotic the act's implementation, she said, it achieved its twin goals of weakening the tribes and opening up prime agricultural and timber land to non-Natives.

As the years progressed, the bad news got worse, according to Stainbrook. After allotment, Native people as a whole were declared incompetent to manage their affairs and all Indian land was taken into trust by the federal government; the Native owners had what is called beneficial title, or the right to use the land. Some individual Natives were then deemed "competent" to manage their own affairs independently of the federal government. A small amount of Caucasian blood might cause a tribal member to be declared competent, for example, at which point the person's land passed out of trust and was instead owned outright. That may sound like a good thing, but it also meant the land became subject to local real estate taxes. Too often, Natives were not informed of this change and learned that they owed back taxes as their land was sold at auction to pay the debt.

Military service also conferred competency and citizenship, which caused a Native soldier's land to be taken out of trust. Tribal members who served in World War I returned home to find they had lost their land, said Stainbrook. Others were murdered for their property, including during a widely reported and investigated reign of terror on the oil-rich Osage Nation Reservation in Oklahoma.[17]

In later years, tribal members' disadvantage persisted. The trust status of the land restricted the landowners' ability to sell or borrow on it, since the federal government's involvement as a trustee meant a bank could not repossess the property if the borrower failed to make payments. Farming remained out of reach. "We didn't have the capital and couldn't go to the bank," said attorney Lance Morgan, a Winnebago Tribe of Nebraska member and head of Ho-Chunk Inc., the tribe's economic development arm. "The usual pattern for farmers is obtaining bank loans for seed and other necessities in the spring, then paying them off after the harvest. That wasn't open to us. As a result, we stopped farming at Winnebago, even though we Indians invented corn."[18]

In the end, using, selling, or borrowing on the land—even bequeathing it—became difficult to impossible for Indian landowners. "You take a look at any one hundred and sixty acres on Pine Ridge. I defy you to say you can make a living there," said Stainbrook. Patrick Adakai observed that qualifying for a bank loan or mortgage secured with allotted land is out of reach for him and his Navajo relatives. "I can't point to my acre, or even my square inch, of our family allotment," Adakai explained. "It's not like one of us owns this hilltop or that canyon. Each of us has a percentage of the whole."

On the tribal level, allotment has been a drag on economic

development. Most reservations are a crazy quilt of Native and non-Native ownership, making it difficult for tribal governments to plan. Just siting a housing development can be challenging.[19] Judge Willett claimed Native people were not vanquished on the battlefield. "We were defeated on paper," she said.

Helping Native people make a living and order their lives was not the federal government's goal, though. In a 1901 message to Congress, President Theodore Roosevelt made this clear when he praised allotment of the reservations as "a mighty pulverizing engine to break up the tribal mass."[20] By the time he became president, the idea of assimilating those "pulverized" peoples had become popular as an alternative to extermination, especially among non-Natives who called themselves "Friends of the Indian."

The *Congressional Record* features discussions of how far certain tribes had come in that process. In 1885, an Indian agent in Oregon reported to Congress that 504 tribal members he supervised were "wholly clad in citizen's dress," while 123 were still "partly" clad.[21] In Oklahoma in 1897, an agent despaired of his Cheyenne and Arapaho charges. Despite the agent's "unyielding firmness," they persisted in sharing food and shelter. If a Native were to "assume the role of the white man," the agent said, "he must shut his door to the hungry horde of visiting relatives ... and must smother his inherited propensity for hospitality."[22]

While the General Allotment Act was supposedly turning Indian adults into farmers and property owners, their children were being transported to government- and church-run boarding schools. At the notoriously violent institutions, religious and lay staff used beatings and degradation to eradicate heritage languages and cultures and replace them with English and Christianity. In doing so, they fulfilled a directive to "kill the Indian, and save the child."[23]

The boarding schools lasted until the 1970s, when most were closed down or turned over to the tribes. Many Native people today who are over age sixty attended the schools. One is Patrick Adakai, who believes that the boarding schools were intended to distance children from reservation land they might inherit, among other goals. "We had vocational training, so after graduation, it made sense for many of us to go to cities to find jobs," he said. "But then I, like others, found my way home. They didn't think we'd come back, but we did."

Breaking reservations into grids of privately owned plots also broke up traditional land-use patterns, which involved communal, rotating, seasonal use of the land. Disrupted hunting, fishing, farming, and gathering economies no longer provided a steady living. Those who have never lived off the land may think it a meager livelihood, marked by hunger and privation, and may assume that the European-style alternative was necessarily an improvement. However, while on a reporting trip to cover Election 2014 in isolated Alaska Native villages, I saw that it can be a life of great abundance. Subsistence hunting and gathering traditions are still robust in the remote Bristol Bay region, and family and village feasts offered delicious preparations for salmon, walrus, moose, and other heritage foods from the tundra and sea. When visiting people's homes, I saw armfuls of medicinal herbs drying on racks; counters covered with pans of jerked salmon and pots of meat, fowl, and fish stews; and freezers packed with tundra berries, some familiar and others the intensely flavored delicacies of the region.

By the early decades of the twentieth century, some ninety million of the acres that supported the subsistence life had been lost. That made up about two-thirds of what the tribes had retained through the treaty process.[24] Losing land is culturally as well as economically devastating for Native people, according to Patrick Adakai: "Our land is essential to our sovereignty and who we are. It holds the bones of our ancestors."

The nineteenth-century Oglala Lakota chief Red Cloud is widely thought to have remarked in his later years, "They made us many promises, more than I can remember, but they kept only one. They promised to take our land, and they did." In 1870, the *New York Times* reported Red Cloud saying something similar in a speech at the Cooper Union for the Advancement of Science and Art, in New York City. Red Cloud had just come from Washington, DC, where he and twenty-some additional Sioux leaders had met with President Ulysses S. Grant. Speaking through a translator, Red Cloud told the cheering, handkerchief-waving crowd packed into Cooper Union's Great Hall that government interpreters had misrepresented the treaty the Sioux had signed with the United States just two years before. "When I reached Washington, the Great Father explained to me what the treaty was and showed me that the interpreters had deceived me. All I want is right and justice," the *Times* reported Red Cloud saying.

Cooper Union founder and Indian Commission chairman Peter Cooper also spoke at the event. Word in Washington had been of inevitable war on the frontier. Cooper told the assembled throng, "We have before us the very men of whom but yesterday we were assured that nothing could be expected but merciless war!" He considered Red Cloud's grievances: "We have recognized in solemn treaties the Indians' claims to the hunting grounds upon which they have from time immemorial enjoyed the rights of 'life, liberty and the pursuit of happiness.'" It was too late to deny this claim, except as "banditti or free-booters," Cooper said. Red Cloud finished by saying, "I hope you will think of what I have said to you. I bid you all an affectionate farewell."[25]

Red Cloud's and Cooper's pleas for reason and cooperation were made in vain. Four years later, an expedition led by Lieutenant Colonel George Armstrong Custer found gold in the Black Hills, which were part of the Great Sioux Reservation, established by the 1868 treaty with the Sioux tribes.[26] This set off a gold rush and accompanying violence. The most famous military encounter, in 1876 at Little Bighorn in Montana, ended badly for Custer and the Seventh Cavalry. The most notorious of numerous massacres took place at Wounded Knee, on Pine Ridge. In an interview in 2011 in Wounded Knee village, Oglala Lakota elder Walter Littlemoon told me that his grandfather had described to him the gunfire and screams in December 1890, as the Seventh Cavalry killed some three hundred Miniconjou Lakota men, women, and children camped nearby, surrounding them, raking them with Hotchkiss guns, and running down survivors in the snow.[27]

BY THE EARLY TWENTIETH CENTURY, the Native population had dropped precipitously from the many millions that scholars estimate inhabited what is now the United States before contact with Europeans.[28] Massacres, incarceration, disease, and deadly removals from traditional homelands, including the Cherokees' Trail of Tears and the Navajos' Long Walk, had cut their numbers to a few hundred thousand individuals. The combination of continual catastrophes and massive land loss alarmed even Congress. It commissioned a study, issued in 1928 as the *Meriam Report,* that found extreme poverty, rampant disease, and desperate conditions on the reservations.[29] Federal policies had been shockingly effective. In response, in 1934 Congress passed the Indian Reorganization Act, or IRA, which provided some tribal self-governance, restored some lost land, and stopped the process of breaking up reservations.[30]

Ramah Navajo weaver Katie Henio assesses the fleece of a Navajo Churro sheep. The treasured breed has made a comeback since the federal government's 1930s "stock reduction," during which hundreds of thousands of the sheep were shot or incinerated, destroying Navajo traditions and the economic independence of tribal women, who owned the sheep. (Joseph Zummo)

Soon, federal tactics would whipsaw in another direction. As both a cost-saving measure and a further attempt to push Natives toward assimilation, the Eisenhower administration formulated its so-called termination policy, touted as "emancipation" for Natives. During the 1950s and 1960s, the federal government declared certain tribes able to survive without federal services and withdrew their recognition as political entities. These tribes' homelands were broken up, parceled out to individual tribal members, and often subsequently snapped up by non-Native interests. Tribes lost land and in some cases their treaty rights, such as water and hunting and fishing rights; they also lost jurisdictional rights as governments. Individual tribal members no longer qualified for certain kinds of government assistance, as they were no longer Indians in the legal sense, that is, members of a federally recognized tribe.[31]

For the once self-sufficient Klamath Tribes, termination in 1954 meant losing the valuable Oregon timberlands their financial independence had relied on. In the 1980s, they regained tribal recognition, though little of their former homeland, and began the arduous process of rebuilding an economy, including through gaming.[32] The Menominees, whom we met in the introduction, accomplished their woodland magic despite also being terminated—from the mid-1950s until their restoration in the mid-1970s.[33] Additional tribes reestablished themselves after termination, often through expensive court battles, while others disappeared entirely.[34] In 1969, the Native professor, author, and rights advocate Vine Deloria, Jr. termed "bizarre" the concepts that underpinned termination. "Indians were such an unknown commodity," Deloria wrote, "that the ridiculous made sense, the absurd was normal."[35]

More than one million acres of Native land were lost during the termination era, which President Richard Nixon ended in 1970. Evoking the treaties and other "solemn obligations," he told Congress that obliterating the relationship with tribes was "no more appropriate than to terminate the citizenship rights of any other American." Embarking on an era of self-determination in Indian affairs, Nixon declared, "It is long past time that the Indian policies of the federal government began to recognize and build upon the capacities and insights of the Indian people."[36]

Today, remaining Native lands sit atop valuable oil and gas reserves and feature large swaths of rich agricultural land. While the total revenue generated by corporations and others already operating on reservation land must add up to a very large sum, apparently no one knows what this figure might be, according to several economists and government agencies, including the BIA. In an era when the American economy is calculated and modeled every which way, Indian country's contribution to gross domestic product, job creation, taxes, and other economic measures is a black hole. "If you find out, let us know," the BIA spokesperson said in an interview.

Figures for some subsets of Indian-country business activities are available, but they offer only glimpses of the whole. In the agriculture sector, the US Department of Agriculture has determined that on average non-Natives farmers and ranchers operating on reservations have larger—sometimes much larger—operations than their Native counterparts on the same reservations.[37] However, agency figures do not specify how much of the non-Native farm sales are derived from reservation land and how much from non-tribal land, such as their home farm. As a result, there is no bottom-line figure for the contribution that tribal land makes to the agriculture sector or the economy as a whole. All the USDA can say is that outside agriculture operations that lease reservation land generate higher overall sales than their Native counterparts.

The non-Indian farmers and ranchers appear to be paying tribes and tribal members the usual rock-bottom BIA-engineered fees. On the Omaha Reservation, in Nebraska and Iowa, chief of tribal operations Carroll Webster said that a decade ago external agricultural operations paid the tribe $400,000 per year to lease land that grossed the outsiders $30 million in sales of corn, soybeans, and other products. I have heard of similar spreads between lease income and sales value elsewhere. The Omaha have worked to narrow the gap. By 2016, the tribe had its own farm on some of its land; it was also receiving $1 million per year for leases on other acreage.[38] Still, there is a long way to go before the Omaha and other tribes are receiving the real worth of their land's productivity.

Meanwhile, the Trump administration has been eyeing those valuable tribal assets, circling Indian country like the "coyotes" surrounding aged Mary Tom. Shortly after the election, a presidential advisory committee declared support for "privatization" of Native energy resources.[39] One committee member later claimed the idea had been misunderstood, but it continued to circulate.[40] Judge Willett was dismissive, saying: "Their theory is that Indians will quit being poor if others get their oil lands. That is the equivalent of telling me that someone wants to blow up my house to get rid of termites. Indians are poor due to improvident, underfunded federal policies and programs and because the government always lets everyone cheat Indians, including the government itself. That's it in a nutshell."

SOME MAY IMAGINE THAT in times past, indigenous people wandered the land, enjoying its bounty while blissfully unaware of anything as practical as well-ordered economic activity and stable property rights. Not so, says Arizona State University professor Robert J. Miller, who has written of finding hundreds of historical examples of prosperous, entrepreneurial tribal economies. Continent-wide, indigenous people had demarcated property rights, specialized professions, and long-distance trade networks; accumulated reserves allowed for leisure time.[41] Sophisticated astronomical-mathematical installations throughout the hemisphere indicate that first peoples had the time, resources, and expertise needed to support intensive inquiries, extending over centuries, into the nature of the universe. Among many such sites are Tikal, Monte Albán, and other complexes in Mesoamerica;[42] rock-outlined circle-and-spoke arrays, including the mountaintop Bighorn Medicine Wheel, a national historic landmark in Wyoming;[43] and monumental earthen-mound groupings in the US Midwest.[44]

Precontact agricultural fields, portions of streams, and other resources were associated with a particular person or family, permanently or semipermanently, Miller writes. These could be passed along to heirs. Tribal law and customs protected these rights, which were rooted in ideas of stewardship and renewable use of the lands.[45] "Land ownership and rights have always been as sacred to us as they are to Europeans," Willett said.

A related misperception is that the Europeans had no concept of sharing resources when they arrived on American shores. To the contrary, Europe had a well-established tradition of communal access to land for agriculture and other purposes. On this continent, the idea survived in town greens like Boston Common, which was established in the 1600s as a shared grazing area. It was a meeting place as the American Revolution got underway and survives to this day as a public park that is communally held by the people of Boston.

Soon after their arrival here, however, land fever overcame the settlers. "Europeans were not interested in Indian conceptions of property," University of South Dakota law professor Frank Pommersheim writes, "only in identifying individuals with the real (or apparent) right to transfer property that would then be protected and interpreted under English (or other European) law."[46] According to Martin Case, director of the Indian Treaty Signers Project, an undertaking of the Indian Land Tenure Foundation, the bounty of the land was quickly divorced from its value. In early America, property was cherished not necessarily for what it could provide but for the cash it would bring when it was sold. Looked at this way, the prominent families of early America—with venerated names like the Washingtons and the Jeffersons—were little more than opportunists, nabbing immense land grants and making fortunes by flipping them.[47]

When the United States emerged as a nation, the plunder of Native land rushed onward, with non-Natives scooping up vast acreage through congressional acts, court decisions, fraud, and other means. The Land Ordinance of 1785 greased the wheels by dividing the country into a checkerboard oriented to the cardinal directions.[48] You have seen it if you have flown over or looked at maps of the Midwest and West. Called the Jeffersonian grid after its originator, Thomas Jefferson, it carved varied ecosystems and landforms into real estate parcels that would appeal to buyers who did not care what they were—rolling grasslands, parched deserts, rich riparian bottomlands, or rugged hill country—as long as they could be resold at a profit. Later, the grid facilitated selling off the 1803 Louisiana Purchase.

WHILE CONGRESS AND THE EXECUTIVE branch of the federal government were devising means to shift Native land and resources to others, the Supreme Court was redefining what the tribes were in law. The tribal nations had struck treaties and other agreements that were enshrined in the Constitution's Article VI as among "the supreme law of the land." In the 1800s, the Supreme Court began chipping away at these expressions of a sovereignty that predated the United States. In a series of decisions, the court styled tribes as "domestic dependent nations," "in a state of pupilage," and "wards" of the federal guardian—all the while describing Natives in virulently racist terms. "[T]he Court, over the decades and centuries, imagines its Indians as was necessary to reach its holdings," writes attorney Matthew L. M. Fletcher, a professor in the Michigan State University College of Law. Early Supreme Court justices called Natives "fierce savages" with "inveterate habits," who were "restless," "warlike," "prone to massacring," "gradually sinking," and "low," according to Fletcher.[49]

This attitude persisted into modern times. Justice William Rehnquist wrote in a 1980 minority opinion regarding a Sioux Nation matter that the Sioux tribes had been treated badly but that their claim was tainted by their own "villainy." Better yet, Rehnquist had proof! He quoted an historian on "the Plains Indians" (which most schoolchildren know include more tribes than the Sioux): "They lived only for the day, recognized no rights of property, robbed or killed anyone if they thought they could get away with it, inflicted cruelty without a qualm, and endured torture without flinching." On the other hand, the hyperventilating historian extolled "the Plains Indians" as "fine physical specimens" who were "gaily dressed."[50] Whoever they were, they had managed to inflict and endure all that villainy while looking marvelous.

"Denigration is a prelude to deterritorialization," said Willett. "Our rights don't change. Only other people's view of them does—always with the view in mind of taking our land and resources."

The fictions that underlie the high court's opinions and decisions should be rejected, not perpetuated, according to the Pawnee attorney Walter Echo-Hawk. He observes that this reassessment did occur in relation to black Americans, for example when *Brown v. Board of Education* and other cases rejected earlier claims that they were racially inferior and that segregation was not harmful. It is time, Echo-Hawk writes, for another look at the dubious claims underlying court decisions that have become precedent and are repeatedly applied to contemporary Indian-law cases.[51]

In a law journal article, Lance Morgan, of Winnebago and Ho-Chunk Inc., doubts that the solutions will come in federal courts. Morgan, who is a managing partner of Fredericks Peebles & Morgan LLP, a national law firm, calls federal Indian law a "web of restrictions grounded in racism, paternalism, and exploitation." He points to an important drag on tribal economies created by the courts—another instance where hobbling tribes works to the advantage of non-tribal interests: that is, courts have allowed states to reach into reservations and create a race-based taxation system, levying taxes on non-Indians doing business and/or making purchases there, such as tobacco and gasoline. Morgan observes that outside of the purview of federal Indian law, the power to tax is based on territorial jurisdiction, not on race.[52]

Massive sums bypass the tribes. The Tulalip Tribes have sued Washington State over $40 million in annual taxes they felt the state had improperly collected, while the Mandan, Hidatsa, and Arikara tribes, known as the Three Affiliated Tribes, have reportedly paid North Dakota $1 billion in taxes over three recent years for oil extracted from the reservation portion of the Bakken. Tribes countrywide complain that states do not return the monies in the form of services, from plowing roads to maintaining schools, that they provide their non-Native communities.[53]

Tribes cannot easily make up the difference. They are loathe to layer their own levies on top of a state's for fear of driving away the businesses and customers they have managed to attract, according to Choctaw Nation tribal member Gavin Clarkson, a former Interior Department official and a New Mexico State University finance professor. That leaves most tribes without a tax base and the money with which governments typically fund the infrastructure—roads, water systems, schools, hospitals, etc.—that other Americans take for granted, even in the poorest inner city.[54]

Photographs of broken-down trailer homes are among the most widely used Indian-country memes. Media outlets of all kinds employ them as a handy stand-in for poverty, apathy, alcoholism, and more. I asked Rosebud Sioux civil-rights leader O. J. Semans what those images tell him. He responded, "Those photographs are intended to show that we can't take care of ourselves." The lack of a tax base, along with other ways Indian country is segregated economically, is entirely out of the frame— beyond the scope of a photographer looking for a quick hit. In an interview, Lance Morgan noted that these economic barriers put tribes at the mercy of the federal government. Meanwhile, the Unites States provides meager support for health care, education, and other needs, despite treaty obligations. Trump administration budget plans look to cut this even further.

How do you fight this? Morgan asks in his law journal article. He answers his own question: "This is America! Legal, economic, and political issues are almost always fought with money." He points to the growing ability of some tribes to bypass the restrictions, saying, "At some point, tribes will be too big to steal from, too powerful to push around, and too smart to play the losing game of mindlessly obeying federal Indian law." He provides examples of tribal and intertribal enterprises that have taken advantage of their sovereignty and their own laws, manufacturing their own products on their own land and trading among themselves in ways that allow them to avoid state taxation and thereby charge their own levies.[55]

IN THE MEANTIME, FEDERAL COURT decisions still have an enormous impact on Native lives, and understanding them is part and parcel of survival for tribal members. The tribal man in the street, or person on the prairie, if you will, can parse legal documents with a clarity and precision that appears to outpace the abilities of many in the legal profession. Tribal members responded in force in 2016 when the Interior Department asked for comments on new leasing and right-of-way rules, for example; individual landowners were concerned that the federal government was using the changes, touted as modernization, to diminish even further their ability to control their land.

Similarly, on a visit to the Yankton Sioux Tribe's South Dakota reservation in 2001, the talk over soup and buffalo burgers at the tribe's casino restaurant was all about *Nevada v. Hicks,* which had just been handed down. The Supreme Court had decided that tribal courts did not have authority over state officials, in this case game wardens, acting on a reservation. In some situations, the court held, "States may regulate the activities even of tribe members on tribal land."[56] Tribal members were alarmed by the ruling's erosion of tribal sovereignty and elevation of the power of states, which are often at odds with tribes within their borders. For a dramatic example of this animosity, think of North Dakota's violent response throughout most of 2016 to the Standing Rock Sioux's objection to an oil pipeline being built through their water supply.

On the Yankton Reservation in 2001, the tribe was in the midst of a fight for survival. This battle would also wend its way to the Supreme Court. The dispute began in 1994, when the tribe tried to stop construction of a solid-waste dump on its land. The state of South Dakota took the opportunity to claim that Congress had "disestablished" the reservation through various actions; in other words, it no longer existed. A ruling in favor of the state of South Dakota would have thrown tribal members' lives into turmoil and might also have implied that other Indian reservations did not exist either.[57]

In advance of any court decision, the Yankton homeland was removed from state road maps. When I prepared to head for the reservation on a reporting trip, I could not locate it on a map I acquired (this was well before the days of online maps). I was momentarily bewildered. Had I imagined the Yanktons? I called the tribal hall and got directions. I flew into Sioux Falls, drove south down the interstate that parallels the state's eastern border, then headed west on two-lane country roads. After about two hours, I hit the border of the county that surrounds the reservation and came upon a police car, the first one I had seen since arriving in South Dakota. I saw several more police cars during the remaining three-quarters of an hour it took to get to the reservation. For miles, it was just me, acres of crops, and the long arm of the law.

Animosity ran high in white communities surrounding the reservation. Near the Yanktons' hotel, where I would stay, a police officer was parked on the state highway where it intersected the main road out of the reservation. I learned that this was a spot where non-tribal police could easily intercept Yanktons. "They sit there and wait for us," a tribal member told me. The tribal newspaper, the *Sioux Messenger,* reported continual arrests of Yanktons for offenses like dusty license plates or failing to return a rented video on time. The fines were set prohibitively high, and tribal members might spend several days in jail before they could resolve their cases. This meant constant disruption of normal life, including the ability to hold down a job, get children to school, and so on.[58]

Beyond the state of siege, the reservation itself was lovely, with grazing buffalo, cottonwood-lined gullies, rolling hills, and majestic crenellated bluffs overlooking the Missouri River. A sense of movement pervaded the scene. Breezes stirred purple-flowering echinacea and prairie grasses. The pale scents of mint and sage wafted by. Deer and coyotes disappeared into thickets, around boulders, and down draws. Even the land was in motion; because the heavy clay soil is highly malleable, its deep brown folds and swells expand, collapse, and reemerge from year to year. Eagles, hawks, and vultures wheeled overhead, surfing the thermals or diving so close to the ground, it was tempting, though obviously inadvisable, to try and touch them as they rocketed by.

The great inverted bowl of the northern plains sky added high drama, as blazing sun alternated with ferocious thunderstorms and gigantic lightning bolts crashing into the earth. And everywhere was the quivering of butterflies—yellow, white, mottled brown and gray, bright orange and black—hovering above puddles, fluttering between blossoms, perching on trees. This is nothing, people told me, you should be here during the butterfly migrations.

As courts issued contradictory decisions on the disestablishment lawsuit over the years, law-enforcement jurisdiction over various tracts of land flipped back and forth between county and tribal cops, causing uncertainty about which officers should respond to which calls. This drove a long-running public-safety crisis that benefited no one but the criminals.[59]

The suit went to the Supreme Court twice, before resolving in the tribe's favor in 2011, when the high court refused to rehear the case.[60] When word arrived, as chance would have it, I was again on the Yankton Reservation, reporting other stories for *Indian Country Media Network*. The cloud that had hung over Yanktons' personal lives and tribal institutions for seventeen years had lifted. I contacted my editors and began doing interviews about the decision. Bobby Cournoyer, then tribal chairman, said that the tribe could get back to normal business, including resolving important issues like purchasing land lost over the years and placing it in trust status. I got tribal attorney Charles Abourezk on the phone. He sounded both thrilled and stunned, not just because he had been part of an important win in the highest court in the land but because a case he had been fighting for a good portion of his adult life was suddenly over.

"Now the state is going to have to issue new maps," Abourezk quipped, adding that he hoped settling the issue would usher in a new era of tribe-state cooperation. Shortly after the state erected a welcome sign on the reservation's newly defined boundaries, the tribe's neighbors in the surrounding county chopped it down and shot dead a tribal member's horses.[61]

WITH FEW BUSINESSES ON RESERVATIONS, tribes and tribal members must look to surrounding border towns for goods and services. The result of this is that a high proportion of Native dollars flow away without changing hands on the reservation and thereby creating jobs and income as they circulate. Economists call this phenomenon "leakage."[62] Said Roberta Tovar, "The little money we work for goes to Gallup." The local Walmart's aisles are jammed on the first and fifteenth of each month, when paychecks and benefits arrive. "You won't be able to get through with your basket," Tovar said. Another Walmart has set up shop outside Pine Ridge. Again, the store is crowded when reservation residents have money to spend and nearly empty, with few vehicles in the parking lot or shoppers in the aisles, when they do not, a manager there told me.

Some of the businesses on reservation borders are predatory. To control alcoholism, tribes may prohibit alcohol and declare their homelands dry. You can often tell when you have passed the external boundary of one of these reservations because you see a bar or liquor store perched there that would be illegal on tribal land. If you circumnavigate the dry Pine Ridge Indian Reservation, you will see that it is ringed by bars and liquor stores. Until recently, these included four beer stores in the most notorious town, Whiteclay, located in Nebraska about 250 feet from the reservation's southern border and a few minutes' walk from the main population center in Pine Ridge village.

With no other towns for miles around and a population of around a dozen, the dismal settlement existed primarily to bootleg liquor onto the reservation. It was heir to the whiskey ranches set up there in the late 1800s for the same purpose, according to Frank LaMere, a Winnebago Tribe of Nebraska activist who has long marched, protested, and advocated to get rid of the stores. For more than a century, the town contributed to an epidemic of alcoholism and fetal-alcohol syndrome, with one in four children born with the devastating condition in recent years.[63]

However, Whiteclay's beer stores also created wealth locally and around Nebraska, making them difficult to close down. They paid taxes and, along with liquor manufacturers, distributors, and trade groups, donated to Nebraska political candidates. A Whiteclay shopkeeper told me his store was a "gold mine in hell." Reservation residents called the town a parasite and termed the situation a public-health crisis.[64] After decades of work on the part of LaMere and fellow activists, the tribe and its attorneys announced in September 2017 that the Nebraska high court had finally closed the stores down.[65]

Other economic restrictions are more subtle. On past trips to South Dakota, I have observed that tourist locations like Rapid City

Regional Airport and Badlands National Park offer maps of western South Dakota showing a narrow slice of the state along the western border, guiding visitors to state and national parks and neatly eliminating the reservations. At the national park, I asked if I could get a map of adjoining Pine Ridge, and only then was one provided.

While policies like these and rapacious businesses drain the strength of tribal homelands, the reservations themselves act as giant funnels, pouring federal benefits and business earnings into state and regional economies. Reservation enterprises contribute mightily to those economies. Tribes purchase goods and services and pay salaries and related taxes for tribal members and others hired in gaming, additional businesses, tribal government, tribal schools, and other entities. Tribal employees, in turn, make purchases, putting more money into circulation, and pay taxes. In Nebraska, the Winnebago Tribe is the biggest taxpayer in its county, according to attorney and tribal member Lance Morgan.

Economic studies demonstrate this phenomenon. In *The Rights of Indians and Tribes*, author and attorney Stephen Pevar cites research showing that from 1979 to 2002, the state of Wyoming received $283 million more in taxes from Wind River Indian Reservation mineral production than it returned in services and other funding. Pevar notes another study calculating that Connecticut tribal casinos created sixty-five thousand jobs and, in 2005, contributed $1 billion to the state budget.[66] Economist Steven Peterson, a professor at the University of Idaho, found that in 2009, five Idaho tribes together contributed nearly $1 billion in economic activity to the state, while creating ten thousand jobs and paying nearly $25 million in state and local taxes.[67] Seventy tribes in Alaska's interior estimated their local impact at $300 million in 2010.[68] Tribes and tribal entities have been shown to be economic boons in California, North Dakota, Oregon, and Washington State, among others, contributing hundreds of millions, or billions, of dollars to their regions and the nation.[69]

The money pours outward, leaving many reservations impoverished. Given the structural nature of the problems—frozen in place by more than a century of government policies and ineptitude—one has to marvel at the faux seriousness of federal programs devised to assist. All the job-training programs in the world will not help if there are no jobs to be had. "We have so many resources on our reservations, so much that others use or take," said Leona Gopher. "Yet we also have so much poverty."

NATIVE LANDOWNERS HAVE ALSO SHOWN in court that they have gotten not just a raw deal but a fraudulent one. While serving as treasurer of the Blackfeet Nation during the 1980s, tribal member Elouise Cobell discovered irregularities in the Interior Department's accounting system for disbursements to Native people. After years of trying to persuade the federal government to fix the problems, in 1996 she became lead plaintiff in a class-action lawsuit that exposed improper records for more than a century's worth of payments to many tribes. Billions of dollars were missing—as much as $140 billion, according to Stainbrook. Documents had disappeared, including some that the court discovered federal officials destroyed during the time the case was being heard.[70] "I have never seen more egregious misconduct by the federal government," US District Court Judge Royce C. Lamberth announced.[71] A court-appointed investigator reported that Navajos were getting twenty-five to forty dollars per rod (16.5 feet) for rights-of-way across their BIA-supervised trust land; similar land off the reservation garnered ten to nearly twenty times as much.[72]

In 2010, Congress approved a $3.4 billion settlement for the *Cobell* case. The settlement included $1.9 billion for tribes to buy back individuals' land interests and place them in trust for the tribe. This arrangement was needed because the federal government's trust oversight had eliminated traditional tribal means of bequeathing land, via the family or clan.[73] The federal involvement meant that when allottees passed on, their property remained intact, and the beneficial title was divided among all Indian heirs. (Other assets were subject to state laws for those who died without a will.) With each passing generation, the number of owners of a plot of land multiplied, each possessing a unique percentage of the whole.[74]

The process of unending subdivision is called fractionation.[75] This makes economic decisions very difficult for the co-owners. "When I give talks to non-Indians, I ask them to imagine sitting around the table at Thanksgiving dinner with two hundred relatives and trying to make a decision about how family property will be handled for the coming year," Stainbrook said.

As a result of fractionation, the BIA's workload is continually multiplying. Economists Thomas Stratmann and Jake Russ of George Mason University looked at the BIA's efforts to track ownership. "In 2010, there [were] 4.6 million ownership records maintained by BIA for the entire trust land base," they wrote in a paper on the subject, "which puts BIA's total recordkeeping costs at $575 million annually." And it all keeps growing. The number of ownership records on the twelve reservations Stratmann and Russ studied in detail doubled over a recent eighteen-year period, with implications for ballooning costs nationwide.[76]

Since fractionation is now understood as a problem, and individuals' plots are the ones that fractionate, federal policy has recently tended to encourage tribes to buy members' property. Theoretically, this should reduce costs while helping tribes reconstitute their "pulverized" land bases. So far, these efforts have proven to be more about running in place than winning the race against fractionation. Through *Cobell*-funded buybacks, about 1.7 million acres became tribally owned land by the end of 2015, according to the Interior Department. However, even this substantial transfer from individuals to their tribes reduced the number of fractionated interests by less than 10 percent. "Fractionation remains a significant problem," says the Interior Department.[77]

Lance Morgan, of Winnebago, described the buyback fixes as "like being handed a Band-Aid after getting stabbed in the aorta." In Morgan's view, the *Cobell* buybacks are simply onetime windfalls for individuals who sell and an ongoing annual bonus for their tribes, which then have more land to lease. The program doesn't create any long-term assets, according to Morgan.

Individual landowners may also feel coerced into giving up their interests. "A buyback program is a way to undo the allotment process and restore tribal ownership," said Stainbrook. "But people who invest time and effort in their property, then are targeted by a buyback, feel that it is a taking." Courts have declared some buybacks unconstitutional, holding that they ran afoul of the Fifth Amendment, which protects Americans from loss of property without due process and just compensation. Before the courts made these determinations, though, thousands of Native landowners lost property, according to Montana State University professor Kristin T. Ruppel.[78] Restoration of the properties took decades, said Stainbrook.

In another attempt to slow fractionation, the Department of the Interior now encourages Natives to write wills and designate heirs. Yet this is another federal disconnect from facts on the ground. Tribal members have little access to the specialized attorneys and estate planners who understand the complex regulations governing such documents, which differ from the rules for non-Native wills. The Indian Land Tenure Foundation estimated in 2012 that less than 10 percent of Native landowners had a valid will.[79]

THE ROSEBUD SIOUX, IN SOUTH DAKOTA, have long worked to expand their land base and control their economic destiny. One way has been a buyback program of their own devising, tailored to their own needs, and this in turn has made it a success story. Set up in 1934, the Tribal Land Enterprise seeks to acquire land interests and reduce the reservation's checkerboard land-ownership pattern, while making tribal members happy. TLE does not necessarily purchase land outright, as *Cobell* does. Instead, it allows individuals a choice. The land they hand over is exchanged for shares that can be converted to either money or other property they find more desirable, said tribal member and buyback plan director Ann Wilson-Frederick. Over the years, TLE has acquired about a million acres this way.

Strategic purchases, with the tribe looking to obtain majority then total control of certain tracts, have facilitated the development of popular projects, and that has helped ensure TLE's success, according to Wilson-Frederick. The projects include a grocery store in a region where there are few and six hundred units of badly needed housing. The program puts more land at the disposal of Rosebud Indian Reservation's ranchers and farmers, so they can increase production. With purchases of contiguous sites, the tribe can put business and environmental regulations in place over more acreage, according to Rosebud tribal member Wizipan Little Elk, CEO of the tribe's economic development corporation and a former Interior Department official. The community can also choose to set aside land for spiritual and ecological reasons. "Our animal and plant brothers and sisters deserve protection as well," he said.

Rosebud is participating in yet another imaginative project that former president Bill Clinton called one of his "favorite commitments" at Clinton Global Initiative (CGI). The Oceti Sakowin Power Authority (OSPA) aims to turn wind into electricity and obstacles into assets. Oceti Sakowin means "Seven Council Fires of the Great Sioux Nation"[80] and is a collaboration of the Rosebud, Oglala, Cheyenne River, Crow Creek, Yankton, and Flandreau Santee Sioux Tribes, all in South Dakota, and Standing Rock, which straddles South and North Dakota. They are in a reliably breezy region that some have called the Saudi Arabia of wind power. The power authority's vision encompasses the possibility that even more Sioux nations in the United States and Canada might join in, using the wind, which they consider sacred, to provide their communities with clean, renewable power and sustainable economic development.

"We tribes see ourselves as custodians of the environment," said OSPA board member Dan Gargan, from Rosebud. "Producing clean energy is something we've wanted for a long time." OSPA's capacity is currently estimated at about two gigawatts, making it a utility-scale project and the first joint power authority formed in this country in decades. Its size is what makes it viable, unlike small individual-tribe wind farms, which have generally stalled. "Working together, we tribes can build on a larger scale, find collateral for loans more easily, and identify bigger purchasers," Gargan said.

Finding advantageous financing and major purchasers demanded out-of-the-box thinking. The consortium devised a strategy that will give it ownership of its facilities and access to major markets. The biggest financing hurdle was the tribes' tax-exempt status and resulting inability to take advantage of the federal tax breaks that private-equity investors can use when developing a wind farm. To be competitive without tax breaks, OSPA will offer bonds, similar to the municipal bonds with which local governments finance anything from a new fire truck to a major construction project. "The bonds would be purchased, probably in large chunks, by institutional investors such as pension funds," said Caroline Herron of Herron Consulting, which has been involved in OSPA since its beginnings.

Another hurdle was identifying potential buyers for the electricity, said Gargan. Local cooperatives providing electricity throughout South Dakota purchase minimal green energy, so OSPA turned to the far larger national wholesale market. This gives the authority a long list of potential customers in more than two dozen central and western states: investor-owned and public utilities, call centers, warehouse distribution centers, and huge energy-hungry corporations, like Amazon and Google, that purchase green energy as part of their corporate mission. The big companies' market share keeps expanding, said Herron: "In 2015, corporations bought more than fifty percent of wind energy for the first time, which was even more than the utilities."

When OSPA is up and running, President Clinton told a CGI conference in 2013, more tribes will see that green energy can allow them to earn substantial money, invest in their communities, and diversify their economic base. They will contribute to national energy independence while building a better future for their children, Clinton announced: "The potential for this is staggering."[81]

Said Little Elk: "We like to say we have a one-thousand-year plan."

2.

On the Voting-Rights Frontline

THE ELECTION OF 2016 WILL NOT go down in history as a victory for rights and justice, except in Indian country. By the time reservation polling places opened that year, hard-fought voting-rights lawsuits and negotiations, along with vigorous get-out-the-vote campaigns, had resulted in greater access to the ballot box in portions of several western states with substantial Native minorities. These included South Dakota, North Dakota, Montana, Nevada, Utah, Arizona, and Alaska. The most recent litigation followed up on scores of Native-rights suits brought since passage of the Voting Rights Act in 1965.[1] In the second decade of the twenty-first century, the nation's first peoples are still fighting county by county for equal access to registration and voting, acceptance of the types of identification they can readily obtain, such as tribal IDs, redrawing of gerrymandered districts, and the opportunity to show up at the polls without fear of harassment.

Participation means empowerment, according to O. J. Semans, the Rosebud Sioux codirector of the civil-rights group Four Directions, whose work since founding the nonprofit in 2003 with his wife, Barb, has been central to increasing Native enfranchisement. I first met Semans in September 2010 when he was in Hot Springs, the seat of Fall River County, South Dakota, to present a demand at a meeting that voters on Pine Ridge Indian Reservation be allowed the same access to the ballot box as voters in white communities.

Hot Springs is a dusty little resort town, where big pickups chug slowly down the main drag, past sandstone buildings housing shops and hotels. In the nearby Black Hills, buffalo graze in pine-rimmed meadows, and the cliffs are studded with rose quartz and tourmaline. The white-majority county's officials, who run elections on an outsourced basis for most of neighboring Pine Ridge, had quit in a raucous meeting three weeks before, leaving

Advocates sue to obtain voting rights for Native people. Gathering in Portland, Oregon, ahead of a 2014 hearing for the federal lawsuit *Wandering Medicine v. McCulloch* are, from left, Michaelynn Hawk, Crow, of Indian People's Action; South Dakota rancher Bret Healy, with Barb and O. J. Semans, Rosebud Sioux, all three from Four Directions rights group; Northern Cheyenne spiritual teacher Mark Wandering Medicine and his wife, Ilo; and Tom Rodgers, Blackfeet, of Carlyle Consulting. (Joseph Zummo)

the reservation with no way to vote in person—on Election Day, or during the forty-six-day period when the state's voters can cast ballots ahead of the day. Fall River's white voters would be fine, as the officials had retained that portion of their duties.

The large Oglala Sioux Tribe has thousands of registered Democratic voters—easily enough to swing elections in this sparsely populated state—and very few registered Republicans. As a result, the state's Republican establishment, which holds sway in Fall River, has long been leery of allowing Oglalas near the ballot box. Convenient early voting has been shown to increase participation dramatically on the South Dakota reservations that have managed to offer it, just as it does in any community in the United States.[2] Trying to keep early voting off Pine Ridge was just one technique to sideline the Native vote, though. Also hobbling Pine Ridge was the fact that Help America Vote Act reimbursements would not be available until the month after the election, which meant that the state's most destitute jurisdictions (its Indian reservations) would not be able to afford full-fledged elections.[3]

The state's GOP also turned up the heat on Democrats' campaign events on Indian reservations, charging that these frybread fests traded food in exchange for votes. At the same time, the Republicans were curiously closemouthed about the hot dogs they were handing out to predominantly white voters at their own rallies, or about the doughnuts Democrats served up in white communities—making it clear that the vote-trading accusation was leveled at the Native community and intended to appeal to the worst in the non-Native electorate. After the GOP demanded an investigation of the purported frybread scandal, Democrats said they welcomed one, and that was the end of that.[4]

Before heading to South Dakota, I interviewed a Fall River County official about election issues a couple of times by phone, then arranged to meet Semans in Hot Springs, along with his cowboy partner in the voting-rights struggle, South Dakota rancher Bret Healy. Semans, short and muscular with close-cropped iron-gray hair, arrived dressed in jeans, running shoes, and a plaid flannel shirt that flapped open over a T-shirt proclaiming "Homeland Security Since 1492." Healy, in a gray suit and cowboy boots, was tall and slim, with brown hair slicked back from a widow's peak. He had his laptop open throughout our conversation and forwarded me relevant documents as Semans ran down the concerns. "Equal rights make it possible for us to improve ourselves and to protect the earth," Semans told me. "People always say we have to better ourselves, and this is how we'll do it. If you don't vote, you're not at the table when decisions are made. Keeping us from the ballot box is a way of preventing us from improving our lives, our communities, and our economies."

After the Fall River County officials jettisoned their Pine Ridge electoral duties, South Dakota's Republican secretary of state offered Pine Ridge mail-in ballots as a substitute for real voting booths. Semans called this a ruse. He pointed out that because there were no more election officials for Pine Ridge, there was no one to count any mail-in ballots that happened to arrive at the county courthouse in Hot Springs. Semans described the hullabaloo that the walkout created as a distraction that allowed Fall River County and the state of South Dakota to pull a rabbit out of the hat: "Presto! No voting for Oglalas!"

Three attorneys from the Justice Department showed up at the meeting in Hot Springs. Tall and imposing in their severe black suits, they quietly and meticulously explained to the county the requirements of federal voting-rights law, as well as the practical details of holding an election. When county commissioners complained that they did not know how to find the ballot translators they were mandated to provide to Lakota speakers under the law, one attorney suggested that they start by learning whether any of the local Pine Ridge poll workers were bilingual. When the county raised the problem of paying for a Pine Ridge polling place during the additional days of early voting, Semans said Four Directions would donate the necessary funds. In the end, Oglalas got to vote early for a few partial days as well as on Election Day.

On November 2, 2010, I photographed state senator and Oglala Sioux tribal member Kevin Killer and Four Directions legal director Greg Lembrich as they stood in the parking lot of the Pine Ridge voting location, watching youngsters driving around tooting their horns and trailing streamers. One young voter rushed up to me with a brooch beaded with the bright red multipronged tribal symbol on a dark blue background. "It represents all of us," he said. "It's all the districts of the reservation voting today." I took it as a kind of press release in beaded form.

This was not the end of the struggle. To obtain equal access in future elections, Oglala voters eventually had to file a lawsuit, organized by Four Directions; in the process, the county defendants tried to go after the plaintiffs for court costs. As might be expected, this frightened the suit's plaintiffs. It also reduced the likelihood of additional plaintiffs and voting-rights advocates participating in related work going forward. When Semans found out, he asked sardonically, "Think they'll take a check?"

Healy called the county defendants' financial stratagem "breathtaking." He explained, "They have the insurance public officials typically hold to cover lawsuits of many types. Meanwhile, the plaintiffs include single parents, one with an epileptic child, others caring for infirm elders, from one of the poorest counties in the nation. The defendants are really going to do this? God have pity on their souls."

The Oglala lawsuit, *Brooks v. Gant*,[5] was one of four suits that Four Directions helped organize around the concept of expanding access to voting ahead of election day. After *Brooks v. Gant* resolved in 2012 with more voting access for tribal members until the end of 2018, the voting-rights group helped organize another lawsuit in South Dakota, *Poor Bear v. The County of Jackson*;[6] one in Montana, *Wandering Medicine v. McCulloch*;[7] and a fourth in Nevada, *Sanchez v. Cegavske*.[8] The strategy for the lawsuits arose from an experiment by Semans and his wife and Four Directions codirector, Barb Semans. When what South Dakota calls in-person absentee voting came to South Dakota in 2004, the Semanses decided to try it out. They made the eighty-five-mile round-trip from their home on the Rosebud Indian Reservation to their absentee polling place at the courthouse in white-majority Winner, South Dakota. "'Well, that wasn't so convenient,' we said to each other," recalled Barb Semans. "Later, O.J. and I were talking with Bret Healy, and it hit us all—this is a voting-rights issue!"

The Semanses and Healy realized that voter intimidation, ID restrictions, and gerrymandering are just some of the barriers between American Indians and the polling place. All of these had been factors in the many equal-rights lawsuits brought on behalf of Natives.[9] But now the three advocates saw that reservation voters also have a hard time getting access to the contemporary, purportedly convenient ways to cast a ballot that are increasingly offered around the nation. These methods end up widening rather than narrowing the enfranchisement gap for reservations. They include voting by mail, last-minute Election Day registration, early voting, and in-person absentee voting. Often, the last three are available only in distant off-reservation county seats. (Early voting and in-person absentee voting differ in legal terms. Generally, an early voter's eligibility is verified and the ballot counted as it is cast; in contrast, an in-person absentee ballot is verified and counted on Election Day.)[10]

Voting by mail poses extreme challenges for reservation voters, as it is dependent on the poor US mail service typically offered to Native communities. Getting a mail-in ballot can also require steps that are daunting on isolated, impoverished reservations with few computers, printers, photocopiers, or notaries and patchy internet access. The prospective voter generally has to download instructions and a ballot application, photocopy the document, along with identification, and get it all notarized before putting this packet in the mail. When Greg Lembrich of Four Directions was on Pine Ridge one year, he decided to determine whether the mail-in process was feasible for the Oglalas who live there. Lembrich had his laptop with him, but even that head start was not enough. After driving into the neighboring state of Nebraska to find a printer and photocopier, he was convinced that mail-in voting was unworkable for Pine Ridge.

Navajo voters in the Utah county that overlaps the northern end of their reservation had a comparable experience. After San Juan County began using mail-in voting in 2014, turnout dropped among tribal voters. Colorado attorney Maya Kane set out to determine why, as part of her pro bono work providing support to the Lawyers' Committee for Civil Rights under Law. The group, formed in 1963 at the request of President John F. Kennedy, was looking into the mail-in process to determine whether it was not just cumbersome but illegal. At that point, Navajos had already sued San Juan County repeatedly for equal rights and had succeeded four times in requiring the county to redraw its voting districts (at publication time, the county had not yet complied with the last three court orders, in 2015, 2016, and 2017);[11] Navajos had also established their right to federally mandated language assistance.[12]

In Kane's travels around the area and discussions with residents, she found plenty of leaks in the mail-in ballot pipeline.[13] She learned that impoverished tribal members did not have rural postal delivery and often shared PO boxes or used general delivery. These factors lowered the odds that they received essential election communications. Many were able to make the multi-hour trips to distant post offices only every few weeks, so that diminished further their chances of getting materials in time to meet registration and voting deadlines.

Even worse, Kane found that reservation postal services were a patchwork of regular post offices, contract offices, and commercial services, some just a counter in a trading post, which might have unique hours and unique deadlines—say 9:00 AM or 1:00 PM, as opposed to the end of the business day—by which point voters must present ballots in order to get them postmarked in time to count for the election. Some reservation mail services did not postmark at all but relied on catch-as-catch-can transport to offices down the line to frank the items. Once in the mail stream, the ballots could take weeks or months to make their way to the county clerk's office, frequently via sorting facilities in other states. To Kane, reservation postal service was a world away from that most Americans receive. "If a tribal member's only option is voting by mail, this creates voting-rights disparities right out of the gate," she said.

Mail-in elections may be especially unreliable on reservations, but they are undependable even in areas with what is generally considered good postal service, according to Jean Schroedel, a political science professor at Claremont Graduate University. In a 2014 expert witness report for *Wandering Medicine v. McCulloch*, she explained that research shows attempts to vote by mail fail for numerous reasons, including the failure of ballots to get to election officials, the disqualification of ballots because of missing signatures, and other errors that could have been corrected during precinct voting.[14]

After the mail-in elections began in San Juan County, Navajo Nation residents who needed or wanted to vote in person had to travel as many as four hundred miles to do so. That was the round-trip distance between a town called Navajo Mountain and the county's last remaining polling place in the white-majority off-reservation county seat. The trip was time-consuming and so were the preparations. You do not set out across the parched desert and rugged mountains of Monument Valley without tuning up your vehicle, filling the tank, checking the tires, stocking up on food and water, and making certain you have enough money for emergencies, said Terry Whitehat, a hospital administrator living in Navajo Mountain.

Most of Whitehat's reservation neighbors are impoverished and do not have reliable vehicles and the extra cash for gas and other supplies. For them, the trek was out of the question. Navajo tribal member Wilfred Jones said, "Don't penalize me because of who I am and where I live. The government put us on this reservation, and now we can't vote because we live here. We Navajos have a right to vote. This is the twenty-first century. Why has this taken so long?"

Elimination of local precincts in favor of mailed ballots also meant that voters who spoke only, or primarily, Navajo no longer had the translators who had been available at the polling location in each precinct; this made ballot errors common and apparently caused some individual voters to give up and make no attempt to cast a ballot.

San Juan County commissioner Phil Lyman defended the county, saying it made special efforts to remedy mistakes that occurred. When Navajo mail-in ballots arrived with errors, the county's interpreter took them to voters' homes for correction, Lyman said in an interview—"even if that meant a seventy-mile drive." The Lawyers' Committee filed a complaint[15] about the mail-in election in February 2016, and soon after the county announced its decision to reopen some of the shuttered Navajo polling places.[16] About Navajos' determined and protracted struggle for enfranchisement, Kane commented that voting rights are the rights from which all others flow. "The Supreme Court has said this a number of times," she said. "The first instance was in 1886, when the court described voting as 'a fundamental political right, because it is preservative of all rights.'"[17]

IN 2017, O.J. SEMANS BECAME legislative affairs director for the Coalition of Large Tribes. Also referred to as COLT, this influential group includes tribes that have large populations and/or large land bases. When Semans traveled to Washington, DC, during 2017, he found politicians on both sides of the aisle who were willing to listen to a Native perspective. This was despite the dramatic differences between the new administration—headed by a president who freely used "Pocahontas" as a slur during the campaign—and the previous one.

During President Barack Obama's tenure, he signed into law measures intended to help Native communities fight crime, expand employment, and improve health and education. He hired Native staffers and made them part of decision-making at the highest level. He enhanced the federal government's consultation with tribes on projects that affect them and settled tribal lawsuits against the United States. In 2015, the Justice and Interior Departments paid $940 million to settle a complaint that the federal government had fleeced tribes nationwide for work it contracted them to do in law enforcement, forest management, and other government services.[18] The following year, the Justice Department announced that it had paid $3.3 billion to settle 104 claims for mismanagement of tribal resources.[19] Some of the grievances went back more than a century.[20]

Obama's record was not unblemished. His administration's review of the Dakota Access Pipeline plan to cross the Standing Rock Sioux water supply was belated and half-hearted. He did not figure out how to protect Standing Rock demonstrators exercising their First Amendment rights to free speech and assembly as they faced extraordinary violence from state and private security forces during most of 2016. During that year, the Federal Energy Regulatory Commission also issued a presidential permit for a fracked-gas pipeline in Texas.[21] In September, archaeologist David

Keller reported that bulldozers had churned ancient tribal sites in the path of the pipeline into a sea of mud.[22]

In the raging chaos of the Trump administration, many Obama-era policies were questioned or reversed. The new president sought budget cuts and federal policy shifts that would fall heavily on already drastically underfunded tribal health, welfare, housing, law-enforcement, land-management, and education programs. Some of the heaviest cuts were proposed for funds that tribes could direct to programs they felt needed them most, observed former assistant secretary of Indian Affairs Kevin Washburn, in an article on *Indian Country Media Network.* This "takes aim at tribal self-determination and self-governance," Washburn wrote.[23] Executive memos signed in January 2017 encouraged speedy completion of the Dakota Access and Keystone pipelines, both fiercely opposed by tribes.

Voting rights were on the block. Sensitive to his whopping defeat in the popular vote, the forty-fifth president harped on his widely discredited claim that "millions" had voted illegally in the 2016 election, including "thousands" bussed from Massachusetts to New Hampshire. He appointed a Presidential Advisory Commission on Election Integrity, headed by an election-fraud fantasist. House Republicans introduced a bill to shut down the Election Assistance Commission, a government agency that protects the integrity of elections, including against hacking. Likely important to those wanting to scuttle the EAC, the commission funds ballot-box access for marginalized communities, including money to set up polling sites and hire election workers on Indian reservations. On the state level, legislatures nationwide introduced laws to stiffen ID requirements, shorten the time allowed for voting, and eliminate

Election Day registration. In July, the Justice Department withdrew its support for a Texas voting-rights suit that claimed the state's ID requirements amounted to racial discrimination.[24]

The massive forces newly ranged against Native people in 2017, including efforts to suppress their participation in the political process, were daunting. However, Semans, in his role as COLT's legislative affairs director, was determinedly optimistic. He credited the attention he got in discussions with senators and representatives to strides made in Native voting rights. "Our elected officials know that we now have more registered voters and more access to the ballot box," Semans said. "If a measure or policy will affect Indian country, they can bet we'll turn out." Native Americans are not just voting, though; they are also being elected to office. In July 2016, Shoshone-Bannock professor and pundit Mark Trahant wrote that seventy-three American Indians, Alaska Natives, and Native Hawaiians were serving in nineteen state legislatures, while two more American Indians held congressional seats.[25]

The nationwide attention to Native issues and the empowerment of Native people by the pipeline resistance at Standing Rock may have an impact at the ballot box in upcoming elections. The gathering there strengthened alliances and information sharing across hundreds of tribes and tribal organizations, many thousands of tribal members, and thousands more non-Native supporters. After the focus at Standing Rock shifted in late 2016 to the courtroom fight against the pipeline, indigenous people and their allies began turning up at disputes and actions in other parts of the country. In April 2017, when tribal members led the Climate March in Washington, DC, Judith LeBlanc called their prominence a "major movement moment."

LeBlanc is a member of the Caddo Nation of Oklahoma and director of the Native Organizers Alliance, which helps indigenous advocacy groups build their organizations. At the start of the march, LeBlanc stood outside the Capitol Building and watched tribal members assemble with signs reading "Honor the Treaties," "Keep It in ihe Ground," and "Mni Wiconi" (Lakota for "Water is Life"). She credited the Standing Rock resistance with improving public understanding of indigenous struggles, partly because the effort had been what she called the largest continuous protest in US history and also because the Sioux and their supporters communicated demands that encompassed far more than Standing Rock's local needs—protection of its Missouri River water supply, as well as its health, environment, and economy. The larger concerns included safe water for the millions of people downriver, environmental justice, action on climate change, and sensible energy policy for the nation and the planet.

If you are not convinced that this level of engagement will be enough to overcome the burgeoning challenges, Semans will probably remind you of the Battle of the Little Bighorn, when another Native coalition turned out. "And you know how that went," he told me.

FOR AMERICAN INDIANS, GAINING citizenship and suffrage in 1924 was the first small step toward meaningful ballot-box access, according to University of Utah political science professor Daniel McCool. "To achieve that, Indians would have to overcome a panoply of state laws, constitutional clauses, and court decisions that blocked the way," he writes in *Native Vote: American Indians, the Voting Rights Act, and the Right to Vote.*[26] Those restrictive measures were rooted in racial animosity and official policies that veered between massacring and "civilizing" Indians. Those in favor of the former were candid and unrepentant. L. Frank Baum, author of the children's classic *The Wonderful Wizard of Oz,* ran a South Dakota newspaper during the late 1800s. In an editorial, Baum called tribal members "a pack of whining curs who lick the hand that smites them." Five days after Sioux spiritual leader Sitting Bull was killed and just nine days before the massacre at Wounded Knee, Baum asked his readers, "Why not annihilation?"[27] McCool quotes a Nebraska newspaper that responded to Custer's massacre of a Cheyenne village by trumpeting: "Exterminate the whole fraternity of redskins."[28]

Those who declared themselves "Friends of the Indian" in the late nineteenth and early twentieth centuries hoped for a tidier form of annihilation: cultural erasure. They supported enfranchisement for Natives who embraced "civilization." Along these lines, some states offered the vote to Native people if they could demonstrate that they had renounced tribal ties or owned "white" clothes, furniture, and houses. After World War II, Native veterans accelerated the demand for equal rights. A Navajo veteran said, "We went to hell and back for what? For people back home in America to tell us we can't vote?"[29]

Passage of the Voting Rights Act of 1965 did not guarantee that Natives could cast a ballot. In South Dakota in 1977, then attorney general William Janklow called the act a "facial absurdity" and advised the state's top elections official to ignore it.[30] Native people did not vote in some parts of the state until the

1980s. When South Dakota polling places were finally opened to Native Americans, they faced official harassment. Before the 2002 general election, the state sent agents to Indian reservations to question newly registered voters and root out voter fraud; no one was ever charged.[31]

On June 25, 2013, the Supreme Court created a new barrier to equal rights for American Indians. On that day, which happened to be the 137th anniversary of Custer's defeat at Little Bighorn, the court struck down Section 4 of the Voting Rights Act, which had been used to protect minority enfranchisement. The court did so while claiming in *Shelby County v. Holder,* "our country has changed." The majority opinion did not mention Native voters and their current efforts to participate in strikingly unchanged civil-rights struggles.[32]

"The decision is a great loss for Native Americans," attorney Judith Dworkin told me the following day. Dworkin was coauthor of an *amicus* brief submitted on behalf of the Navajo Nation, O. J. Semans, and others, explaining why the court should uphold the law. "I went through the decision to see if there was any mention of Native people and found no references. It was very disappointing."

Until the *Shelby* decision, Section 4 of the Voting Rights Act had provided the formula for applying preclearance procedures, outlined in Section 5, to state and local governments with a history of discrimination. If preclearance was required, a jurisdiction had to go to the Department of Justice or the courts to obtain advance approval of new voting laws or practices. These places included Alaska and Arizona, which have large Native populations, and certain South Dakota counties that overlap reservations. The *Shelby* ruling eliminated preclearance until Congress came up with a new formula for it, which has not yet occurred. Immediately after the decision was handed down, states began devising new ways to limit enfranchisement, including gerrymandering and restrictions on allowable voter identification. "Native people have gone to the courts many times to sue for access that the Voting Rights Act and the Fourteenth Amendment, guaranteeing equal protection, say they should already have," said Greg Lembrich of Four Directions. In an instant, the *Shelby* decision made that work harder and more critical.

THE NEXUS OF DISTANCE AND POVERTY prevents tribal members from getting to white-majority towns and their court-house polling places, but so does fear. "They are today the poorest, most isolated and, in some quarters, the most racially castigated population in the country," sociologist Garth Massey, a University of Wyoming emeritus professor, wrote in an expert report for the *Wandering Medicine* lawsuit.[33] In 2000[34] and 2007,[35] the US Commission on Civil Rights held hearings that uncovered hate crimes, murders, and police shootings of Natives in states with sub-stantial Native minorities, such as Montana, South Dakota, and New Mexico. The commission has produced several reports on Native issues and the often desperate conditions on reservations. It heard from community members and experts about high lev-els of violence against indigenous people, along with a sense that there was a significant undercount of the attacks. Those who tes-tified said that Native people report little of the violence to police, because they mistrust law enforcement and because the incidents are so common the victims have come to consider them normal.

Racial animosity is easy to observe in the West. One Blackfeet official told me that a person could walk into most bars in the region and hear derogatory comments about Natives. However, it is not necessary to hang out in saloons to hear the vitriol. I have found that in areas near Indian homelands, all I have to do is say that I am traveling to or from a reservation to unleash a stream of venom. The hostility pervades the civic institutions of the West and, in turn, has an impact on voting rights. Bret Healy has observed that the seat of Rosebud County, Montana, where Northern Cheyennes must go if they wish to register or vote ahead of Election Day, is named for James William Forsyth, the Seventh Cavalry officer who directed the Wounded Knee massacre. The official who ran Rosebud County elections until a few years ago was married to a Custer descendant. In South Dakota, a county is named for Alfred Sully, another Union officer who went west to fight Indians after the Civil War.

This sense of antagonism fuels a variety of efforts to chill Native turnout. During the 2004 election, a federal court in South Dakota stopped Republican operatives from following tribal voters from the polling place and writing down their license plate numbers so that they might be "improperly dissuaded from voting," in the words of the judge hearing the case.[36] After the 2012 election, *Colorlines* news site reported what it called Bull Connor–style harassment of Tohono O'odham voters on their Arizona reservation—a reference to the Birmingham, Alabama, segregationist who encouraged violence against 1960s civil-rights advocates.[37] Also in 2012, on the Blackfeet Indian Reservation in Montana, Bret Healy confronted a Republican operative who was harassing tribal voters. The operative's aggressive questioning of the voters caused them to fear they would be thrown in jail for casting a ballot.

Greg Lembrich, also of Four Directions, was a twenty-four-year-old Columbia University law student when he first volunteered to poll-watch in South Dakota. When he arrived from the East Coast in time for the 2002 election, he had the impression he had landed in the Wild West. He heard allegations of cops tailing Native Americans to the polls and rumors of dragnets for tribal members. As a poll watcher, he confronted improper voter challenges and white ranchers making intimidating statements to Native people lined up to vote (as in, "I know where you work, I can get you fired").

Since then, for each federal election, Lembrich has organized dozens of attorneys and law students armed with voting-law manuals to poll-watch in reservation voting places throughout the state on Election Day. There is no lack of work to do. In 2014, during the period when South Dakotans vote early, Pine Ridge get-out-the-vote coordinator Donna Semans snapped a photograph of a white county sheriff slouched in the doorway of the reservation polling place. With his ten-gallon hat and drooping mustache, the lawman looked like he had been sent over from central casting. He also effectively intimidated tribal members, who became too frightened to cast a ballot.[38]

I met Greg Lembrich and Donna Semans at the tribe's casino. "Voters walking to the polling place would see the sheriff and veer off," Semans told us. "If I was driving them to the polls, they'd spot the sheriff's vehicle out front and tell me, 'No way. I'm not going in there.'" The moccasin telegraph began working overtime. "Word spread like a grass fire." When I talked to tribal members, they confided that they worried about why the sheriff was there and what charges he might bring if they dared enter the polling place. The number of Pine Ridge residents contacting Semans's get-out-the-vote operation for rides to the precinct dropped from more than one hundred a day into the teens. Lembrich began contacting and visiting federal, state, county, and tribal officials to talk about the sheriff's presence and the effect on voters.

I went to the polling place to interview the Fall River County election official who runs balloting for Pine Ridge. She told me she had asked the sheriff just to "pop by" periodically. She acknowledged that she had done this during past elections and that she'd heard the officer's presence scared off Native voters, but she said she did not understand why.[39] I also spoke to the sheriff, who seemed more embarrassed than enthusiastic about being told to show up at the polling site; he downplayed the need for a law-enforcement presence.[40]

Were tribal members' concerns far-fetched? Not at all, said O.J. Semans, who is Donna Semans's father. "For us, there's a lot of history behind the sight of a white man in a uniform. You'll also find that in states with large Native populations, the disparity between Native and non-Native incarceration rates is extreme, which means that we are commonly arrested and prosecuted unfairly. People have a lot of experience with being hauled in by law enforcement for no good reason. It's like the Old South, except it's happening in the twenty-first century. And on Pine Ridge, you can't ignore memories of the Wounded Knee massacre, which happened within miles of the polling place." The Justice Department got involved, telephoning the county official[41] and placing monitors in the polling place to guarantee that voters had proper access.[42] The sheriff went back to his usual patrols, and Pine Ridge turnout rebounded to previous levels.[43]

COUNTIES RUN ELECTIONS IN MOST of the United States, and the county officials who keep turning up in these tales of voter suppression are part of a thin white line that holds the fort against Native enfranchisement throughout the West. They help ensure that non-Natives keep setting the agenda. Explanations I have heard in several states for not providing equal access to the ballot box are many and varied and show a kind of bristling resentment at having to provide equal enfranchisement—the officials are too busy, setting up another polling place is too difficult and complicated, the trip might be dangerous, reservations are too far away, and, finally, the reservation voters who live all those miles from the county-seat polling place just have to try harder.[44] That means that county officials, though low on the nation's political food chain, can have an outsized impact on civil rights. "Keeping polling places in county seats and away from reservations is a simple and efficient way to disenfranchise us," O.J. Semans said.

When visiting the jurisdictions that are determined to suppress the Native vote, one struggles to see how they can afford the million-dollar, or even multimillion-dollar, lawsuits they must fight in order to accomplish this. Rural hamlets with empty main streets, tattered town greens, few businesses, and aging populations seem hardly likely to generate these impressive sums. As it turns out, in some cases they do not have to.

In South Dakota, the state taxpayer-funded insurance pool for governing bodies—towns, counties, and the like—has been the big spender in local crusades against Native voting. In the normal course of business, the South Dakota Public Assurance Alliance offers jurisdictions coverage for litigation concerning anything from a slip-and-fall case to allegations of hiring discrimination. The alliance also pays for the legal costs of defending against voting-rights lawsuits. In September 2015, the South Dakota blogosphere and conventional media were alight with commentary about the alliance's role in backing opponents of the Native vote.

The Sioux Falls *Argus Leader* published an investigation into the alliance's payments to Jackson County, South Dakota, to help it shoot down the voting-rights lawsuit, *Poor Bear v. The County, of Jackson*. The county overlaps the northeastern portion of the Pine Ridge Indian Reservation, where Oglala residents wanted the same number of days and hours of voting that off-reservation residents got at the county courthouse. The county refused, and tribal members, including Tom Poor Bear, then vice president of the Oglala Sioux Tribe, became plaintiffs in the lawsuit.[45] The insurance alliance was picking up the tab for the county's defense.

The *Argus Leader* story included a quote from an alliance official who called the Native lawsuit "frivolous" but "just one of those things you have to put up with." The story went on to show that when the reporter interviewing the official followed up by pointing out that federal money in the form of Help America Vote Act funding was available for the requested polling place, the official quickly pivoted. He told the reporter that this could mean the insurance alliance would pressure the county to settle. The article also noted that the judge presiding over *Poor Bear* had scolded the county for trying to have it both ways—claiming that it could not afford a full-service polling place for its part of Pine Ridge while at the same time admitting that it knew all along about the federal funding.[46]

The *Dakota Free Press* news site scoffed that Jackson County was "happy to stick taxpayers with the lawyer bill for defending their racism,"[47] while the *South DaCola* blog mocked the alliance for spending huge sums to help the county avoid paying out "already set aside federal dollars."[48] When I interviewed Jeff Barth, a commissioner from South Dakota's Minnehaha County, he compared the insurance alliance to an auto-insurance company that persists in covering a habitually drunk driver. "Why would we spend one or two million dollars to defend Jackson County against using federal funds?" Barth asked. "Clearly, Jackson County doesn't want Native Americans to vote."[49]

Some called the funding fracas a smoke screen for other important issues. "The Voting Rights Act doesn't allow a jurisdiction to grant voting rights to one group and deny or burden the voting rights of another group," said the nation's leading civil-rights attorney, Laughlin McDonald, longtime head of the Voting Rights Project at the American Civil Liberties Union (ACLU), author of *American Indians and the Fight for Equal Voting Rights*,[50] and a veteran of more than three decades of voting-rights litigation in Indian country. "People must be treated equally,"[51] he added. O.J. Semans described the defendants as "modern-day wannabe Indian fighters who would rather spend millions of taxpayer dollars fighting equality than one thousand dollars implementing it. They, like Custer, are on the wrong side of history."

THE NATIVE VOTING LANDSCAPE was looking more hospitable in several states by the time the 2016 election rolled around. In October, Paiutes won an eleventh-hour judgment expanding ballot-box access on two Nevada reservations, where tribal chairmen and members had sued to obtain it.[52] After just two days of Nevada's early-voting period, turnout on the Walker River Indian

Reservation nearly equaled that of the last presidential election, in 2012, according to the tribe's chairman, Bobby Sanchez.[53] On the Pyramid Lake Indian Reservation, the number of ballots cast in two days was already double the 2012 total, according to Vinton Hawley, Pyramid Lake's chairman. "It's been great," Hawley said. "We have a voice. We're involved."[54]

In another step forward in 2016, a North Dakota federal judge blocked a new state law that rejected the types of identification that Native voters usually carry.[55] These included tribal ID cards from reservations that lack numbered named streets, which is very common. The new law had banned cards without such data; it did allow tribal voters to obtain alternative IDs, but many live far from offices where they are available. On Standing Rock, some residents have a 120-mile round-trip to the nearest office that issues drivers' licenses. The election safety net of past years was also gone; North Dakota voters without acceptable ID no longer had such options as signing an affidavit attesting to their identity. The federal judge's order came in a ruling on a lawsuit brought by the Native American Rights Fund.[56]

By 2016, voting-rights lawsuits recently litigated in South Dakota and Montana had improved Native ballot-box access in several counties. The access was not entirely equal to that of off-reservation voters, but it did mean more days and longer hours than before the legal actions. Natives did not have to sue in Dewey County, South Dakota, which overlaps the Cheyenne River Sioux homeland. For several election cycles, the Dewey County election official has deputized tribal members to run polling places there. The unusual trust and cooperation prompted O. J. Semans to call the county the "gold standard" in equal rights.

Several Minnesota counties were similarly welcoming. When Bret Healy made polling-place requests on behalf of Minnesota tribes during the summer of 2014, he was surprised and pleased at the reaction. "The belief expressed at one county commission meeting was that every eligible voter should be able to vote. You could have knocked me over with a feather," Healy said. The Minnesota legislature had approved no-excuse absentee voting the year before, but long trips to the courthouses where it was offered kept the option out of reach for reservation residents. Since tribal members already go to their own capitals to do business and pick up mail—just as non-Natives may go to the county seat for the same reasons—putting offices in tribal capitals helped solve the equal-access problem.

In Alaska Native villages, voters have been using newly available early voting, language assistance, and ballots in their traditional languages since 2014. The Voting Rights Act requires translations for members of language minorities who are not proficient in English. However, it took two major federal lawsuits to ensure this assistance in Alaska—*Nick v. Bethel*, settled during 2009 and 2010, then a second trip to federal court, *Toyukak v. Treadwell*, in which the judge made an oral decision in 2014. A settlement for the case was negotiated in 2015.[57]

Alaska Native voters had long struggled with the English-language text of the state's ballot, according to James Tucker, one of the attorneys who argued *Toyukak*. When I interviewed lead plaintiff Mike Toyukak in his home in Manokotak, Alaska, he told me through an interpreter that Native voters had been upset by a badly translated referendum that resulted in them allowing alcohol to be sold in their villages when they intended to

During the 2014 national election, election workers helped voters get to the polls in To-giak, an Alaska Native village in the remote and pristine Bristol Bay region. (Stephanie Woodard)

ban it. Lists of candidates, the convoluted legalese of referenda, and detailed instructions for signing, folding, and other manipulations of the ballot that had to be done perfectly for the vote to count added more confusion for those whose first language was a traditional tribal one.

The state's half-hearted attempts to comply had been little help. Translators, whose credentials were apparently not verified, had made blunders. During the trial, the press continually reported the gaffes, which were reiterated in hours of embarrassing testimony and many pages of court documents.[58] A ballot measure about parental consent for minors' abortions had been mistranslated for Natives as requiring parental permission to become pregnant. "Absentee voting" was rendered as the equivalent of "voting for a long time." About one mistranslation, a state worker emailed, "What the heck, it's a similar word and hope that it goes right over their heads!☺" At times, the state's interpreters tossed in English words when they did not know the equivalent in a Native language, even though it was obvious that non-English-speaking voters would not understand them.[59] Tucker said that without correct translations and language assistance for those who wished it, casting a ballot was "a Hail Mary play" for Native voters.

After the judge's decision in favor of the tribal plaintiffs, the state of Alaska was thoroughly flummoxed by the loss and by its officials' experience in court. When Alaska Native leaders sat down with state officials and simply announced that they would bring early-voting capabilities to their villages, the officials acquiesced immediately. "It was the perfect political storm," recalled Nicole Borromeo, general counsel of the Alaska Federation of Natives, or AFN. "We said, 'We will sign up the locations,' and the state agreed. Eleven days later, we had added one hundred and twenty-eight locations."

In Alaska, the ability to cast a ballot ahead of Election Day can mean the difference between voting and disenfranchisement. In isolated Alaska Native settlements, subsistence hunting, fishing, and gathering activities are in full swing in the weeks leading up to the election, as people put up food for the long Arctic winter. During Election 2014, I saw voters casting ballots while still wearing their waders or hunting gear. In Manokotak, election official Arline Franklin described the demanding yearly round of fishing, berry picking, and bird hunting in spring, summer and fall, followed by seal, moose, and walrus hunting as winter sets in. "As we speak, my son is headed for the lake to fish and to see if there are any ducks left," Franklin said. "Our hunters go out several times a week, and the rest of the time we're processing what they bring in."

There are no other viable food sources in the distant villages. A tiny store in Manokotak stocks a few shelves' worth of supplies, including four-dollar cans of beans and twelve-dollar boxes of breakfast cereal that villagers cannot afford on a regular basis, or at all. This means that hunters who are on the trail of a catch that will feed their families for days or weeks cannot drop everything to go to the polls on Election Day, Franklin said. Yet Alaska Natives see political participation as a critical way to play a role in governmental decision-making and protect their traditional lands and lifeways. The opportunity to vote ahead of the day expands their options and, in the name of equality, gives Native voters the same access to the polls that the state's white-majority urban voters have.

During the 2014 election, Alaska Natives enjoyed their newly affirmed rights and participated with enthusiasm. Turnout soared. In some villages, virtually all eligible voters cast a ballot.[60] Voters in Togiak, Alaska, on the shore of Bristol Bay, started filing into the election office when it opened at 7 AM. At midday, the voice of village resident Rose Wassillie crackled over the local open-mic VHF radio: "Go Togiak! It's just noon, and one hundred and twenty out of five hundred have voted! Let's make those numbers climb!" Most voters were speakers of Yup'ik, the language most often heard around town, and wanted either a Yup'ik ballot or an interpreter, as federal law allows. The translated ballot was a big driver of turnout, according to Togiak city administrator Clara Martin. "In the past, I never felt my vote counted," Martin said after the polls closed. "It seemed that people who didn't know anything about our way of life were making decisions for us."

Togiak is distant from the centers of power and decision-making. I got there via a tiny aircraft that flew between, not over, the snow-covered shoulders of jagged mountains and above crystal-blue seas. When the pilot pointed out the safety gear in the back of the plane to the four passengers who barely fit, packed in shoulder to shoulder, I found it hard to believe that the gear would make any difference if the plane ditched in the frozen expanse. For Alaska Natives, enfranchisement bridges this huge geographical gap. "The new ballot tells us our vote means something. Someone out there is listening," Martin said.

Togiak celebrated the conclusion of the election with a feast created with ingredients from the surrounding Bristol Bay region. Residents lined up in the village hall and scooped onto their plates pungent stewed seal; domino-like rectangles of black whale meat and white whale blubber; beaver and moose meat in sweet-and-salty sauces; caviar-like herring roe on fronds of kelp; baked, dried, and jerked salmon; and several versions of *agutak*, a chilled dessert of tundra berries and fat. Thanks to tribal voters' active participation, they helped elect a Native lieutenant governor, raise Alaska's minimum wage, and create barriers to placing a copper, gold, and molybdenum mine in the watershed of the bay. "We live in exciting times," Martin said. Said Nicole Borromeo of AFN, "Our people have a hunger to vote. They go to huge lengths to do so and overcome barriers no one else in the country faces. Now, Native people feel included. This feels different."

The 2014 turnout pattern was similar in South Dakota, where the only places to see increases in participation that year were four counties that overlapped reservations. Native voters were credited with helping raise the state's minimum wage, renaming a county after its majority Oglala Lakota population, electing tribal mem-

Casting a ballot in Togiak, an Alaska Native village in the Bristol Bay region. In some villages, ballot translation and easier access to polling places meant nearly 100 percent of voters voted in 2014. (Stephanie Woodard)

bers to that county's commission, electing or reelecting Native representatives to the state legislature, and replacing the white sheriff who had been parked in the doorway of the Pine Ridge polling place. A Native candidate won the sheriff's badge with 80 percent of the vote.[61] "The voters made their voices heard," said South Dakota state senator Kevin Killer. These victories have profoundly affected American Indian voters' view of what is possible when they assert their rights as citizens, according to Killer. For him, having *Oglala Lakota County* on the nameplate on his desk in the legislature was a particularly meaningful, and indeed emotional, change.[62]

Native voting-rights advances of the last several years were aided mightily by the Obama administration's Justice Department, which undertook numerous efforts to support voting rights nationally. Starting in 2009, the department submitted *amicus* briefs and statements of interest supporting Native voting-rights lawsuits in South Dakota, North Dakota, Montana, Utah, Nevada, and Alaska. To prevent voter intimidation and other problems, Justice Department attorneys monitored elections in counties with significant Native populations. In an unusual move, the department also proposed legislation of its own to remedy Indian-country access issues. The measure, which was not enacted, would have placed at least one election office in each tribal community that requested it.[63]

Though the Obama administration was often supportive of Indian country, it would be a mistake to think that Democrats are necessarily the heroes of Native voting-rights sagas.

ON THE AFTERNOON OF MARCH 9, 2014, the Montana Democratic Party leadership was holed up in a small stone building in the state's capital, Helena. Inside were the state party chairperson, members of the party's executive board, and two Democratic National Committee members. Across the street was the state capitol, and on its lawn was the larger-than-life bronze statue of Montana's first territorial governor, Brigadier General (and Democrat) Thomas Meagher, astride a warhorse and brandishing a saber—forever in command.

For today's Democrats inside the building, the mood was decidedly less so. They were talking to Northern Cheyenne spiritual teacher Mark Wandering Medicine and representatives of additional Montana tribes and tribal groups, who were trying to persuade the Democratic leadership to throw its support behind the voting-rights lawsuit for which Wandering Medicine was lead plaintiff. The press was barred, so I was outside on the sidewalk, along with photographer Joseph Zummo, who was shooting my article for *Indian Country Media Network*, and a separate documentary film crew. No local or national mainstream newspapers had shown up.

"They said no," Michaelynn Hawk called out, as she ran down the building's front steps about an hour after the start of the meeting. A Crow tribal member, she is on the board of Indian People's Action, an advocacy group in Butte, Montana. As the sunny afternoon wore on, Democrats began exiting the building as though on a perp walk. They hurried down the front steps, chins tucked, grimacing. They refused to comment on their rejection of Wandering Medicine's request. Zummo caught party officials bolting out the back door. "Look, there goes another one!" exclaimed William "Snuffy" Main, Gros Ventre tribal member and former chairman of Fort Belknap Indian Community. Apparently, it was embarrassing—if not surprisingly impractical—for the Democratic Party to rebuff equal rights in the second decade of the twenty-first century, in an election year, for a large number of people of color who were almost entirely Democrats.

Just as Oglalas had already done on Pine Ridge, in *Wandering Medicine v. McCulloch* Montana Natives were suing for the ability to vote ahead of Election Day. They wanted satellite voting offices on their reservations during the state's monthlong in-person absentee-voting period. This would give reservation residents the same ballot-box access as those living in mainly white-inhabited county seats, where voters can register and cast ballots in the courthouse during that month. For some Montana tribal members, including Wandering Medicine, the journey from home to the courthouse was as many as two hundred miles round-trip.[64]

The lead defendant in the lawsuit was Montana's secretary of state and top elections official, Linda McCulloch, a Democrat. The other defendants were a mix of Democratic and Republican county officials. The Department of Justice joined the suit on the side of the Native plaintiffs and asked University of Wyoming geography professor Gerald Webster to quantify the barrier that distance creates for American Indian voters in Montana. Webster's study showed that residents of three of the state's reservations traveled two to three times farther than non-Natives to get to the polls in their county courthouses. They were also less likely to have a vehicle or sufficient gas money for the trip.[65]

At Fort Belknap, one of the reservations in Webster's study, tribal member and former councilman Ed "Buster" Moore told me that if he had to travel to the county courthouse to vote that very day, he could not afford it. He would have to save for a few weeks to make sure he had enough cash for the trip, while during the travel day, he would lose the income he earns making crafts and selling them locally and via the internet. Fort Belknap is part of a rural transportation system, but unpredictable connections meant that if Moore were to use it, instead of a private vehicle, he would have to carry enough money to cover a night in a motel, in case the trip took more than one day. "Without on-reservation access to early voting, Indians in big rural states like Montana have one day to vote, and everyone else has many days, with the exact number depending on the state," said Snuffy Main. Four Directions legal director Greg Lembrich called the extra costs Native voters bear to get to the ballot box a "backdoor poll tax."

The Montana Democrats did endorse an alternate resolution promising Native Americans early registration. An early draft of the party resolution provided to Wandering Medicine, as lead plaintiff, showed the word "equal" crossed out and "equitable" inked in above it. Later in the document, the word "equality" did appear, as in "continuing to fight for equality in voting access." This seemed to advocate a process that could result in equality, but fell short of supporting equality itself. O. J. Semans was furious. "I wasn't there back when the treaties were written, but now I see how it worked," he said. "Democratic party operatives and their lawyers know perfectly well what means what. They guaranteed us early registration—which we already have in Montana! They thought, 'Those dumb Indians will never figure it out.' They had the temerity to treat us the way they did two hundred years ago, twisting the English language and the law with intent to deceive us."

Bret Healy was admitted into the building along with the Native voting-rights advocates. He was not allowed to speak, but he could observe. "They couldn't even say the word 'equal' to an Indian," he said afterward. "Did they really think they could ignore federally recognized tribes, tribal leaders, tribal associations, Native spiritual leaders, *and* Native combat veterans? The meeting was a disaster for the party. It was like watching a wreck occurring in slow motion."

Later, when I asked a state party official for a comment on the meeting, he was indignant. He told me that questioning the Montana Democrats' commitment to Native voting was "presumptuous." He pointed to the party's promise to fight for equality.[66] When I called the Democratic National Committee, in Washington, DC, its spokesman backed the state operatives, saying that in theory the national party approved of the tribal request for satellite voting offices. However, the party official said, the DNC believed that "technical logistics" were the real problem. They prevented the counties from setting up the polling places. Patience was necessary.

"The heart of the question in Montana from the Democratic perspective is how do we get to where we all want to be," the DNC spokesman explained. "It has to do with technical questions, who has the authority to do it, and who will write the check." Still, the official stressed, American Indians are a "core Democratic constituency." He said he had consulted with the party's Native advisors just that week. He could not recall their names.[67]

"That's what's been going on throughout this lawsuit," Wandering Medicine said. "Double-talk and dragging out the process." As a matter of recognized constitutional law, "technical questions" don't override equal rights, Laughlin McDonald of the ACLU commented: "Administrative inconvenience cannot justify practices that burden the fundamental right to vote." When I checked with Snuffy Main in 2017, he said that polling sites were open for more days on his Montana reservation during the 2016 election than they were before the *Wandering Medicine* lawsuit, though unevenly, with more days offered in the northern portion, which was closest to the county seat, than farther south, where people have the greatest distance to overcome if they have to register or vote in person. No part of the reservation had the same number of days as, say, one of the state's white-majority cities.

Wandering Medicine said that Montana tribes have many concerns that require political participation, including energy development, jobs, rural transportation, education, and health care for veterans. About the Northern Cheyenne Tribe's interests, he added, "We're facing massive coal and methane development in the Powder River Basin. What will be the cultural, economic, and environmental impacts on us? Will our tribal members be able to get jobs there? We need to participate in the electoral process to be a part of the decision-making." Nevertheless, Wandering Medicine remained optimistic, describing the delay as "a stumbling block to progress, but only that."

Keeping voting inconvenient for Natives is a peculiar choice for the party of Bobby Kennedy, Lyndon Johnson, and Barack Obama. What would Martin Luther King do? I asked Healy. He responded, "About Native voting? He sure as hell wouldn't dither about technicalities. Read Dr. King's 'Letter from Birmingham Jail' on the subject of waiting for rights." In the 1963 letter, Dr. King decries the person "who paternalistically feels that he can set the timetable for another man's freedom." He writes that "wait" almost always means "never."

The Democratic obstructionism in Montana did not appear strategic. In a state of hard-fought elections and razor-thin victory margins, Native Americans make up 8 percent of the population and register and vote overwhelmingly Democratic. In 2012, the Obama-Biden ticket received more than 90 percent of the vote in seven reservation precincts. The state's Democratic senator, Jon

Tester, credited his win that year and in 2006 to the Native vote.[68] Those weren't the only times American Indians decided a national election. In South Dakota, Democrat Tim Johnson held on to his US Senate seat in 2002 by five-hundred-some ballots, which included 92 percent of Pine Ridge ballots, out of nearly three thousand cast there. In the 2002 Arizona governor's race, Navajo turnout helped Janet Napolitano eke out a victory. "Without the Native American vote, I wouldn't be standing here today," Napolitano told the 2004 Democratic National Convention. Other senators and former senators with decisive tribal backing have included Washington State's Maria Cantwell, Heidi Heitkamp of North Dakota, Al Franken of Minnesota, and Mark Begich of Alaska, all Democrats.[69]

Democrats cannot take Native voters for granted, though, Professor Daniel McCool said. He described tribal members as acutely aware, issue-specific voters who have supported Republicans as well. These have included Arizona's Senator John McCain and Alaska's Senator Lisa Murkowski, who beat back a 2010 Tea Party challenge with a long-shot write-in campaign that benefited from Native support.

Blackfeet tribal member Tom Rodgers, the founder of Carlyle Consulting and the whistleblower in the Jack Abramoff scandal, suggested that the Montana Democratic Party's 2014 shenanigans were part of a balancing act. Rodgers speculated that the party wanted some Native votes to help push national candidates over the top but worried that having too many tribal members lining up at the polls would rile constituents in areas near reservations, thus alienating the Democratic base. If Native voting turnout were to increase substantially, the balance of power would shift in rural areas, Rodgers said. Tribal voices would be heard when decisions were made.

A Northern Cheyenne tribal member who served for a time on his local county commission agreed. Danny Sioux pointed out that you cannot vote without registering and that putting election offices on reservations would embolden tribal members to take that essential first step. "We could explain voters' rights," said Sioux. "On the Northern Cheyenne Reservation alone, our current four hundred active registered voters could become three thousand and impact elections all the way up to the federal level."

That would mean a sea change in Native participation and inevitably well-being, said Glacier County commissioner Michael DesRosier. "More people would have to deal with us when we want to talk about our issues. Otherwise, all they recognize is our 'plight.'"

WE AMERICANS LIKE TO THINK OUR COUNTRY was founded on democratic concepts. Not so, said Laughlin McDonald in an interview for my article marking his thirtieth year of fighting on behalf of Native voting-rights. "It was actually founded on principles of aristocracy, with voting originally restricted to white male property owners over age twenty-one." Though the franchise was eventually extended to African Americans, American Indians, and women, he said, states have continued to pass new suppression measures. "Those in control have shown great willingness to adopt a whole range of discriminatory measures so they can stay in charge, ranging from literacy tests and poll taxes to whites-only primaries and outright intimidation. We at the ACLU Voting

Rights Project see increased participation by minority voters on the one hand and efforts to stymie it on the other. It's an ongoing process, with progress despite setbacks."

According to McDonald, some of the hurdles Natives face can be ascribed to the sense of apartness, of separation from the mainstream, that we see in other ways in other chapters. This results in a knowledge gap, local and national. "Indian country is a blank for most non-Native people, whether they live far from a reservation or right next door. Many have little knowledge of the concept of sovereignty, or even that Indians are US citizens," McDonald said. He described a case he argued in Fremont County, Wyoming.[70] "I took a deposition from a county commissioner who had driven through the Wind River Reservation but had never stopped, never visited, never gotten to know tribal members. She was embarrassed to realize she knew nothing about many people in her district, and she wasn't the only county official in this position."

Wandering Medicine compared the Native fight for voting rights to his people's flight from prison in Nebraska in January 1879. In a four-hundred-mile trek that Northern Cheyenne youngsters retrace in a spiritual run each winter, the tribe faced bitter cold, starvation, and death in order to return home to Montana. "Back then, thanks to the wishes of a greater force, our ancestors succeeded against great odds in preserving our way of life. Securing our voting rights will also be good for us." And it will be good for America, Wandering Medicine said. "Survival depends on sharing."

Snuffy Main, of Fort Belknap, said that attaining equal rights will empower Natives to define their own needs and find their own solutions. Inclusion in the political process will allow them to pursue self-determination. It will also bring their ideas and energy to the nation. "There will be more Native elected officials and a greater involvement for us in our traditional lands, which, taken all together for the US tribes, encompass the United States of America. We volunteer for the armed forces in a greater percentage than other groups,[71] which means many of us are veterans. We have fought for this country, and we want to be part of taking better care of it."

3.

Gods and Monsters

ARLY ON THE MORNING OF MARCH 28, 2014, an email
with the subject line "URGENT" snapped around the
Bureau of Land Management.[1] The BLM is the powerful
subdivision of the US Department of the Interior that administers
more acreage than any other federal agency. It controls one-tenth
of the surface land of the United States, along with the mineral
rights underlying one-fourth of the nation. These tracts include
approximately 80 percent of Nevada,[2] where an international mining company needed to reassure investors about the expansion of
a gold mine there.

Approval of the expansion, called a record of decision,
was complicated by the fact that the mine sat in the middle of
Tosawihi, a cultural landscape in northern Nevada that is covered
in ancient sacred sites and revered by the Western Shoshone and
other tribes. Federal historic preservation and environmental laws
require reviews of such projects and consultation with the affected
tribes, even when the threatened lands—like these—are not on
a reservation.[3] A similar situation made headlines in September

Joseph Holley, an official of the Battle Mountain Band of the Te-Moak Tribe of Western Shoshone Indians, points out an abandoned mining structure, one of many marring an ancient multi-tribal cultural landscape in the northern Nevada desert. (Joseph Zummo)

2016, when private security contractors used dogs to attack demonstrators at Standing Rock; the tribal members and others had gathered at a pipeline-construction site because they had heard about the recent destruction of such an area, which included burial sites, ancient stone cairns, and prayer places.[4]

Tribes view protection of sacred sites as critical to identity and survival. For Native people, the health of the natural world is interwoven with their own well-being. Their spiritualities are anchored not in written texts, as they are for Christianity and other large, portable religions, but rather in the land—localized in features like mountains, springs, and rivers, in processes like pilgrimages along primordial routes, and in ancestral burial sites that define a place as home for descendants. Indigenous people are who they are because of the places they treasure and care for.[5]

The Nevada tribe that was front and center in March 2014 was the Battle Mountain Band of the Te-Moak Tribe of Western

Shoshone Indians. The group has about five hundred members, about half of whom live on a small reservation outside Battle Mountain, Nevada.[6] Generations have struggled to hold their own on the land and in court with the Bureau of Land Management and a succession of multinational mining companies. The BLM is yet another federal agency that has been described as managing public lands to accommodate corporate interests,[7] something agency spokesperson Greg Deimel denied when contacted. He said that view was the result of "bias that is untrue and runs contrary to the values of Bureau of Land Management employees [who manage] public lands for the benefit of current and future generations, supporting conservation as we pursue our multiple-use mission."[8] Though issuing permits for corporate activity is an important function of the agency, many Americans have probably heard of it because of its helicopter roundups of wild horses in the West, widely condemned as inhumane but defended by the Department of the Interior's Office of the Inspector General, which said the agency was "doing its best to perform a very difficult job."[9]

When I first began talking to the Battle Mountain Band's then chairman, Joseph Holley, in late 2015, he was already a veteran in the fight to protect Tosawihi. He was brought up in it and learned by watching and listening to his parents, aunts, uncles, and grandparents. Nowadays, his children and grandchildren watch and listen to him. It is a costly fight that requires hiring high-powered lawyers to repeatedly confront formidable outside interests. At the time, Holley had an idea that recalls the interplay of sovereignty and increasing economic clout that Winnebago Tribe of Nebraska attorney Lance Morgan describes in the preceding chapter. Taking advantage of the Battle Mountain Band's status as a sovereign nation, Holley (like many other tribal leaders across the country before him) was working to develop a casino on the tiny reservation. It would bring in far more income than the tribe's small smoke shop, which sits along a nearby highway, selling tobacco products and T-shirts and producing barely enough to pay the costs of defending the sacred landscape.

For tribes, safeguarding the sacred does not just drain scarce tribal resources. It can also be a painful process involving disclosure of closely held information to agencies and corporations that may not treat it with respect. The incident involving attack dogs at Standing Rock occurred shortly after the tribe filed information with a federal court on sites in the path of the pipeline so that they could be protected. Tribal members were not the only ones who were outraged when they were bulldozed instead. More than 1,200 museum directors and scholars condemned the action in a letter to President Obama and the federal agencies overseeing the project.[10]

In Nevada, after the BLM official emailed colleagues with the "urgent" request for a decision on the gold mine, an agency geologist replied on the email thread, "I do not believe we have completely satisfied Tribe concerns." Other agency staffers dismissed this objection. One reported that she had received a call from the international mining firm's legal counsel: "They are requesting that the ROD and approval be signed or dated no later than March 31. March 31 is the end (last day) of the first quarter for their financial auditing and reporting that they have to provide to their investors."[11] By the end of March, in what may be a record-setting sprint for a federal agency, the record of decision was signed, sealed, delivered.[12] The mining company announced a "significant permitting milestone" for the project.[13] A BLM spokesperson later told me the process was "robust" and "not hurried," with full consideration for tribal concerns under the law.[14]

Many Western Shoshones consider Tosawihi the spiritual heart of their traditional homeland. It encompasses scores of square miles, where they have camped, hunted, gathered, and participated in ceremonies for millennia. Northern Paiutes and members of other tribes revere and use the area as well. Tosawihi (pronounced *dos*-a-wee and also referred to as Tosawihi Quarries or Tosawihi Complex) is named for a Western Shoshone band whose name translates as White Knives. The group was famed, and feared, for carrying razor-sharp blades made from the area's white flint.[15]

The landscape is within the Great Basin, so called because all of its precipitation stays there, as though contained in a giant vessel. Rather than running off into the Pacific Ocean or Gulf of Mexico, snowmelt and rain flow into the Great Basin's lakes and rivers and soak into its aquifers. The boundaries of this area encompass most of Nevada and portions of adjoining states. It includes rugged pinyon- and juniper-dominated mountains running north to south, as well as brush-covered high and low desert. The temperature range is as daunting as the setting: from higher than one hundred degrees Fahrenheit in the summer to well below zero in winter.

For Western Shoshones and others, one of Tosawihi's most important resources is the white flint, or chert, found throughout it. A type of rock that breaks to form extremely sharp edges—even finer than those on steel scalpels—it can be made into arrowheads, knives, scrapers, and other edged items. Western Shoshones also utilize it in ceremonies, with their traditional healers relying on it for its healing properties. "That stone is sacred to us," said Holley, who is now a Battle Mountain Band council member. "We use it every day and have done so for millennia, for tools, ceremonies, and healing. The stone, the water, the entire place is sacred."

Ongoing usage by tribal members leaves traces on the land. When Holley showed me around Tosawihi, I saw that it was covered with artifacts, scatters of stone flakes left from toolmaking, shelters, and ceremonial places. It was clear that Tosawihi has long been a very busy place. At first glance, it may have appeared to be a vast and sere and empty place—a desert. A closer look revealed how lively it had always been. Archaeologists have dated the beginning of the human occupation here to something like fourteen thousand years ago,[16] or nearly eleven thousand years before the founding of Rome.

Reggie Sope, a medicine man from the Shoshone-Paiute Tribes, saw far earlier connections. "Interesting you should ask," he said, responding to a question about when his people began riding horses. According to Sope, their first mount was not the Spanish mustang that some other tribes acquired starting in about the sixteenth century but a multi-toed equine that lived in the area until about ten thousand years ago. "First they were little, and we hunted and ate them. As they evolved into animals the size of a dog, we used them to pull travois [joined poles forming a sled used for transport]." Later, they were big enough to ride. "And we were lords of the plains," said Sope, miming the gesture of drawing a bow.

Traditional lifeways were meticulously sustainable. The site of an old winter camp can be seen by tree-sheltered warm springs

In preparation for a ceremony in the Nevada desert, Joseph Holley (right) of the Western Shoshone's Battle Mountain Band, and medicine man Reggie Sope, of the Shoshone-Paiute Tribes, cover a sweat lodge frame with tarps. (Joseph Zummo)

and near rock walls that radiate the sun's heat. "We cultivated the riches of the land by taking a little here and a little there—hunting and gathering roots, seeds, and medicinal plants," Sope said. When the rabbitbrush turned yellow in the fall, that was Nature's signal that it was time for a trek to the mountains to pick pine nuts, a dietary staple that would be roasted and stored for later use. Sope gestured toward nearby sagebrush bushes. "A home or sweat lodge could be made with hides thrown over a few of them. Nothing was overused, nothing went to waste."

Western Shoshones may have occupied Tosawihi for a long time, but that does not make the place "prehistoric," according to Ted Howard, chairman and former cultural resources director of the Shoshone-Paiute Tribes, whose reservation falls in northern Nevada and southern Idaho. Today's tribes are living cultures, he said. "We visit these places and practice our traditions. Our so-called ancient and prehistoric sites are actually contemporary."

The fight to protect Tosawihi is as current as the place. Gold lies underneath the chert, and mining companies want it. Decades of mining have left multi-acre scars on the land. Tribal members say that if the BLM followed federal law, including historic preservation and environmental regulations, damage by the mines could be minimized. In a court filing, the BLM called Western Shoshone accusations of unfettered mining-related destruction not a valid legal argument but simply the product of a "differing world view." [17]

The disagreement revolves around two relationships to the land that have clashed from the first arrival of Europeans. The indigenous people they encountered interacted with the land as they would with a relative; it was a repository of ancestral burials, sacred places, and benevolent spirits. It was cherished and cared for. The newcomers saw it as an opportunity, either because it could produce commodities for sale or because it was itself a commodity, to be bought and sold at a profit. For them, caring for property could be conceived of in monetary terms, rather than cultural ones; decisions about an improvement could be made based whether it increased the market value of the goods produced or of the land itself.[18]

As tribes and tribal members lost land through abrogation of the treaties and other schemes to separate them from their property, their sacred places increasingly fell outside reservations. One of the best-known examples is the federal government's seizure and parceling out of the Black Hills, in South Dakota, which are Sioux treaty land that is considered holy ground by several northern plains

STEPHANIE WOODARD · *115*

tribes.[19] Biker bars and adult entertainment haunts have sprung up in the area. People at prayer can hear pounding music and the roar of motorcycle rallies.[20] After the Supreme Court declared the Black Hills seizure unconstitutional in 1980, the federal government tried to pay the Sioux tribes for the land. Despite being some of the poorest people in the country, they have refused to accept the money, which sits in an interest-bearing account and has grown to more than $1 billion. The sacred is never for sale, they say.[21]

For the Western Shoshone, the expanse they claim was wrongfully taken is massive. In 1863, their tribal heads and United States representatives signed the Treaty of Ruby Valley, which declared friendship between the parties; the tribes also reserved a homeland that encompassed most of Nevada and chunks of Idaho, Oregon, California, and Utah. The federal government seemed to ignore the agreement for decades, though there were distractions—Lincoln needed more Electoral College votes to win his next election so Nevada was rushed into statehood, the Civil War broke out, Lincoln was assassinated, and gold rushes meant struggles to protect settlers invading various Native homelands. After the United States woke up to the gigantic gap in the national map, it tried unsuccessfully for decades to pay off the Western Shoshone tribes; in a last-ditch effort in the early 2000s, Congress voted to make payments to those who were at least one-quarter Western Shoshone, though not necessarily tribal members. According to traditional Western Shoshone chief Raymond Yowell, some refused to accept the money.[22] Some did not find out in time that they were eligible. Tosawihi and other sites revered by the Western Shoshone and additional area tribes are on these disputed, now-federally managed, tracts.

Federal laws presumably protect sites on federally managed land, but agencies vary—one to another and even state to state within one agency—in the degree of zeal with which they apply the rules.[23] There are also fundamental disagreements about how the places should be understood. For tribal members, places like Tosawihi or the Black Hills are traditional cultural landscapes. The term is recognized in national historic preservation law and signifies a place that has been subtly shaped by the activities of a heritage lifeway, with its hunting, gathering, food preparation, medicine-plant cultivation, and ceremonies. The importance of such an area is determined by oral histories and other knowledge of traditional tribal experts, as well as by physical evidence. These proofs can make a site eligible for inclusion on the National Register of Historic Places. This does not protect the place in perpetuity, but it does make destroying it more cumbersome.[24]

Locations like Tosawihi can also be viewed in a more limited way as archaeological places, defined by the objects, such as arrowheads or pottery sherds, that archaeologists find there. Howard accuses the Nevada BLM in particular of cherry-picking federal law and thereby confining its reviews to the narrowest of archaeological conclusions, while ignoring the context provided by cultural evidence. Howard notes that Section 106 of the National Historic Preservation Act, a National Park Service program under which agencies typically commission studies to evaluate the importance of a place, relies on archaeology to determine eligibility for the National Register of Historic Places.[25]

Tosawihi provides excellent examples of this conceptual mismatch. There, BLM-commissioned archaeologists have done studies and identified "loci" that have more than a certain number of artifacts, such as stone tools, per square meter. This density made the spots eligible for preservation, according to BLM archaeological standards. The agency has marked these loci on maps, drawn lines around them, and told miners to stay a certain number of meters away.[26] The by-the-numbers approach to preservation pushes aside tribal expertise and places, such as vision sites, that are not defined by objects, according to Howard. He said that the BLM overlooks other portions of the National Historic Preservation Act that do protect such places, as well as presidential executive orders[27] and the Native American Graves Protection and Repatriation Act, which safeguards items of cultural patrimony as well as burials and grave goods.[28]

The dispute has raged for decades. A 1993 National Park Service publication, *Traditional Cultural Properties: What You Do and How We Think*, noted that the protection of subtle but nevertheless important cultural properties was included in the original National Historic Preservation Act, passed in 1966, as well as in its 1992 amendments. The 1992 provisions also established tribal preservation offices. One author in the 1993 publication declared that there is no substitute for talking to the people who value a place and learning how they understand it.[29]

According to Paul Loether, chief of the National Register of Historic Places, most preservationists today recognize the concept of the traditional cultural landscape; however, he said, it is still harder for some to comprehend fully than a conventional building or other structure.[30] In Nevada, the register of historic places includes twentieth-century hotels and a 1937 railroad underpass that was deemed historic for improving Las Vegas traffic flow—but not the whole of Tosawihi.[31] Loether, like Howard, believes that archaeological studies, with their emphasis on physical evidence, have their limits in evaluating places that are important to indigenous people. "The result [can be] like seeing the Mona Lisa's smile, but not the rest of the painting," Loether said. "You can't understand its beauty and meaning without considering the entire thing." In Howard's view, archaeologists' dependence on material evidence makes them uniquely unqualified to assess complicated traditional-spiritual Native landscapes.

JOSEPH HOLLEY AND HIS GRANDSON sat companionably side by side in canvas camp chairs. We were in a small Tosawihi valley hugged by rolling hills. A carpet of golden grasses, gray-green sagebrush, and splashes of bright yellow rabbitbrush stretched to craggy mountains on the horizon. In their left palms, Holley and his grandson each held a piece of rough black stone resting on a small leather pad, and in their right hands, a length of deer antler. More tribal members had set up camp nearby, and they were chatting, cooking, and watching the pair work. A jackrabbit hopped by. Heads turned. "Breakfast," someone said. Mule deer dashed into the distance.

Granddad was teaching seven-year-old Julius Jr. flintknapping, which refers to chipping stone in order to fashion it into useful forms. Since prehistoric times, knappers worldwide have turned out arrowheads and spearheads (also called points), blades, hide scrapers, drills, and other items. By participating in his people's stoneworking tradition, Julius was learning lessons that were cultural as well as practical. Because he was a beginner, the pair was working with obsidian, a shiny black stone that is more brittle and easier to work than the chert that is so plentiful in this landscape. Chert's extreme hardness made it their ancestors' favorite material, but that also means it is better handled by experienced makers. And because obsidian is not available in Tosawihi, the flakes they left behind would not be mistaken for ancient workings.

After using fist-sized hammerstones to rough out chunks of obsidian, grandfather and grandson used the deer antler pieces to shape them further. After Holley finished his arrowhead, he made a tiny fishhook and one more arrowhead, which snapped. "As a child, when I sat flintknapping with my dad, he would counsel patience," he recalled. "As you work a piece of stone, you learn its characteristics, its hard places and weak places. You treat it with respect, and prayer goes into every stroke." The attention to detail means an experienced flintknapper can find an old arrowhead and

Joseph Holley gives his grandson Julius a lesson in flintknapping, which refers to shaping stone into useful items such as arrowheads, fishhooks, and sewing and cooking tools. (Joseph Zummo)

read the intentions of the ancestral maker. "I can see what the person, who may have been male or female, was thinking by the way the stone is fractured, the choices made, the final form, the desire for perfection," Holley said. Creating points was traditionally altruistic and community-oriented as well as meditative, according to Holley's late father, Glen, a celebrated Western Shoshone activist. "My dad told me a point might save your life, feed you, or clothe you. Or you might store it away in a cache somewhere in the landscape to save for another time. If someone else happened to find it first, it saved his life or fed and clothed his family."

The place where you learn is as important as what you learn, said Holley. It's all about context. That day, Julius was sitting in a camp in his people's sacred landscape, surrounded by his relatives. Everything around him and his grandfather informed their work as they shaped the rock—the jests, the stories, the aroma of cooking meat, the plants, the animals, the nearby sweat lodge, the easygoing lesson, and the tactile interaction with the stone. "When Western Shoshone children flintknap here at Tosawihi, they might see an old dwelling off to one side, a stream where ceremonies took place, and flakes chipped off by ancestors when they worked stone," Holley said. "The children can then look at our modern camp and see that it reflects the old one, with places to sleep, cook, gather, work, and pray. They understand that they are part of the entire story."

The next day, Holley took Julius and another grandson, four-year-old Wanbli, for a walk around Tosawihi. Holley is a big man, tall and broad-shouldered, and the kids mostly stuck close to him, like little sprouts in the shade of a giant oak. They occasionally scampered away to climb hills, scramble down steep-walled ravines, and play in ancient rock shelters formed under arched stone outcroppings. They found arrowheads and scatters of flakes—missives from a past that was very much a part of their present. Items seen around Tosawihi also include domestic implements: grinding stones for the nuts and seeds that dominated the people's diet, bowls, axes, awls, sharpeners, hide scrapers, personal ornaments, and sewing tools such as thread gauges, with graded holes for measuring the diameter of willow bark strips and other basketmaking material.[32]

Where they are found tells a story. Broken arrowheads around a spring or along an animal trail show that ancient hunters waited in those places for their prey.[33] A spray of flakes shows that someone sat here to craft a stone item. Holley told us that when archaeologists remove items, they divorce them from the cultural context and degrade the wider meaning of the landscape. He recounted watching archaeologists spot a finished arrowhead and exclaim, "This is a major find!" Not so, Holley said. "Many activities occurred here, all aspects of which are significant." Standing on a rise overlooking a magnificent expanse of Tosawihi sweeping up to a vision-quest site across the valley, he indicated a scatter of flakes. "An ancestor sat right here and worked stone. That tells us a great deal."

"Look, just like mine!" Julius exclaimed. He held up a small partially finished white chert arrowhead made by an unknown ancestor. The piece, with its tapered shape, finely chipped edges, and surface grooves, was nearly identical to the black obsidian point Julius had worked on earlier with his grandfather—a profound and effortless connection across time. The piece of worked stone sat at the intersection of land and culture, with a child essential to the ongoing well-being of both. After finding the arrowhead, Julius placed it back where he found it. Without being told, both children left behind items that caught their eye, ensuring that future generations will know that they, too, are part of the story. When it comes time for these two youngsters to be part of efforts to save their sacred sites, the knowledge they have acquired in the places will be part of them—not theoretical, not learned in bits and pieces in a classroom, but "entire."

Tosawihi had another lesson to offer that day. A faint trail was etched into the land where centuries ago an ancestral doctor walked, singing and gathering medicinal herbs. As we walked around the site, Joseph Holley traced the doctor's steps and showed us where he practiced. As the healer passed by, people heard his song. Those who needed cures followed him to a grassy meadow where he held bleeding ceremonies or to a small pool created by setting rocks in a stream threading its way through a rocky ravine. Here, the doctor bathed them. Holley pointed out rock shelters with small, flat terraces that faced the treatment areas, like ancient waiting rooms.

The healer's trail was intact there, but a large portion of it was bulldozed during the summer of 2016. That June, a federal court refused to stay the above-mentioned mining company's construction of a power line until a way could be found to save the trail, which had been determined eligible for the National Register of Historic Places.[34] The Battle Mountain Band appealed the ruling, but mining company employees immediately fired up their bulldozers—even with the issue still being before the courts, which should have kept construction activities on hold, according to Rollie Wilson, the attorney handling the matter for the band.[35]

Within days, the miners had bulldozed a twelve-mile road, along with fifty-foot-wide gashes for the bases of utility poles. They gouged a trench into the side of the hill used for vision quests and obliterated much of the ancestral doctor's trail, along with the natural pharmacy he cultivated alongside it.

By the time an appeals court got around to considering the band's request for an injunction, it called the request "moot" because the power line was already built, according to Rollie Wilson. Tanya Reynolds, an official of the South Fork Band of the Te-Moak Western Shoshone, called the destruction "beyond words, beyond what is possible to fix."[36] The BLM continued to defend the permit it issued for the work, with spokesperson Greg Deimel claiming in 2017, "It was permitted in a sound manner."[37]

Demolition of irreplaceable ancient artifacts usually merits outrage, or at least notice. The Islamic State, or ISIS, was widely condemned in June 2016 when photographs and video footage showed the group's yellow bulldozer demolishing the Gates of Nineveh, in the remains of an ancient city in Iraq.[38] Major media outlets had reported shock worldwide when ISIS thugs smashed museum exhibits and destroyed other precious places and artifacts in the preceding months, as well as when the Taliban blew up the Buddhas of Bamiyan, in Afghanistan, in 2001.[39] In contrast, portions of Tosawihi have vanished in a national, and international, blind spot. "We don't understand their need to destroy," Holley said. "We are realistic. We know we can't stop them entirely, but we want them to partner with us. They need to listen when we flag endangered cultural resources. They need to follow their own laws."

Though the second half of the twentieth century saw passage of federal historic preservation and environmental laws, an older law continues to undercut modern efforts to protect the nation's resources. In 1872, Congress passed the General Mining Law in order to lure settlers west. The measure offered mining patents for a few dollars per acre, with no royalties due to the federal government (unlike in other extractive industries) and no cleanup required.[40] According to the BLM, the law "declared all valuable mineral deposits in land belonging to the United States to be free and open to exploration and purchase."[41] The law poured billions of dollars' worth of public resources into private hands, including foreign companies in addition to American ones. With no environmental controls, miners typically walked away when claims were worked out, abandoning hundreds of thousands of mines across the country. The BLM reports that unwary tourists have died after falling into deserted mine shafts or breathing toxic gases, while explosives left behind hinder rescuers.[42]

The devastation is immense and continuing. The Environmental Protection Agency's 2011 Toxics Release Inventory shows that mining accounted for 98 percent of the 529 million pounds of toxins released in Nevada that year. Long after the digging stops, cyanide, arsenic, and other mining-related poisons continue to wash into rivers, soak into the aquifers, and evaporate into the atmosphere, with taxpayers picking up the tab for remediation. The American taxpayer will pay as much as $72 billion to clean up the old mines across the nation.[43] Cleaning up today's operations will cost additional billions.[44]

STEPHANIE WOODARD · *125*

MINING IS NOT THE ONLY ACTIVITY that has plowed a destructive path through Tosawihi and other sacred places around Indian country. Archaeology, the discipline that federal agencies typically use to evaluate sites for protection, has demolished beloved sites as well. A photograph that Ted Howard took at the Nevada State Museum's Indian Hills Curatorial Center shows shelves of boxes labeled "Tosawihi." The cartons—342 of them, according to the museum's curator of anthropology[45]—contain objects collected by archaeologists under Nevada Bureau of Land Management auspices to satisfy preservation law as the gold mine was beginning operations in Tosawihi. The collection includes as many as 1.5 million items. These are mostly flakes (chips produced while working stone) and soil samples, along with a stunning list of archaic treasures—a fluted Clovis-era point that is more than twelve thousand years old, large stemmed spear points, additional finished and partially finished stone points and tools, elk antler tools, and buffalo scapula digging implements.[46]

Battle Mountain Band elder Colleen Burton cried when she saw the photograph. "It's sickening," she said. "I have been to meetings with federal agencies for years, and no one said they took those items. Why has no one ever come forward?" Joseph Holley's mother, Kathleen, was hurt and angry as well. "How dare they keep those materials!" she exclaimed. "They belong to us, and they should not be kept in a building." An archaeologist who gathered the collection defended it, saying its contents came from areas that were to be utterly wiped out by the planned mine; in the end, though, some of the places were not destroyed.[47]

The 342-box collection is a fraction of what has been removed from the Tosawihi environs. A pipeline project supervised by the

Federal Energy Regulatory Commission resulted in nearly seven hundred thousand items being taken during 2010 and 2011. These materials include a preponderance of flakes and soil samples, along with two-thousand-plus points, more than eight thousand implements including hundreds of articles such as drills, mortars, and pestles, and a massive stone bowl.[48] These items were also deposited in the state museum.[49] Innumerable additional studies commissioned by the BLM, the Forest Service, and other agencies have scooped up unimaginable numbers of indigenous objects in Nevada and beyond. Oglala attorney Brett Lee Shelton called museums yet another extractive industry preying on indigenous people.[50]

The practice of collecting Native possessions in the name of research, cultural tourism, and morbid curiosity has a long and sordid history. During the 1620s, the newly arrived Pilgrims found graves while reconnoitering their environs. The first time the colonists found a burial site, they decided to leave it alone, as it would be "odious unto them to ransack their sepulchers." However, they could not resist the second grave. "We brought sundry of the prettiest things away with us, and covered the corpse up again."[51] Thomas Jefferson is known to have dug into Indian mounds in the 1770s to learn about tribal burial customs; this makes him the father of American archaeology[52] or a grave robber,[53] depending on your perspective.

In the late 1800s and early 1900s, the economic and demographic collapse of tribes that had been newly confined to reservations created opportunities for collectors with cash. New York City investment banker Gustav Heye scoured Native villages countrywide. The approximately one million items Heye acquired in his travels became the foundation of the National Museum of the American Indian's collection.[54] Harvard's Peabody Museum of Archaeology and Ethnology is another repository of Native history. It boasts that it is the "steward" of 1.2 million objects, five-hundred thousand photographic images, and many archival records, mostly from the Americas and Pacific Islands.[55]

Over the centuries, an untold number of sites have been looted, vandalized, and purposefully or mistakenly destroyed across the country.[56] Important pieces of Native patrimony have been sold worldwide to institutions and individuals. Auction houses in Paris made headlines in recent years when they put on the block treasured Hopi religious statuary known as kachinas. During the 1990s, Marcella LeBeau, of the Cheyenne River Sioux Tribe, traveled to Glasgow, Scotland, to ask for the return of a Ghost Dance shirt that was taken from the massacre at Wounded Knee in 1890. Such shirts were thought to protect the wearer from harm; dancers wore them while doing a spiritual dance form that swept the West during a very difficult time for the tribes. Representatives of the Glasgow museum that had ended up with the shirt made the journey to South Dakota to return it, according to LeBeau.[57]

In 1990, Congress passed the Native American Graves Protection and Repatriation Act, which requires federal agencies and US museums receiving federal funds to return to tribes related human remains, funerary objects, and items of cultural patrimony. Many agencies and institutions subsequently complied, if reluctantly in some cases. A twenty-year court battle and DNA analysis were required to return to Northwest tribes a nine-thousand-year-old skeleton that was variously called Kennewick Man or the Ancient One.[58] Speaking in Tosawihi, the epicenter of his plundered universe, Joseph Holley said that curators, archae-ologists, and others have a sense of cultural superiority that leads them to believe they are entitled to take what they want and define other peoples' cultures for their own purposes. "What about our context and the importance of our children seeing their patrimony in place?" he asked.

The American Indian Religious Freedom Act, and other government declarations, support Holley's assertion. Signed by President Jimmy Carter in 1978, AIRFA acknowledges indige-nous people's right to pray at their sacred sites and retain posses-sion of their sacred objects—something that federal policy had discouraged or even forbidden up to that point. A 1996 execu-tive order by President Clinton further directed federal agencies to "avoid adversely affecting the physical integrity of such sacred sites."[59] Yet that is exactly what federal agencies do when they have sites studied and allow their contents to be altered or removed.

In the meantime, the communities that love the lost objects and ruined places are bereaved, according to Holley. They mourn important aspects of their culture, once encountered as naturally and easily as the familiar-looking arrowhead picked up by Holley's grandson. They suffer harm to health and well-being. "How are we going to pray in these places when they've been destroyed and their contents taken?" Holley asked. "How are we going to pass on our culture to our youth? How are they going to attach themselves to our identity?"

Tribal youngsters agreed. I learned from Jonathan Holley that Western Shoshone history is not taught in his local public school. "Nothing. Not a word," he said. "When we are at Tosawihi, we can visualize and understand. It also changes our perception of what we have been told [by outsiders] about our past." Kiana Vance asked, "How can we have a future without a past?" Referring to the materials that had been scooped up and interred in boxes at the Nevada state museum, she said that an entire generation has missed learning from those things.[60]

Kathleen Holley is eighty-three. She has been coming to Tosawihi all her life. "It's worse than ever," she said, looking out over the dry hills, which were turning gold in the cool days of advancing autumn. "I see disrespect everywhere. So many of the animals are gone. What will be left for the children?"[61]

DURING 2016, MEMBERS OF THE Standing Rock Sioux Tribe expressed related concerns about an oil pipeline crossing the Missouri River, which is their main water source. Originally planned to cross the Missouri north, or upsteam, of Bismarck, North Dakota, the pipeline was moved downstream to Standing Rock when Bismarck residents complained. When Standing Rock citizens objected in nonviolent demonstrations, the state of North Dakota reacted with astonishing levels of force. For the better part of a year, the world watched, aghast, as social media, then increasingly conventional media, showed law-enforcement officers and private security contractors employing military-style surveillance and weapons against unarmed civilians. The state and private forces used dogs, rubber bullets, beanbag rounds, chemical gases, sound cannons, batons, water cannons in sub-freezing temperatures, and more against the water protectors, as the Standing Rock resisters called themselves for their defense of the sacredness of water. The demonstrators were dragged from ceremonies, beaten, and arrested. More than one hundred were hospitalized.[62] The force applied was extreme, even by military wartime standards, according to former US Army ranger Griz Grzywa. He served for fifteen years, including one tour of duty in Somalia and three tours in Iraq, and had come to Standing Rock in December 2016 to help shield the demonstrators from harm. "They are using a level of force against women and children here that our military would hesitate to use," Grzywa said in an interview at Standing Rock.

The North Dakota legislature added fuel to the fire in January 2017 when it considered, though eventually failed to pass, a measure that would have allowed motorists to kill protesters. The bill's all-Republican cosponsors were frank about it being a response to the anti-pipeline demonstrations, which had occasionally spilled over into public roadways. Had the bill become law, motorists who "negligently" killed or hurt anyone obstructing traffic would not have been liable.[63] Soon after the bill was introduced, North Dakota civil-rights lawyer and former US attorney Tim Purdon told me the proposal was a "new low" that "sends a message that we are going to dehumanize those with whom we disagree."

The imbalance at Standing Rock, with a heavily armed force in riot gear on one side and unarmed civilians on the other, made the protest a contemporary exemplar of nonviolent resistance. "The seemingly powerless here at Standing Rock have kept their wits about them and held on to their peaceful values. They have turned out to be infinitely more powerful than the bullies going after them," said Jeremy Freer, another vet who had traveled to Standing Rock in December 2016; a marine combat engineer, Freer had served in Iraq.

Eventually, the US Army Corps of Engineers, which was the supervising federal agency for the project, decided that the plans for the pipeline had not been fully scrutinized. It ordered just what the tribe had been saying needed to happen: a full environmental impact statement, which looks at the effects of a project on human life as well as on the natural world. In December 2016, the corps asked the pipeline's builders to halt work until that could be done.[64] The mood in the camp that day was cautious —more wait-and-see than optimistic. Things seemed to be truly looking up when the Obama administration convened meetings of federal officials and tribal leaders to examine tribal consultation procedures and decide whether they had been properly applied. In early 2017, however, the corps backtracked, and the Trump administration ordered a speedy completion of the Dakota Access Pipeline. The focus of the controversy then moved to the courts.

Seen through Native eyes, the wanton brutality at Standing Rock was nothing new. In fact, it was a generations-old policy, according to Wendsler Nosie, former chairman of the San Carlos Apaches and a longtime Native-rights activist. "Federal and state involvement with us has always been military, from the days when we Native people were prisoners of war until this very day," said Nosie, whose Apache Stronghold movement was striving to protect Oak Flat, a tribal cultural landscape in Arizona threatened by mining.[65]

There are myriad examples of contemporary state-sanctioned violence toward Native people. During the 1960s and 1970s, unarmed members of Northwest tribes were shot at, beaten, and arrested while seeking recognition of treaty-guaranteed fishing rights, said former Puyallup Tribe chairwoman Ramona Bennett.[66]

For decades, Nebraska law enforcement roughed up and arrested protesters from Pine Ridge Indian Reservation as they tried to shut down Whiteclay, the tiny border town that existed almost exclusively for more than a century to bootleg alcohol onto the dry reservation.[67]

The Yankton Sioux Reservation has been the site of standoffs between unarmed demonstrators and large contingents of police. For example, in 2008, South Dakota sent state highway-patrol officers to help local police arrest tribal members demonstrating against construction of a concentrated animal feeding operation, or CAFO. "The violence toward us is embedded in our history," said Nosie. "The message they are sending in these situations is, 'We did it to you before, and we can do it again.'"

Worldwide support for Standing Rock has meant that its Native-led expertise has moved outward to help other communities protect their land and resources.[68] In late 2016, Frankie Orona, from the Borrado, Chumash, and Tongva people, led actions against the Trans-Pecos Pipeline, which would run from West Texas to Mexico. For months, he and others danced and prayed in the path of the line. In December, after consulting with the Indigenous Environmental Network, which was instrumental in organizing the Standing Rock resistance, Orona decided to establish an encampment in Texas, using the one in North Dakota as a model. People from the Standing Rock camp came to help out. Under the rubric Society of Native Nations, he built an indigenous/non-indigenous support system, similar to that at Standing Rock, with backing from local environmentalists and ranchers. One rancher hosted the camp on her property. Orona called them "allies," a term frequently used by advocacy groups of all kinds nationwide as they find they share values with a wide range of supporters.[69] Standing Rock was also evoked in Florida and New Jersey, where Natives and non-Natives united in 2016 to resist construction of the Sabal and Pilgrim pipelines, respectively.[70] In 2017, additional resistance camps emerged in western Massachusetts[71] and elsewhere. Orona said that the power of unity is one of Standing Rock's most important lessons. "Hundreds of indigenous nations from all over the country and the globe stood together, along with supporters, and that idea endures."

Standing Rock inspired wider interest in Native struggles, according to Judith LeBlanc, director of the Native Organizers Alliance and member of the Caddo Nation of Oklahoma. "People everywhere are talking about Standing Rock, which has magnified the reality of other situations like it," she said. She called the awareness a "Flint moment" for Indian country. She was optimistic, noting that tribal struggles are ever more successful, including an international effort to persuade banks, city councils, and others to divest billions of dollars from Energy Transfer Partners and its financial backers that has been a major coup. The divestment concept is also moving outward and being used by other resistance groups, Native and non-Native.[72] As Shoshone-Bannock professor and pundit Mark Trahant has written, the end of these stories is no longer inevitable, with Native communities always losing to outside interests.[73]

SINCE TAKING OFFICE, THE TRUMP ADMINISTRATION has tried to shovel vast and pristine portions of the United States into the maw of mining concerns and fossil-fuel companies and other extractive enterprises. An attempt to cut back the size of national monuments including Bears Ears, a Utah monument replete with tribal sacred sites, in order to allow oil and gas drilling has garnered much publicity and the threat of a tribal lawsuit. The reversal of Obama-era prohibitions against oil drilling in the Arctic and Atlantic Oceans has already been challenged by a lawsuit by the Center for Biological Diversity, the Native organization Resisting Environmental Destruction on Indigenous Lands (REDOIL), and additional conservation groups. Iconic national landmarks are under siege. Oil-well pump jacks inched closer to Chaco Canyon,[74] the remains of a one-thousand-year-old Puebloan village in New Mexico, and the US Forest Service has reopened the possibility of uranium mining in the watershed of the Grand Canyon, the age-old homeland of the Havasupai Tribe.[75]

Also in the administration's crosshairs is Bristol Bay, an expanse of Alaskan land and water that supports a $1.5-billion salmon fishery. The bay underpins the subsistence lifeways of surrounding tribes while providing some fourteen thousand jobs and pumping associated spending and taxes into the state and national economies. In 2014, after years of scientific study and public comment on a proposed copper, gold, and molybdenum mining operation for the watershed of the bay, the Environmental Protection Agency found that Pebble Mine would devastate the area.[76] Fast-forward to May of 2017. Within hours of meeting with Pebble Mine owners, according to a CNN report, the Trump EPA suggested withdrawing Clean Water Act restrictions on the mine and opened a public-comment period on the concept. Administrator Scott Pruitt said the EPA did not seek "a particular outcome" for this turnaround but wished to be "fair" to the mine.[77]

The agency and the mine face fierce opposition that cuts across all ethnicities and relationships to the water in Alaska, said Alannah Hurley, the Yup'ik executive director of United Tribes of Bristol Bay, which represents fourteen tribes. Commercial and sport fishermen have joined indigenous people as they rallied, petitioned, and spoke out against the mine.[78] When opposition to Pebble Mine was gathering steam in 2004, tribal members realized they needed to learn more in order to combat the project effectively. The environmental nonprofit Earthworks helped them reach out to Western Shoshones to learn about modern large-scale mining, as they had experienced it in Nevada. Starting in 2008, groups representing tribal communities around Bristol Bay visited Wendsler Nosie in Oak Flat, Arizona, and traveled to Nevada, said Bonnie Gestring, an Earthworks staffer who went on these trips.[79]

In Nevada, the Alaska Natives toured mines and did flyovers. "Flying above large mines let people see the landscape-level environmental disturbance," Gestring said. "And seeing the operations close-up on the ground familiarized them with the processes and their terminology, so they could understand what exactly was meant when companies back home threw around technical language." The Alaska Natives also talked to the area's indigenous communities, including members of the Elko Band of the Te-Moak Tribe of Western Shoshone Indians. "They could ask whether promises—about jobs or effects on the environment and subsistence lifeways, for example—had been kept," Gestring recalled. The answer was generally "no," she reported. The environmental impacts are crushing, the visitors from Alaska learned.[80]

For a vivid example of the damage a mine creates, we can look at the southern border of the Fort Belknap Indian Reservation, in northeastern Montana, where a gold mine opened in 1979. To get at the precious metal, the miners lopped off the peak of Spirit Mountain, a place where tribal members had sought visions and collected healing plants since time immemorial. All that remains is an immense yellow scar on the horizon, from which orange, ochre, and blue-gray streams carrying arsenic, lead, and other heavy metals bleed down onto the reservation.[81] Former tribal chairman and cultural leader William "Snuffy" Main stood overlooking a spring in a deep valley at the base of what is left of the mountain, as a curious herd of horses—bays, chestnuts, and a calico foal— watched us. "The frogs have disappeared," Main said, gesturing toward the spring. "So have the fireflies and silver-striped minnow." He thought human health had been affected as well. "They get cancer, and in a few months they're gone." For years, tribal members have called for studies of the mining waste's effects on human and environmental health.[82] In November 2017, the tribe joined with conservation groups—Earthworks, Earthjustice, and others—to call on Montana to stop the mining company from doing this again in another still-pristine part of the state.[83]

During the 2014 national election, two-thirds of Alaskans voted to create barriers to the opening of Pebble Mine in Bristol Bay. The opposition won in every precinct in the state.[84] "Nothing has changed about the project and the objections to it," Hurley said about the Trump EPA taking another look at the agency's decision. "The only change is the political leadership of this country. This administration puts profits before human beings and before science. It is willing to create a humanitarian, environmental, and economic crisis in Alaska so that a mining company can reap profits. If the administration succeeds, a huge sustainable resource will be destroyed." In late 2017, Hurley was traveling around Bristol

Bay, letting isolated communities know what was going on so they had the information they needed to submit comments to the EPA. "We want to make sure our voices are heard," she said.

As at Tosawihi, Standing Rock, and other sites of indigenous resistance, the Alaska Native struggle involves youngsters working alongside their elders. Tribal members as young as thirteen testified before the EPA when it was gathering information for its 2014 report, according to Kimberly Williams, who is Yup'ik and the former director of Nunamta Aulukestai (a Yup'ik phrase meaning "caretakers of our land"). "Issues like this keep arising, and our children need to be prepared. They may be fighting Pebble Mine or similar operations when they're adults, and they understand that," she said.[85] According to Hurley, "This involvement is expected of our young people. We see it as part of our responsibility to our people and our lands."[86]

Carina Miller, from the Confederated Tribes of Warm Springs, in Oregon, agreed. Tribes in her locale have objected to Nestlé Waters drawing water from area springs, bottling it and selling it. The tribes have invoked treaty rights and the springs' function in underpinning an ancient way of life. "In the past, it was so difficult to think that tribes could have a real voice," Miller said. "Now, our younger generation is empowered because of the healing work that has been done and the conversations we have had about the historical trauma that has impacted us generation after generation."[87]

IT IS NOT ONLY NEW industrial activities that threaten the ecosystem of Indian country. One of the world's largest environmental disasters-in-waiting lurks on the bottom of the Great Lakes.

Tribes have warned of it, but the response has been slow. "An accident waiting to happen" is how Chairman Aaron Payment of the Sault Sainte Marie Tribe of Chippewa Indians, in Michigan, described aging, mussel-encrusted pipelines carrying 540,000 gallons of oil and natural gas daily through the Straits of Mackinac, which connect Lake Huron and Lake Michigan.[88] "It's very frightening," agreed Stella Kay, vice chairwoman of the Little Traverse Bay Bands of Odawa Indians, also in Michigan.[89] The resource threatened is massive. The five Great Lakes together contain 20 percent of the planet's fresh surface water, providing millions of people with drinking water, supporting a vibrant tourism industry, and offering bountiful fisheries.

On the lake bottom are twin pipelines dating to the 1950s. Called Enbridge Line 5, they are part of a system that burst in 2010, dumping 840,000 gallons of oil into the Kalamazoo River in Marshall, Michigan—the nation's largest land oil spill to date.[90] "Half of the pipelines in America predate our current environmental laws and protections," Aaron Payment told Obama administration officials in one of a series of tribal listening sessions in 2016. "Aging pipelines with substandard welds and steel, old coating technology or nonexistent coating, and decades of corrosion are not subject to environmental or safety rules. This is appalling."[91] University of Michigan videos show scuba divers swimming along pipes weighted down by encrustations of barnacles and reveal that bags of grout have been used to support the pipes.

According to Kay, a rupture in the straits would be devastating in good weather, but if it happened in winter and the damage were frozen under the ice for weeks or months, the effect on the sensitive environment and the regional economy would be unimaginable.

Adding to the concerns, figures from the Pipeline and Hazardous Materials Safety Administration, a US Department of Transportation agency, show that detection systems and the employees running them do not discern most of what the agency calls "significant incidents." Of the more than four thousand significant incidents reported to the agency over a six-year period, detection equipment recognized less than 10 percent, while the general public and techniques like ground and aerial patrols spotted the rest.[92]

Enbridge procedures have changed for the better since the Line 5 break, according to company spokesperson Ryan Duffy. He called the accident "transformational for us." Duffy said that Line 5 is now constantly monitored from an "enhanced" control center that would automatically shut it down, should a break occur. That would presumably prevent what happened on the Kalamazoo River, when an Enbridge employee assumed detection equipment readings showing a breach were errors and pumped even more oil through the broken Line 5, worsening the spill. Duffy described today's inspection techniques as high-tech and continual with divers, robotic vehicles, and MRI-like scanning devices searching for corrosion and cracks.[93]

Despite continued calls for replacing the line, however, the company has resisted doing so. A task force has been studying alternatives for the line, ranging from no change to replacing it to transporting its products by another method altogether. The public has less hesitation coming to a decision. Memories of the Kalamazoo River Line 5 accident are still fresh in the Great Lakes area, and when the Michigan Petroleum Pipeline Task Force asked for public input for its 2015 report on Line 5, the consensus was clear. Most respondents said, "Shut it down."[94]

According to Payment, Line 5's weaknesses threaten the tribes' court-affirmed treaty right to fish within the waters of the Great Lakes. If natural resources are destroyed, that agreement is meaningless. "To exercise the treaty right to fish, there have to be fish in the waters, and the fish have to be safe to eat. The US government does not have the right to give away our court-affirmed treaty rights to those who threaten them with environmental disaster." The damage would be to lifeways as well as to economies.

Some may think of treaties as dusty documents that are no longer relevant in the modern day. Not so, said Indian-law attorney Rollie Wilson. They are contracts between governments and are enshrined, along with federal law, as "the supreme law of the land" in the US Constitution's Sixth Article. "In these contracts, tribes reserved lands, rights, and resources and made agreements with what was a fledgling government," Wilson said. "The tribes did not anticipate that the United States would keep coming back for more, or that as the United States gained power, it would unilaterally break treaties and impose new agreements on tribes." Regardless, treaty rights are legally binding, as has been shown repeatedly in court. "Tribes exercise treaty rights every day, and they are the foundation of the government-to-government relationship between the United States and tribes."[95]

On January 4, 2017, the Bad River Band of the Lake Superior Tribe of Chippewa Indians, in Wisconsin, added a serious obstacle to the continued existence of Line 5. The tribe decided not to allow the line to cross through reservation land in which it had ownership interests, explaining that even a minor spill could be disastrous. Said Bad River tribal council member Dylan Jennings,

"We are standing firm. We are not prepared to leave our future generations to deal with this pipeline and what could be the end of our way of life."[96] In November 2017, Enbridge spokesperson Duffy emailed to say that the situation was still unresolved, adding, "Enbridge respects Bad River's sovereignty and authority over its lands. We remain committed to the mediation process and will continue working with the Band and its experts."

In the Navajo homeland, disaster has already struck. One August day in 2015, a river that is central to the tribe's economy and way of life turned a ghastly orange and became one of the nation's latest Superfund sites. The San Juan River, which runs down into the Navajo reservation from mountains in Colorado, joined the more than one thousand locations on the Environmental Protection Agency's list. One-quarter of them are on Indian reservations. This means that about 1 percent of the United States population sustains a massively disproportionate 25 percent of the environmental and related cultural damage.

The disaster occurred as a result of EPA activities at the Gold King Mine in Colorado, one of many abandoned operations along tributaries of the San Juan. While attempting to draw off contaminated water, EPA construction crews triggered the collapse of a portion of the mine and a three-million-gallon blowout of sludge laced with lead, mercury, and other toxins. Even worse, the agency did not tell the Navajo Nation that the poisons were headed for tribal members' homes and farms until nearly two days later.

In a lawsuit filed against the EPA in August 2016, an infuriated Navajo Nation described the damage to the river as causing anguish "akin to the loss of a loved one." Ceremonies that use sand and water from the river and pollen from once productive

cornfields have been interrupted. Tourists have stayed away, causing more economic pain. Tribal member Mark Maryboy lives in
Montezuma Creek, Utah, a tiny Navajo Nation village on the San
Juan River. "We still can't drink the water or farm, more than a
year later. The spill brought Navajo farming and the area economy
to a halt," said Maryboy,[97] a board member of Utah Diné Bikéyah,
the grassroots group that in 2010 initiated the process of designat-
ing the Bears Ears National Monument.[98]

The EPA has worked to clean up the spill and has announced
that 2015 data showed the river "trending" toward its pre-spill
condition.[99] "Navajo people don't believe them," said Maryboy.
"We have been exposed to dangerous materials, including uranium from Cold War-era mining in this area, and have cancer and
other diseases that result from those exposures.[100] Our goal is to be
sure that nothing like this happens again."[101]

ON AUGUST 17, 2017, IN THE Nevada high desert, the narrative was changing for the Battle Mountain Band of the Te-Moak
Tribe of Western Shoshone Indians and the cultural landscape
it had fought to protect. Preparations were underway for a ceremony and feast the following day. Trucks delivering supplies came
and went along the circular drive around which tribal member's
houses and trailers were clustered. Some tribal members were
cooking or setting up an elevated viewing stand. Others were
in the tribe's small public park, erecting tipis that would shelter visitors arriving from other tribes. Inside the community center, long tables were set up, soon to be draped with white cloths
and brightened with red bandanna decorations. The occasion was

the gift of 3,629 acres of nearby ancient sacred sites from a gold-mining company, Klondex Mines, an international firm with headquarters in Nevada.

Band chairwoman Lydia Johnson, who also chaired the over-arching Te-Moak Tribe, had just returned from meeting with Klondex representatives to sign off on the transfer. "It's done," she said, looking both elated and exhausted.[102] Council member Holley said his people were discussing not placing the gift in federal trust, as most tribes do for the exemption from local real-estate taxes. He supported the idea as a declaration of tribal sovereignty. "A lot of us are saying we should pay the taxes on the new land and keep the federal government out of all decision-making there," Holley said. The new casino the tribe had planned was moving toward becoming a reality, and that would help make the payments possible, he added.

The band was eager to work directly with Klondex. "We have seen for decades that we can't count on the Bureau of Land Management to protect our sacred places, and putting the land in trust would put them in charge of it," Holley said. "But we are not naïve. We also know that we can't halt mining altogether. So, we choose to work cooperatively with a company that wants to do this." Tribal members were not planning to relax their vigilance, though, vowing to keep Klondex under the same scrutiny they have always applied to any entity working in their ancient cultural landscape.

When Klondex's chief executive officer, Paul Huet, took over the open-pit mine in Tosawihi in late 2016, he was determined that his company's tenure would be different.[103] Earlier in his career, he had worked at the same site as general manager for another firm and had given mine tours as part of his job. Western Shoshone elders who took the tours told Huet about sacred sites that were central to their culture, yet threatened by mining expansion and other development. For tribal members, the holy place was filled with personal memories of hunting and gathering, prayers and visions, in addition to artifacts and ancient locales. Huet drove out to see what they were talking about. He was thunderstruck. "I had no idea that such a beautiful spot, with a rushing creek and trees, was tucked away in Nevada. I had never seen anything like it in the state. It was obvious it should be in Western Shoshone care."

To buy the tract and make that happen, he had to raise nearly a million dollars. "I'd never done anything like that in my life," Huet confessed. "I am a third-generation miner who started out in the mines as a janitor three days after my high school graduation." He recalled a tribal official exhorting him, "You can do it!" Huet plucked up his courage and flew to South Africa and then Canada to lobby the company's top brass. To his delight, he got the money and bought the land in 2009. However, before the tract could be turned over to the Western Shoshone, the company went bankrupt. The acreage was caught up in legal proceedings, and the gift was in limbo until Huet returned in late 2016, this time as CEO of Klondex. Huet's plan would face one more trial, by fire this time. A lightning strike in mid-July of 2017 ignited a wildfire that consumed 220,000 acres surrounding the sacred sites. They were among the millions of acres that burned that year in one of the nation's worst wildfire seasons.

Holley took me and photographer Joseph Zummo out to see the Klondex gift on August 17. On the way to the place, the land around us was black—scorched to the horizon. When we got to the sacred sites, we could see that substantial portions of the area had been spared the inferno. The flames left untouched land enclosed by prayer circles, raging up to the edge of a grouping of three hill-top rings and stopping. The fire leapt sweat lodge frames, which are made of willow and covered with boughs. In some spots, native plants were barely singed, rising laden with seed from the black-ened earth. Cheerful green shoots poked through the ash, sug-gesting springtime more than loss or destruction. Back at Battle Mountain later that day, Zummo showed his photographs of the place to medicine man Reggie Sope. He was not surprised at how much had escaped the flames. "The strength of the prayers pro-tected those places," he said.

August 18 dawned cloudless and cool. Medicine man Johnny Bob of the Yomba Shoshone Tribe sang a sunrise service as an orange sun rose from behind distant mountains into a pink sky. Tribal members donned brilliantly colored regalia and walked or rode horseback to the plaza fronting the community center. Several explained the iconography of the traditional dress and the meaning of the colors and shapes used. Images of the land, with its blue water and jagged mountaintops, were interwoven with evocations of community, as many of the pieces were gifts cre-ated by family or honors bestowed in thanks for service on behalf of others.

Leaders and elders from Nevada and South Dakota tribes joined Klondex representatives on the viewing stand to applaud the gift. The land would change lives and make people happy, Huet said in his speech. He hoped the effort would be a model for more positive interactions in these contentious times. "Others will see what we're doing and understand that groups that have been at odds can work together if they listen to each other. The important thing was that we listened."

Huet's good intentions extend to Klondex's mining methods at the gold mine in Tosawihi. The company has pledged that, going forward, it will work underground only, using precision hand techniques. Holley has been hired as the company's senior community-relations supervisor, with responsibility for a team of tribal cultural specialists who consult with the miners on an ongoing basis.

"The Klondex gift was meant to be," said Battle Mountain tribal member Marleine Knight. "Now, we can camp, tell stories, and take care of the place properly."[104] Plans for the new land include a complex of small cabins near a pond, where elders will teach youngsters Shoshone language and customs in the natural environment where they arose.

"After everything that tried to deter us—churches, the cavalry, alcohol, drugs—we still walk our path," Holley said.

4.

Rough Justice

OREY KANOSH BLED TO DEATH in the Utah desert on an October night in 2012. A police officer shot the unarmed Paiute after chasing the car in which Kanosh was a passenger, mistakenly thinking it had been stolen. Dashcam video shows cop-car and ambulance lights flickering over the gruesome scene, as Kanosh lies facedown in the dirt while officers and medics mill around. Eventually, the medics can be seen on the video checking Kanosh for a pulse. They do not detect one, but testify in a subsequent investigation that this does not necessarily mean that the individual is dead. Kanosh lay in the desert until morning. He never received care for his wounds, and no one knows when the traditional dancer and father died. His relatives continue to ask questions, including why police went after him but not the car's white driver. The investigation cleared the officers of wrongdoing.[1]

Two years later, Suquamish Tribe descendant Jeanetta Riley, a thirty-four-year-old mother of four, was shot dead outside a Sandpoint, Idaho, hospital, after staff summoned police. The official account of the incident reports that her husband sought help at the hospital because Riley—homeless, pregnant, and with a history of mental illness—was threatening suicide. She had a small knife in her right hand and was sitting in the couple's parked van. Dashcam video shows officers quickly closing in on Riley. Wearing body armor and armed with an assault rifle and Glock pistols, they move down the sidewalk and across the roadway toward her. Soon they are within the distance at which a knife can be considered potentially lethal. They shout instructions—to walk toward them, to show her hands. Cursing them, she refuses. "Drop the knife!" they yell, continuing to advance, then open fire. They pump two shots into her chest and one more into her back as she falls to the pavement. Fifteen seconds have elapsed from the time they exited their vehicles. The officers' actions were later ruled as justified.[2]

On a January morning in 2016, Puyallup tribal member Lisa Earl's telephone began to ring with condolence calls. She was shocked to learn of reports that police had shot dead her thirty-two-year-old daughter, Jacqueline Salyers, a mother of four. "They shot my baby, they shot my baby," she kept saying to relatives. The Tacoma, Washington, officers were not seeking Salyers, but rather her boyfriend, who was not a tribal member. After one patrolman shot Salyers at close range in the head and arms while she was driving, both officers took cover, they testified in the ensuing police investigation. From protected positions, they watched the boyfriend "climbing around in the front of the vehicle," "attempting to retrieve something from the rear," screaming, "You fucking killed her," clambering over the "apparently shot female," exiting the car on the driver's side, and running away into the surrounding residential neighborhood, armed with a rifle. The boyfriend was apprehended two and a half weeks later. The officers were cleared of wrongdoing.[3]

Puyallup tribal member Lisa Earl mourns her daughter, Jacqueline Salyers, shot dead by police in Tacoma, Washington, in 2016. Salyers's family and tribe have mobilized the wider community to march and advocate for police training and accountability. (Joseph Zummo)

As a consequence of their encounters with police, Kanosh, Riley, and Salyers joined the ranks of Native Americans killed by law-enforcement officers. In February 2017, Attorney General Jeff Sessions halted Justice Department investigations of police departments suspected of civil-rights violations. These inquiries have been called "pattern or practice" investigations because they look into whether the problems are a result of an ongoing pattern or regular practice. Obama-era analyses of this type had revealed systemic racial and ethnic discrimination in excessive use of force, false arrests, shootings, and other measures by several police departments, including Seattle and Albuquerque. Both cities have substantial Native populations.[4]

It is not just modern-day individual interactions of this sort—a shooting on a road or sidewalk somewhere—but long-term national policies that have made Native Americans the group most likely to be incarcerated in this country, as well as the most likely to die at the point of an officer's gun. From the beginnings of our republic, vindictive laws and attitudes have exposed indigenous people to criminal-justice and extra judicial penalties, including death, far more than other citizens. For juveniles, the situation is appalling, with Native children three times as likely to be under lock and key as white kids. In the thirty-six states in which Natives have been overrepresented in the prison system, their incarceration rates have ranged from 1.2 times that of whites in Missouri and Tennessee to a high of 14.5 times greater in Nevada.[5]

The Bureau of Justice Statistics has the numbers to prove the disparities. The bureau reported in 2015 that Native Americans were 38 percent more likely to be under correctional supervision than other Americans, adding up to about seventy-nine thousand Native individuals behind bars, on probation, or on parole that year. They faced relatively tougher sentences in federal court than the rest of us. They were 3.4 percent of the federal prison population, while making up about half that proportion of the United States population. According to the bureau, Native prisoners' average age was seven years younger than that of the general prison population. About half the Natives had little or no criminal history before ending up in federal prison, as opposed to the rate in the general population, where less than a third had clean or minimal records. The Natives were also more likely to be women—20 percent as opposed to 10 percent of the general population. We can see from these numbers how frequently relatively young, relatively vulnerable people with little criminal background leave the reservation for the promises of a nearby city, only to be sucked into a criminal justice system that continually trades them up the line to ever more serious punishments.[6]

Native Americans are more likely than others to appear in federal court for what Kevin Washburn calls "routine, local and simple cases." According to Washburn, a citizen of the Chickasaw Nation of Oklahoma as well as a distinguished law professor at the University of New Mexico, and the former Department of the Interior assistant secretary for Indian affairs, the crimes, though they may be very important to the communities in which they occur, would be considered "common street crimes," were it not for their Indian-country origin.[7]

"Once they're accused, they're gone," was how Mark Wandering Medicine summed it up for me in 2016. He said he sees tribal members, often youngsters, disappear into federal prisons for years or decades. This may happen even after a minor, isolated brush with the law, Wandering Medicine said. I met the Northern Cheyenne spiritual teacher when he was lead plaintiff for a voting-rights lawsuit discussed in Chapter 2 and communicated with him over the following years about a range of human-rights matters in which he was involved—improved health care for Native Americans, veterans' issues, and, in this case, criminal justice.[8]

A lay advocate who works with parties appearing in the Northern Cheyenne tribal court, which sits in the tribe's capital in Lame Deer, Montana, Wandering Medicine was well familiar with the distinctive, and ultimately malevolent, way that the law applies to Native Americans. They can be prosecuted in tribal, state, or federal court, depending on where a crime occurred and who was involved. Charges are generally federal for tribal members accused of committing serious crimes on reservations, including murder, assault, and rape; charges are usually tribal when Natives have allegedly committed other, minor crimes on reservations. Off-reservation charges are prosecuted in state court.[9] Because Natives are federally charged for on-reservation crimes that would otherwise be prosecuted in state court, they are more likely than others to face the federal system's longer sentences, mandatory sentencing guidelines, court procedures that favor the prosecution, rare use of diversion, probation and other mitigating actions, and almost complete lack of Natives (that is, peers) on juries.

How did Native Americans end up more liable to face federal charges than the rest of us? This aspect of the nation's criminal-justice system arose in the aftermath of the 1881 killing of a Brulé (or Rosebud) Sioux chief, Spotted Tail, by another Sioux named Crow Dog in what is now South Dakota. Although the killing was resolved under the laws of the tribe, which required Crow Dog to make restitution to Spotted Tail's family in the form of horses, money, and a blanket, the Dakota Territory's court charged Crow Dog with murder and convicted him. When Crow Dog appealed the conviction to the US Supreme Court, it overturned it, ruling that American Indian tribes retained the right, as an attribute of their sovereignty, to be governed by their own laws; the United States had no jurisdiction over crimes committed among tribal members in Indian country. Following this decision and the ensuing public outcry, Congress enacted the 1885 Major Crimes Act, which extended federal criminal jurisdiction into Indian country for certain enumerated crimes. The list has lengthened through the years.[10]

What was really going on, said South Dakota attorney Matthew Rappold, was that Congress saw an opportunity to create dissension, break up the tribal judicial and social structure, and thereby extend federal influence over more Native land. That motivation arose in the context of shifting federal focus from treaty-making with sovereign tribal powers to forced assimilation and dependency. Rappold, who works in the Pennington County Public Defenders' Office, lived on the Rosebud Indian Reservation and worked in the tribal court there. He explained, "Congress increased criminal prosecution of Indians though they were not even citizens. Congress's action transformed criminal justice as it applied to Indians, but it had no basis in the Constitution to do this. The action was entirely extra-constitutional, which is not how American law is supposed to work."[11] More offenses with which Natives can be charged are now called federal.[12]

Normally, federal charges cover matters of national reach—immigration, voting rights, racketeering, interstate drug cartels, and the like. Not in Indian country. Sitting one day in the Ninth Circuit Court of Appeals in Portland, Oregon, I heard a litany of cases with nationwide implications, along with a Native man's appeal for an assault conviction. Additional drivers of Native incarceration are legal oddities that have been repeatedly approved by the Supreme Court. These include Natives facing greater upward departures (sentence increases) for oft-uncounseled tribal-court convictions,[13] as well as Natives facing double-jeopardy prosecutions in federal and tribal court.[14] [15]

The idea that the justice system should not try an individual repeatedly for one offense goes back to the ancient Greeks and Romans. The concept was recognized in British law and affirmed in the Fifth Amendment to the US Constitution, which holds that no one will be "subject for the same offence to be twice put in jeopardy of life or limb." However, that is not the case if the multiple prosecutions are by "separate sovereigns," each of which may have a crack at the accused. According to the Supreme Court, tribes are just that: sovereign entities in and of themselves and not merely an arm of the federal government; a tribal member might appear in a tribal court, then a federal one, and could serve two sentences for the same offense.

In 1953, several states became exceptions to federal criminal oversight of American Indians. As part of Eisenhower-era cost cutting, Congress passed Public Law 280.[16] It turned over to Alaska, Wisconsin, and other states the responsibility for prosecuting Natives accused of what might be federal crimes elsewhere. Neither the states nor the tribes were happy with the change. It burdened the former with additional costs and degraded the latter's sovereignty and government-to-government relationship with the United States. A few tribes in these states succeeded in returning to the original arrangement. Nevertheless, despite the PL-280 twist, as we have seen, Natives are still more likely to be subject to federal law's more severe penalties, which has been a major driver of Natives' contribution to the prison population.[17]

That's in the context of the highest incarceration rate in the world. Though our incarceration has dropped slightly in recent years, the United States still has more than 20 percent of the world's prisoners, though just 5 percent of the global population. The high number of inmates is largely a result of mandatory-minimum and three-strikes laws that were part of the so-called war on drugs that exploded during the 1980s and 1990s and continued into the 2000s.[18]

State courts contribute to the disparity. Even misdemeanor convictions drive the numbers, said attorney Rappold. That is not just because they are more numerous than felonies, though.[19] Misdemeanors contribute to an individual's downward life spiral. An unregistered vehicle, a cracked taillight, and homelessness are all easy entry points into the justice system. Suspension of a driver's license might mean a person cannot get to work, for example, cannot feed his or her family, and ends up offending again. Convictions for such charges also create prior records that can increase a subsequent sentence. They may lead to obstacles in housing, employment, public assistance benefits, and education, said Rappold. They may also contribute to Native parents losing custody of their children in child-welfare proceedings.

"Many of the accused in the Rapid City courtroom are Native," Rappold said. "When I walk into court, I might be back on the Rosebud Sioux Reservation, where I once worked in the tribal court—as a public defender in 2003 and as the chief prosecutor from 2008 to 2013. A lot of my current clients are hungry people looking for food or homeless people sleeping in someone else's car."

Though Native Americans make up about 10 percent of Pennington County's population, approximately 53 percent of the county's daily jail population is Native—a fact that has apparently not reduced crime or improved related measures, such as community safety, recidivism rates, or the integration of former offenders into society. To help solve these problems, Rapid City's police department has set up a committee that is run by Vaughn Vargas,[20] a member of the Cheyenne River Sioux Tribe, in Eagle Butte, South Dakota. The group is exploring ways to improve police-community relations. These might include arranging for police officers to coach Native children's lacrosse games, setting up cultural-awareness lectures for officers, or assessing policing strategies with an eye toward recommending more culturally appropriate, supportive, and effective techniques.[21]

Tribes, tribal members, judges, and academics have long claimed that Native people face worse outcomes in federal court than people who appear for similar offenses in state court. Federal sentences are not just harsher, though. Those who are convicted almost always serve sentences in their entirety because the federal system has few provisions for parole or time off for good behavior, according to two attorneys writing in the *North Dakota Law Review* in 2013. One of the authors, B. J. Jones, is director of the University of North Dakota's Tribal Judicial Institute and a tribal judge; the other, Christopher Ironroad, is a member of the Standing Rock Sioux Tribe and an attorney with a Washington, DC, firm specializing in Indian law.[22]

Jones and Ironroad cited the case of a young Indian woman whose newborn died; she was charged with neonaticide and received a ten-year sentence in federal court in 2010. Meanwhile, a non-Native woman whose newborn died under similar circumstances at about the same time received three years of probation from a state court. Jones and Ironroad also described the case of an Indian teenager in South Dakota who got forty-eight years for second-degree murder. This was not only much higher than a state court sentence but more than twice the mean sentence for that crime over the preceding five years in the Eighth Circuit, the federal court subdivision that encompasses South Dakota.[23]

In 2003, a US Sentencing Commission panel of federal judges and other experts, called the Ad Hoc Advisory Group on Native American Sentencing Issues, also found striking disparities in certain states. A tribal member convicted of assault, for example, could have gotten twenty-nine months in prison if he or she appeared in state court in South Dakota, but thirty-nine months—or 34 percent more time—if the proceeding were federal. The spread in New Mexico was more dramatic: six months from a state court and fifty-four months from a federal court. The advisory group was unable to get additional reliable data from all states but did recommend that federal sentences be made to conform more closely with those applied by states. The group also suggested that the federal government involve tribes in the effort.[24]

In 2015, the US Sentencing Commission took another look at the issue. It formed a blue-ribbon panel called the Tribal Issues Advisory Group, or TIAG. The group found that in the intervening years since the 2003 group met, the perception that Native Americans were subject to sentencing disparities had not just persisted, it had grown. Federal judges, prosecutors, and defenders, as well as tribal members and leaders, believed that Indian defendants received sentences that were, on the whole, different from those for non-Indians committing comparable crimes. TIAG also noted that federal court features few prosecutions of non-Indians for Indian-country crimes against Indians.[25]

Courtroom procedures are also at fault. University of New Mexico law professor Washburn criticized the composition of federal juries, especially in regard to Native cases.[26] Most American juries are drawn from the community of the defendants, he explained; this makes the juries exemplars of the local focus of American jurisprudence—what the Constitution calls "the right to a speedy and public trial." This is thought to provide a public resolution of a case that benefits both defendants and their communities. In contrast, federal jury pools generally come from large geographical areas that may have pockets of Native population concentrated on isolated reservations. The number of Natives who might be called to serve on a jury is thus relatively small to begin with. This number is reduced further by the use of voter rolls to find potential jurors. Because of long-term civil-rights discrimination—which we looked at in Chapter 2 on voting rights—Natives are less likely to be on these lists.

A related problem is getting Native witnesses into court. This is another result of the intersection of poverty and distance, which we examined in Chapter 2. Just as impoverished tribal voters without ready access to a vehicle or gas money have a hard time getting to distant off-reservation polling places, tribal witnesses often cannot make it to court in a far-off city. The interaction of these forces means that American Indian defendants almost never face juries that are familiar with their homelands or their cultures; the defendants' trials are not the open, factually comprehensive, widely viewed, and well-understood resolutions of a problem that other courtroom proceedings may be. In the end, the defendant's community may have little idea of what transpired when the charges were tested in a court of law.[27]

American Indians continually pay the price. In December 2016, four Alaska Natives were exonerated and released after serving eighteen years for murder. Despite numerous corroborating alibis, they had been convicted of a crime they had not committed.

Long distances between reservations and federal courts mean Natives on trial there almost never face juries of their peers; they also confront more severe sentences than non-Natives, who go to state court, with its more lenient sentences and opportunities for parole, probation, and alternative sentencing. (Joseph Zummo)

White jury members reportedly said that this occurred because they were certain Natives would lie for each other.[28] In an unrelated case, four Yankton Sioux men remain in federal prison today for offenses they were charged with during the 1990s but which they say did not occur. One of the federal judges sitting on a so-far unsuccessful appeal for the case roundly criticized the jury's racist remarks and discussions. In 2017, one of the Yankton Sioux men, Garfield Feather, wrote via email to say that at the start of his legal process more than twenty years ago, he had rejected the prosecution's initial offer of two and a half years in prison in return for a guilty plea. "To this day," according to Feather, "I wake up and can't believe I'm still sitting in prison for a crime that never happened. I actually believed that the courtroom was a true and just system. What a joke that turned out to be."[29]

Even a short prison term can be a kind of life sentence, said O. J. Semans, the Rosebud Sioux legislative affairs director of the Coalition of Large Tribes and the codirector of the voting-rights group Four Directions.[30] Semans observed that most jobs on most reservations are with the tribal or federal government and that a conviction disqualifies a person for employment. If the accused receives a longer sentence, said Wandering Medicine of the Northern Cheyenne, he or she simply disappears, often for a very long time.

PATCHY US GOVERNMENT DATA COLLECTION and general unawareness of Indian-country issues mean the complete tally of Natives who are shot dead by police officers remains elusive. The *Washington Post* and Great Britain's *Guardian* have both developed databases that seek to quantify more accurately Americans' police-related deaths, but even these may misidentify or omit tribal victims.[31] To obtain a clearer picture, Mike Males, senior researcher at the Center on Juvenile and Criminal Justice, looked at data that the Centers for Disease Control and Prevention, or CDC, collected from medical examiners in forty-seven states between 1999 and 2014. Males found that when the statistics on police killings of Natives were compared to their percentage of the

US population, Natives were overall more likely to be killed by police than any other group. Natives twenty to twenty-four, twenty-five to thirty-four, and thirty-five to forty-four years old were three of the five groups most likely to be killed by police. The other two groups were African Americans, twenty to twenty-four and twenty-five to thirty-four. Native Americans were 3.1 times more likely to be killed by police than white Americans.[32]

In 2016, Claremont Graduate University researchers Jean Schroedel and Roger Chin took their own look.[33] In tabulating state-level data between May 1, 2014 and October 31, 2015, they found that in six states—Mississippi, South Dakota, Idaho, Washington, Alaska, and North Dakota—death rates for Native Americans caused by the police ranged from a high of 1.19 down to .27 per 10,000 people. All six were higher than the highest rate for African Americans—in California, at .19 deaths per 10,000.

Yet the Native killings went almost entirely unreported by major US media. Schroedel and Chin reviewed articles about deaths-by-cop published during that period in the ten largest-circulation US newspapers: the *Wall Street Journal*, the *New York Times*, *USA Today*, the *Los Angeles Times*, the *New York Daily News*, the *New York Post*, the *Chicago Sun-Times*, the *Denver Post*, the *Washington Post*, and the *Chicago Tribune*. Of the twenty-nine Native Americans killed by police during the fifteen-month period Schroedel and Chin covered, only one death received sustained coverage. The *Denver Post* ran six articles, totaling 2,577 words, after Paul Castaway, a Rosebud Sioux tribal member, was shot dead in Denver while he was threatening suicide. The killing of Suquamish tribal member Daniel Covarrubias, shot when police apparently mistook his cell phone for a gun, received a total of 515 words in the *Washington Post* and the *New York Times*. The other twenty-seven deaths received no coverage in these major papers.

In 2017, the researchers added another year's worth of data to their study, bringing the analysis up to October 2016. For an article in the peer-reviewed journal *Race and Justice*, they found that the pattern persisted, with a total of fifty-three Native deaths in the period the study covered, and little additional coverage other than a series of dramatic crime stories about one man who was the subject of a manhunt, though he was not identified as Native.

Compare this media blackout with the coverage of the group next most likely to be killed by police. The researchers found that the top ten newspapers devoted hundreds of articles and hundreds of thousands of words to 413 African Americans killed by police from May 1, 2014 to October 31, 2015. Publications also produced copious material about Black Lives Matter protests and, more broadly, about police violence against African Americans. That is largely a testament to the power of the Black Lives Matter movement, which exploded after the August 9, 2014, killing of Michael Brown and continues to advocate strenuously and eloquently for the issue.

The Claremont Graduate University researchers stress that they are not in any way criticizing the extremely important attention paid to the movement for black lives, nor are they diminishing the excellent work done by activists and families to draw attention to this issue. Indeed, they laud the movement's efforts. However, the researchers note, a larger narrative is at play, with racial issues in the United States generally framed as black and white. That was evident in Minneapolis during the fall of 2015, when police killed two young men in separate incidents: White

Earth Ojibwe tribal member Philip Quinn, who was thirty at the time, and African American Jamar Clark, who was twenty-four. Clark's story was well reported, while Quinn's passing, like those of almost all other Native victims, was barely noted.

Nor did major media report on a spate of Native jailhouse deaths in 2015. The statistics on "death by legal intervention," which is the term the CDC uses to describe fatalities at the hands of police, include those that occur in custody prior to sentencing. Whether the deaths are due to police actions or neglect, the department is considered accountable, said Mike Males. "When people are in custody, law enforcement has control of them and a responsibility for their welfare," he explained.[34]

Among the deaths are those described in a 2015 report commissioned by the governor of Alaska. The report announced that Joseph Murphy, an Alaska Native veteran of the Iraq War, died of a heart attack in a holding cell in Juneau in August 2015 while jail staff cursed him and yelled "I don't care" in response to his pleas for help. In January 2015, Alaska Native Larry Kobuk was held facedown by four officers and died, reportedly because his heart condition, which he had disclosed to his jailers, meant he could not survive the stress of the position and the weight the officers applied.[35]

The list of 2015 deaths continues: Sarah Lee Circle Bear, a Sioux mother of two, died in custody in South Dakota, after reportedly complaining of pain and being refused medical attention. Choctaw medicine man Rexdale Henry died in a jail cell in Mississippi after being brought in on suspicion of a minor traffic violation; Alaska Native Gilbert Joseph passed away while in custody in Alaska; and badly bruised Yurok tribal member Raymond

Eacret died in a California jail. On the Cheyenne River Sioux Reservation in South Dakota, an angry crowd marched on police headquarters after the mother of tribal member Phillip High Bear alleged that her son had been beaten to death there. Protesters sang, drummed, and dared police officers, who were cleared of wrongdoing by the FBI,[36] to come out and face them. Members of the crowd shouted taunting references to the 1890 shooting death of Lakota spiritual leader Sitting Bull, which occurred nearby at the hands of Native police officers. Even this dramatic event, with its historical resonance, received little media coverage.[37]

Native Americans' experiences of violence and discrimination may occur in a national blind spot, similar to the "blank" described by ACLU attorney Laughlin McDonald in Chapter 2, but they often parallel the better-known sufferings of African Americans. Federal investigations have found that in towns and cities on the borders of Indian reservations, police and public agencies treat tribal members as second-class citizens in ways that echo the black experience. The US Commission on Civil Rights, or USCCR, an independent government agency, has held hearings on border-town discrimination, including in New Mexico, near the Navajo Nation; in South Dakota, home to nine Sioux reservations; and near the Crow and Northern Cheyenne reservations in Montana.[38]

Incidents aired in USCCR hearings sound like tales from the pre-civil-rights Deep South. They range from denial of service in public places to police brutality and police failure to investigate murders. In northern plains states, USCCR members personally observed staff in restaurants and stores hassling or refusing to serve Natives. In South Dakota, the commission heard testimony about a police department that found reasons to fine Natives hundreds of dollars, then "allowed" them to work off the debt on a ranch. Malee Craft, who was then director of the USCCR's Rocky Mountain regional office, described the situation as "modern-day slave labor."[39]

"We are living a silent, comfortable genocide," said the late Philip Quinn's fiancée, Darleen Tareeq, who is of White Earth and Leech Lake Ojibwe heritage. "Everyone is cool with it—us dying and our cultures being taken away."[40]

PREJUDICE IS ONE DRIVER OF the relatively high rate of police killings of Natives. Another is the comparative dearth of mental-health services for American Indians, said Bonnie Duran, an Opelousas/Coushatta tribe descendant and a professor at the University of Washington School of Public Health.[41] People threatening suicide and experiencing other mental-health crises made up one-quarter of all those killed by cops in the United States during the first half of 2016, according to data collected by the *Washington Post.*[42] However, this group made up nearly half of the Native deaths examined by the Claremont Graduate University researchers.[43]

Distraught people facing stressful encounters with police— such as Jeanetta Riley in Sandpoint, Idaho, or Paul Castaway in Denver—can be particularly vulnerable. Commands from multiple officers in a quickly developing situation can be very difficult to parse, even for someone who is not in crisis, said Jim Trainum, a former Washington, DC, homicide detective who consults on criminal-justice matters.[44] Melissa Russano, a psychologist and criminal-justice professor at Roger Williams University, agreed. "Attending to conflicting signals from multiple sources results in a huge cognitive demand," Russano said. "Split-second responses are required of the individual. He or she has to assess if and to what extent there is a threat, and that may create a certain level of panic."[45]

In Native communities, the lack of mental-health services is particularly acute, according to an analysis of CDC data by the Suicide Prevention Resource Center, or SPRC.[46] This includes a critical shortage of Native professionals who understand cultural factors that should be taken into account when assessing an indigenous patient. Data from the National Congress of American Indians reveals the funding disparity: in 2013, Indian Health Service per-capita expenditures were $2,849, as compared to $7,717 per person for health-care spending nationally.[47] One result of the resource drought is the suicide rate for Natives, which in 2010 was 16.93 per 100,000 people, as compared with 12.08 per 100,000 for the population as a whole, according to SPRC.[48]

Mental-health resources for Native Americans are even scarcer in the so-called urban Indian communities. These are Native enclaves in off-reservation towns and cities, where about half the tribal population lives, according to Professor Duran. There, clinics are funded at a lower rate than reservation facilities, she said. The off-reservation areas are also where the largest share of police killings occur—83 percent of them, according to data collected by Schroedel and Chin.

As funding for mental-health care continues to plummet, police are increasingly the first responders to mental-health crises that they are not necessarily trained to handle. However, improvement may be on the horizon, as police departments find ways to solve this problem. Some departments pair officers with mental-health professionals during calls that clearly involve such issues. Some other departments, though not yet enough according to Roger Chin, give courses in Crisis Intervention Team training, or CIT.[49] This curriculum teaches officers to slow down and seek alternatives to the application of lethal force, according to police trainers for the state of Washington.[50] On the other hand, said criminal-justice expert Trainum, taking a course does not make officers experts at the technique. They have to expand and refresh their skills with regular follow-up training, and supervisors have to be supportive of the method, he said: "Otherwise, it's just a box to check." Research is not yet conclusive about which of these methods works best, said Duran. She stressed that the ideal solution was addressing the problem at the root: better funding for social services.

THE PUYALLUP TRIBE WAS CATAPULTED into the issue of police violence on the night tribal member Jacqueline Salyers was shot. The economically powerful, four-thousand-member Northwest Indian nation has successful casinos, tribal and individual fishing enterprises, a hotel, and a real-estate portfolio of commercial and industrial properties. Its land base overlaps the city of Tacoma, Washington, making it one of the country's few urban reservations. Residents of both the reservation and city include not just Puyallup members but Natives from other tribes, along with a diverse population whose ancestry spans the globe.[51]

After Salyers's death, her relatives began to question the police account of the incident. They hired an investigator to look into the conflicting information and data gaps in the official version. There was no video record: Tacoma officers used no body cams or dashcams at the time, a police surveillance camera overlooking the street allegedly malfunctioned during the event, and police apparently managed to destroy three security cameras that had been mounted on a nearby house. However, in response to a freedom-of-information request, the city of Tacoma provided hundreds of pages of witness statements, detectives' reports, 911 calls, logs of police-vehicle movements, scene photographs, and more. In addition to finding out how the event had unfolded, Salyers's family wanted to help ensure that police in Washington State and nationwide would be held accountable for their actions, no matter who the victim was, Native or non-Native.

The killing of Salyers horrified residents of the Tacoma neighborhood where it occurred. Gary Harrison, an army combat engineer who had served in Desert Storm, was awakened by the gunfire. The shooting happened in front of his home, he said, as he diagrammed what he observed during an interview in Tacoma. "I saw Jackie's car and so many police, for blocks around," he recalled. "Someone said, 'They shot Jackie.'" Harrison had known the young woman. "She always had a smile for you," he said, eyes bright with tears.

It was a terrifying night for the community, as well as a sad one. When an armored vehicle moved into position in front of the house, Harrison worried for the safety of his housemates. "We cleared buildings in Iraq, so I knew a vehicle like that has thermal imaging," he explained. "I told people in the house, don't move around. If you do, the police may think you're going for a weapon. And when they come in, hold your hands up, or you could get shot."

Professor Duran called this country's epidemic of police violence a public-health issue. Yet while we can know, for any given period, how many Americans came down with flu or visited an emergency room, we are not able to determine how many were shot by police, Duran said. She noted a 2015 Public Library of Science, or PLOS, paper contending that law-enforcement-related deaths affect communities' well-being and should be what is called a notifiable condition.[52] That would mean information about them would be disclosed to the CDC and made publicly available, said Duran. Without this data and the policy solutions that could follow, citizens' trust in government becomes "another casualty," the PLOS paper's authors wrote.

At Salyers's funeral, her mother, Lisa Earl, called for justice, not only for her daughter but for all those affected by excessive use of force by law enforcement. The Puyallup Tribe took up the challenge under the banner "Justice for Jackie, Justice for All." Salyers's relatives began meeting weekly at the community center where Earl works, to mourn and then to plan a two-mile protest march from the tribal headquarters to Tacoma's federal courthouse. On March 16, 2016, nearly three hundred people turned out for the protest walk, including non-Native city residents concerned about a range of issues, from workers' rights to the environment, in addition to police brutality.[53]

As time went by, ever more people began attending the family's gatherings. On the evening of June 20, 2016, participants filtered into the community center, hugged, and exchanged bits of gossip. They were Native, black, white, and Latino, young and old.

Wafting over the gathering was the aroma of cooking crab, which Salyers's uncle, James Rideout, had gathered earlier that day from Puget Sound. Participants sat in a traditional Puyallup talking circle. They expressed themselves in turn and without interruption, as they recounted their stories of tragedy and survival. Some could barely speak for crying, while others were angry and defiant.

Each person arrives in a different phase of grieving, said Rideout: "They are in such tender moments." According to Tlingit tribal member and participant Sylvia Sabon, everyone felt welcome. "It doesn't matter what color you are. We are all going through the same thing," she said.

The sense of safety was both psychological and physical. Puyallups had created a welcoming place for those who needed to express their feelings to supportive, nonjudgmental listeners. The participants also felt that they were out of harm's way. Several non-Natives told me that they believed they were physically safer on the reservation than elsewhere. They said that the Puyallup meetings gave them a respite from an ongoing feeling of danger hanging over their lives. Their assertions were visceral and vivid: while in the shelter of the Puyallup talking circle, neither they nor their loved ones could be shot.

At the meeting, André Taylor, who is African American, spoke about what he called the execution of his brother, Che Taylor, whom officers gunned down in Seattle in 2016. Sylvia Sabon described the police-shooting death of a twenty-three-year-old Latino family friend, Oscar Perez-Giron. Young white attendees described their cop-watching activities, which involved observing and videotaping police to help prevent misconduct. Crystal Chaplin, an African American mother from nearby Olympia, Washington, said that in 2015, officers shot both of her sons in the back; Bryson Chaplin was then twenty-one, and his brother André Thompson was twenty-three. Both survived, but Bryson was paralyzed. Lisa Hayes, a white advocate from nearby Olympia, talked about a ballot initiative that sought to bring to the state legislature a bill to make police more account-able under the law; it was eventually succeeded by a ballot initiative that also included a mandate for police training in handling such situations. "I want police violence to be a topic of conversation at every dinner table and on every porch," Hayes said.

"On January twenty-eighth, our family was made part of a circle of families throughout the nation who are living with this issue," said Chester Earl, another of Salyers's relatives. "Until then, I sympathized when I saw a television report that someone had been lost to a police shooting, but I have to admit I didn't do anything. That night, I was shocked off the couch and knew I had to get involved."

"We never asked to be a part of this," added Rideout. "We always want to stress the good narratives—our children succeeding. Right after Jackie died, we wanted to follow our quiet traditional ways of mourning and, after a year, have a memorial giveaway. But now that we are involved in the public aspects of this situation, we must ensure that nothing like it ever happens again."

Though Puyallup people have acknowledged Native Lives Matter as a movement, the thrust of their efforts has been ecumenical. That is where the "Justice for All" part of their slogan comes in. This makes sense to them culturally. The Puyallups' name for themselves in their own language can be translated as "the generous and welcoming people." Rideout explained, "When the police killings happened to people who didn't have a tribe to back them up, they

For this multigenerational group of Puyallups, canoeing is more than transportation. It is an expression of solidarity, cooperation, and caring, as well as of their enduring relationship to the water. (Joseph Zummo)

were alone, on their own out there. When our tribe took a position on this issue, we realized we had an opportunity to take care of them all, to bring them along with us." The idea goes back to heritage lifeways, said Chester Earl, who is president of the culturally important Puyallup canoe society: "We lived in longhouses, and everyone took care of each other, whether they were related by blood or not."

Puyallup tribal council member Tim Reynon called this the original significance of what it means to be a tribe. "Treaties we struck with outsiders meant an imposed definition of what it is to be a tribal member, confinement on reservations, and the breakup of traditional cooperative living patterns," Reynon said. "But long before that, tribes took care of their land and their people as they saw fit." He added that a tribe can be an effective advocate in ways that an activist group cannot. "We have a trust relationship with the federal government, so we are a sovereign nation with the full weight of the United States behind us. We also have the recognition and respect of local governments."

In 2016, Washington State legislative leaders appointed Reynon to a new Joint Legislative Task Force on Deadly Force in Community Policing, a committee drawn from community groups as well as law enforcement. The bill establishing the task force acknowledged the danger that police officers may face as they protect the community; the bill also sought ways to reduce violent interactions between law enforcement and the public. "We have to find a solution that works for everyone," Reynon said. "It will mean change, and change is never easy."

Tribal involvement means the possibility of real and lasting change to Ramona Bennett, a Puyallup elder in her late seventies. "People and movements may fade, but a tribe doesn't go away," said Bennett, a former Puyallup chairwoman who was gassed, shot at, beaten and arrested during the area's 1960s and 1970s fish-ins to affirm treaty fishing rights for Northwest tribes. I met her at her house on the outskirts of Tacoma, where we sat and talked at a picnic table set up under an awning.

The Puyallups endured so much official hostility over the years, in Bennett's telling, that they could be seen as proof of her assertion that tribes survive where other groups might not. Late nineteenth-century presidential proclamations and congressional actions, including the General Allotment Act discussed in Chapter 1, broke up the tribe's communal living arrangements. Tribal members were forced to move into isolated cabins on separate plots, said Bennett. "Certain forms of our fishing and trapping were also outlawed, so the men had to go out at night to obtain food, making the cabins very dangerous. White men would come, kick the doors in, rape and murder the women, and throw their bodies on the railroad tracks, where they'd be run over and called railroad-accident deaths.

Later, Bennett and others discovered a stack of 'railroad death' documents in the tribal enrollment office (an office that tracks the lives and deaths of authenticated tribal members). The documents covered the years from 1912 to 1917. Among them was the death record for Bennett's grandmother Jennie. The Justice for Jackie, Justice for All effort will succeed, Bennett believes: "But I'm still out for justice for Jennie, a girl who has been dead for one hundred and four years."

THE FLIP SIDE OF THE intense police and criminal-justice-system focus on Natives as alleged perpetrators of crime is their failure to investigate and prosecute when tribal members are victims. In 2007, Amnesty International revealed that Native women are raped at several times the rate of other American women. Yet tribal women are caught in what Amnesty

International called a "maze of injustice," with state and federal authorities unwilling or unable to investigate, much less prosecute, such crimes. Complicated overlapping jurisdictions put different police forces in charge at any given place and time, depending on multiple factors, including whether the crime occurred on or off Indian land and whether the alleged perpetrator and victim were or were not Native. The lack of rape kits and other forensic resources for Indian country adds more hurdles.[54] The Violence Against Women Act eventually included Native women in its protections, over vigorous Republican opposition. However, the act has reportedly been rolled out to a pilot project of just a small number of tribes; in 2017, it had reached thirteen out of a total of more than five hundred sixty tribes.[55]

In South Dakota, scores of unsolved murders of tribal members go back decades.[56] The bodies of murdered Natives have been found lying by roadsides, floating in a river, and stuffed in a garbage can. Tribal members have been shot, stabbed, run over, and hacked to death. The few who were convicted of these crimes got very light sentences—as few as two years for murder—when the victim was Native. Also concerning, said the US Commission on Civil Rights, it learned that South Dakota's white leaders and ordinary citizens commonly deny the existence of racism toward indigenous people.[57]

The Oglala Sioux Tribe has long advocated for a closer examination of crimes that occurred on its homeland, the Pine Ridge Indian Reservation. In May 2000, the Minneapolis division of the FBI, which covers South Dakota, attempted to quell suspicions of poor or nonexistent investigations by listing its "findings" for fifty-seven cases it looked into over the years.[58] In 2012, after years of trying to obtain more details about the cases, Tom Poor Bear, then the vice president of the Oglala Sioux Tribe, described the FBI's findings as lacking in "rationality and common sense."

Many of the findings were as short as a sentence or two and offered more confusion than clarity. Examples include a man who died of stab wounds to the face and neck and was ruled a suicide, despite the wounds being a highly unlikely manner of self-harm. Then there was the axe murderer who was not prosecuted because of "a mental condition." The FBI finding did not reveal whether the condition was determined via an official process or was merely a guess on someone's part; nor was it clear whether the axe-wielding assailant ended up with mental-health care, or even adjudication, of any kind. More FBI findings held that several tribal members died of exposure; in some of these examples, family members apparently believed that the dead were beaten, including by law enforcement, prior to being left to die. The FBI report also seemed to imply that the agency did not investigate when federal officers may have been involved in the deaths.[59]

The incomplete, often fantastical, information in the FBI report made the reader feel that any of it could well be suspect. The situation has left people on the reservation feeling unsettled for decades, I learned there from one victim's frightened relative, who asked not to be identified for fear of retribution. "I want to know what happened to my sister, but I'm afraid that if I look into it, someone will come after me," she said. Nevertheless, she felt that somehow "justice should be done."

—

THE GRASSROOTS NATIVE LIVES MATTER movement has been working to bring attention to the enduring patterns of individual and institutional violence against Native Americans, as well as to their social and economic marginalization. Arising in several states at once, mostly during 2014, the movement was inspired by Black Lives Matter, said one of its several originators, Chase Iron Eyes, a Standing Rock Sioux attorney who has run for Congress in North Dakota and was a leader in the Standing Rock anti-pipeline resistance. From the beginning, Iron Eyes's view of Native Lives Matter encompassed numerous issues affecting tribal people, from child welfare to incarceration disparities. Facebook pages and Twitter feeds show that this wide perspective has proliferated across Indian country, with grassroots groups adopting the moniker Native Lives Matter as an umbrella term to advocate for multiple causes.[60]

"Native Lives Matter is a movement for reclaiming our inherent spiritual dignity," Iron Eyes said. "It is a healing and a way to move beyond what has been imposed on us for five hundred years—since the arrival of Europeans. Black Lives Matter brought attention to police brutality and institutional racism, and we Natives were very aware of that when we coined our version of the term. But we also wanted Native Lives Matter to be understood as expansive—advocating for improvement in the many quality-of-life issues that affect our communities, in addition to pointing out police shootings specifically." He called the movement "a comprehensive call to action for social-justice reform."

In December 2014, Iron Eyes and a group of friends organized a rally in Rapid City, South Dakota, to bring attention to what Natives contributed to the local economy. The rally occurred during the popular Lakota National Invitational, an annual basketball tourney that has attracted thousands of attendees and related spending to Rapid City for more than forty years. Tribal members' monetary contribution to the city does not begin and end with the tournament, though. Because the nearby Pine Ridge and Rosebud Indian Reservations have relatively few businesses, their residents shop in Rapid City throughout the year.[61]

However, while Natives support the Rapid City economy, their quality-of-life indicators there and around South Dakota are poor. This situation is compounded by the bitter resentment directed toward them by non-Native people, as one might observe in cities and towns surrounding reservations and other concentrations of Native population. From rural areas to cities like Los Angeles and Denver, non-Natives are quick to rail against Natives, for reasons that are often strangely inarticulate. Non-Natives may cite a range of misinformation, from the fantasy that "Indians pay no taxes" to the idea that tribal members are all living high on the hog on casino money or government funding.[62] "Yeah, we got a great deal," one advocate on a very poor reservation told me. "Just look around."

A Lakota resident of Rapid City named Allen Locke happened to attend the rally that Iron Eyes and his friends organized in December 2014. "The next day was the championship game," Iron Eyes recalled. "I went to buy Christmas gifts, and when I returned to the tournament, everyone's Facebook timelines were going crazy with the information that cops had shot someone in a development called Lakota Homes. Some of us went over and learned it was Allen Locke." Locke's family asked for help dealing with the sudden flood of police and media attention, and Iron

Eyes and his friends agreed to assist. The advocates later shifted their operations to the Rapid City office of the Lakota People's Law Project, where Iron Eyes worked. They held press conferences and produced releases about what had happened. Iron Eyes wanted to document what was occurring and wrote a report, *Native Lives Matter*, that became an early influential description of the movement.

In Minnesota's Twin Cities, two young friends were also influential. Hip-hop and dubstep musician Troy Amlee, from the Standing Rock and Cheyenne River Sioux Tribes, and J. R. Bobick, from Saint Paul, founded a popular Native Lives Matter–related Facebook page in early 2014.[63] Amlee, whose Lakota name is Akicita Sunka Wakan Ska, or White Horse Soldier, recalled his introduction to social action. "In 2011, a lot of *tokala*, who are members of a traditional warrior society, attended the funeral of my uncle Beau Little Sky. He had been in AIM, the American Indian Movement. I was nineteen at the time and observed that they had a consciousness about them. I was curious." The teenager joined AIM, where he brought food to the homeless and participated in cop-watching patrols. This work introduced him to Occupy Minnesota and Idle No More Twin Cities. He wrote on the latter's Facebook page about the December 2013 police-shooting death of a Native teen and went on to collaborate on a new page.

Social media has been essential to the spread of Native Lives Matter. American Indians are tribal people, explained Iron Eyes: "There are few degrees of separation between any of us. We're also highly involved internet users, with the ability to go viral even though we're a small percentage of the US population." He pointed out that tweets about opposition to the Dakota Access Pipeline were trending high on Twitter long before there was much mainstream media coverage. "The world where you had to get a TV network to cover you doesn't exist anymore," Iron Eyes said. "That's old-school."

Marlee Kanosh agreed.[64] She is the sister of Paiute police-shooting victim Corey Kanosh. "Without the internet and social media, each of us would be talking to small communities," said Kanosh. "With online connections, we talk to a larger audience." At first, Kanosh went online to find solace for the 2012 loss of her brother. She discovered what she calls "a whole world" of people suffering similar tragedies. "People whose relatives had been killed reached out to me. The huge community of those affected by police violence embraced my family. Now, I reach out to embrace others and let them know I have been where they are. Whenever a new person or family comes in, we all gather around them."

In early 2015, she began volunteering as the administrator of the Facebook page Native Lives Taken by Police. "I didn't know how to deal with what happened to Corey, other than to use my pain to be helpful to others, to share their stories," Kanosh said. The initial information for each of her posts comes from her large and ever-expanding circle of contacts, including community members, advocates, and groups nationwide. "People message me constantly," she said. "Groups share lists with me. I know relatives of those who died. I know their neighbors. If someone thinks someone who has been killed just might be Native, they send me the information, so I can look into it."

Kanosh's posts plumb the personal side of a victim's story. After she researches an incident, she talks to the family. "I find

STEPHANIE WOODARD · *181*

out more about who the victims were and get permission to use personal photographs and other material." The work invades her dreams. "Each night after I do a story for the page, I dream about it. Today, opening up the page and seeing all the stories there overwhelmed me, and I know there are even more." Though many Native Lives Matter–related pages cover the wide range of issues that interest tribal members, Marlee Kanosh's does not. "I focus on police brutality."

In October 2016, eight Natives reportedly died at the hands of the police. Kanosh's workload for the Facebook page was suddenly heavier. Her notebooks were full of information, and her tabletops were covered with piles of paper. The fatalities apparently occurred around the country—on the Muckleshoot Reservation in Washington State, where a young mother was shot dead in front of her young children during a welfare check, apparently because she was threatening suicide; in Oklahoma, where a homeless Native man met his death at the hands of police; and in Nevada, where an Oglala military veteran was shot after a sudden spate of ineffectual robberies that were by all accounts more of a mental-health crisis than a crime spree. Two more indigenous people appear to have been killed in Oklahoma, while Nebraska, Texas, and North Carolina seemed to see at least one Native fatality each.[65] Kanosh cannot point to a reason for the spike, but noted, as has Bonnie Duran, that poorly funded health care and untreated or under-treated mental issues continue to place Native people in jeopardy when facing police.[66]

Kanosh criticized common police claims that citizens should simply follow orders in order to survive these encounters. "We have a saying here in Utah, 'Comply or Die—It's Not the Law!'"

Kanosh said. "What about our rights? We didn't put up our hands fast enough? What about the man I am aware of who was shot when he instinctively pulled up his pants after cops ordered him to crawl forward on his knees? How can we possibly know instantly what's expected of us in these horrible situations? And because we don't, we *die*?"

This thought is echoed in the dissent Supreme Court justice Sonia Sotomayor wrote in 2017 in *Salazar-Limon v. Houston*.[67] Justice Ruth Bader Ginsburg joined in Sotomayor's opinion. The case turned on a lower court tossing out the claim of an unarmed man, Ricardo Salazar-Limon, who was shot by a Houston police officer. The officer alleged that Salazar-Limon had reached for his waistband, which the officer said he perceived to be consistent with reaching for a gun. The Supreme Court backed the lower court. As a result, a jury will not hear the case.

Sotomayor slammed the high court, writing that as a matter of law, lawsuits can be thrown out only if there is no dispute of fact. But *Salazar-Limon v. Houston* had what Sotomayor called "competing affidavits." In such a case, she wrote, American jurisprudence does not allow a judge to accept the word of one party over the other. "Our system entrusts this decision to a jury sitting as finder of fact, not a judge reviewing a paper record." In a disturbing revelation, Sotomayor wrote that the high court had recently intervened five times to prevent a lower court from allowing the trial of a police officer to proceed. At the same time, said Sotomayor, the reverse was not true. The high court rarely intervened on behalf of victims when lower courts threw out cases against officers.

She noted another alarming trend, writing: "Some commentators have observed the increasing frequency of incidents in which unarmed men allegedly reach for empty waistbands when facing armed officers." She cited a *Los Angeles Times* article reporting that nearly half of individuals shot by that city's police officers after reaching for waistbands turned out to be unarmed. "With these cases becoming increasingly common," according to Sotomayor, it is ever more important "to let the jury exercise its role as an arbiter of credibility."

In *Salazar-Limon,* Sotomayor concluded, "we take one step back today."

IT WAS A BRIGHT MORNING, and photographer Joseph Zummo and I were in a small crab vessel in Puget Sound, north of Tacoma. Jacqueline Salyers's uncle James Rideout was baiting and tossing overboard about a dozen wire-mesh crab pots, as Zummo photographed him. "Crabs travel on the currents, so you try to throw the pot so its door faces into the current," said Rideout, as he stuffed squid into a small bait canister hanging inside a pot. As Rideout worked, the boat crisscrossed the sound, with its forested islands and peninsulas. Beyond them, Mount Rainier's massive snow-covered peak appeared to glide around the horizon, slipping behind one hilly shoreline, then another.

Toward evening, Rideout would return to collect the crabs, so they could be cooked for one of the regular community meetings that have followed Salyers's shooting death. That week, Rideout also gathered crabs for another tribal member's funeral. "Hundreds of our people may attend a funeral and by contributing food, we can take the pressure off the grieving family to organize feeding them all," Rideout explained.

The baited crab pots that Puyallup fisherman and tribal council member James Rideout throws into Puget Sound will provide a meal for those gathering later that day to remember his niece Jacqueline Salyers, who was killed by police in Tacoma, Washington. (Joseph Zummo)

During my visit to the Puyallup tribe, that was one of many examples I saw of the cultural ties that bind tribal members to each other. On another pleasant day, I watched Chester Earl supervise dozens of people, as they practiced for an upcoming multi-tribal canoe journey. Groups sharing a canoe ranged in age from kindergartners to retirees and worked together on technique and strength-building as they plied the reservation shoreline. Earl pointed out that canoeing was historically more than a way to get around. It was an expression of cooperation, caring, and a spiritual relationship to the world. "Our connection to the water kept us alive," Earl said.

In the boat on Puget Sound, Rideout gestured toward the ocean depths, where tribal members dive for a large clam called the geoduck, considered a delicacy. "It's another world down there," he said. "When you come back to the surface after a dive, you're never the same." Rideout evoked the memory of his niece and the feeling that his family and community are similarly struggling to the surface, transformed, after the tragedy. "None of us who have lost family and friends to police violence will ever really get justice, because nothing will bring them back," he said. "But we can work together to ensure that no else ever experiences it."

There is one important requirement as they undertake these efforts, Rideout said. "We must make sure we don't end up with hate in our hearts."

5.

Take the Children

THE SLIDE PROJECTED ON THE screen offered a list of imperatives: *Take Territory, Take Natural Resources, Take Sovereignty* . . . The image was part of a lecture by Terry Cross, a member of the Seneca Nation of Indians and director of the National Indian Child Welfare Association. Cross was using the list to explain how colonialism works, as he addressed a conference put together by the First Nations Repatriation Institute.[1] The meeting took place in a large, open room, with about fifty attendees seated around folding tables at the University of Minnesota Twin Cities in Saint Paul. The group included tribal members and leaders, community activists, officials of child-centered nonprofits, welfare workers, judges, and attorneys. The Repatriation Institute specializes in helping Native adoptees find their way home, so the most important people present, according to founder and conference organizer Sandra White Hawk, were adoptees who had come to share their experiences.

The preceding chapters of this book have laid out the manner in which Native people's homelands, natural resources, sacred places, freedom, and safety have been compromised or destroyed over the years. We have looked at the ways in which these actions continue in the present day with the aid of federal agencies, state and local governments, and the corporations that cozy up to them. In Cross's telling, this dismembering has usurped tribal sovereignty and attacked the spirituality of communities and individuals. Though the losses have tested indigenous identity over many years, the lifeways of the nation's first people have remarkable staying power. The late David McAllester, an anthro-

Yankton Sioux children play lacrosse on an historic fort's parade ground, in southeastern South Dakota. "To save bullets, cavalrymen smashed our children's heads with rifle butts," said Yankton tribal member Kip Spotted Eagle. "Now, our children are transforming this place's memories with laughter and joy." (Stephanie Woodard)

pology professor at Wesleyan University in Connecticut who studied Navajo and Comanche music, was fond of telling his students that culture should not be understood as a fragile hothouse flower. Rather, he said, it is a weed that thrives in many settings and against all odds.

To push forward the effort to sweep away tribal people, one more step was, and continues to be, necessary. The final entry on Cross's slide was: "Take the Children." "The last item is removal of the children to educate them in the language and worldview of the colonizer," Cross told the conference. The strategy is reminiscent of Teddy Roosevelt's "pulverizing engine," described in Chapter 1, but applied to children rather than land. Several Native adoptees at the conference recalled being separated from their families and the effect it had on their lives. White Hawk told the group that she was taken from her family as a toddler on the Rosebud Indian Reservation in South Dakota. It was the mid-1950s. After decades of disconnection from her roots, along with what she remembered as continual warnings against turning into "a good-for-nothing drunken Indian," she found her way home to family, culture, and identity.

White Hawk's childhood experience had its beginnings in assimilation policies conceived in the previous century. Carl Schurz, a Union Army general who served as Interior Department secretary from 1877 to 1881, calculated that killing just one Indian in warfare was costing the federal government about a million dollars.[2] Meanwhile, the emerging alternative—educating a Native child according to "white" norms in off-reservation boarding schools—would set the government back about $1,200 per child over eight years.[3] Schurz realized there was a cost-cutting way to solve what was referred to in those days as the Indian problem; the federal government could give the tribes a choice—extermination or civilization. Another expert of the day declared, "We must either butcher them or civilize them."[4]

If parents refused to relinquish their children, the Bureau of Indian Affairs withheld the food and money allocations the treaties had established in return for tribes ceding land. The idea of forcibly assimilating Native people had its roots in the 1600s but got underway in earnest in 1890.[5] A witness later wrote about how students were recruited for the boarding schools: "The children are caught, often roped like cattle, and taken away from their parents, many times never to return."[6] In the clinical language of federal policymakers, this process was generally referred to as the "collection and transportation, and so forth, of pupils."[7]

The boarding schools offered mainly vocational education.[8] As Teddy Roosevelt directed Congress in 1901, "In the schools, the education should be elementary and largely industrial. The need of higher education among the Indians is very, very limited."[9] The government retained the administration of some schools, but many were parceled out to Protestant and Catholic denominations; in Chapter 1, we also saw this contradiction of the nation's supposed separation of church and state in the evolution of Supreme Court decisions regarding indigenous peoples. Eradicating Native cultures and languages was paramount for the federal government, and it relied on churches to do this.

Since most Native children in those days were monolingual in their tribal language, or at least first speakers of it, it was literally pummeled out of them. Many children did not survive the beatings, crowded conditions, poor food, epidemics, and lack of medical care.[10] Incomplete or lost records mean the number of Native children who died is unknown. Children often had compulsory assignments as domestic or farm workers for white families, essentially slave labor. A tribal member who was in her fifties when I spoke to her in 2012 remembered participating in harvesting and other fieldwork during elementary school. She was surprised when I asked whether her parents had given permission for this, or if she had ever been paid. "I never thought of it, but 'no' to both questions," she responded.[11]

Sexual abuse was rampant in church-run schools, largely because the churches used the institutions as dumping grounds for clerics who had exploited youngsters elsewhere.[12] (Sexual assaults may have been less common in the government-run schools, though there was plenty of physical abuse, according to former students I spoke to who had attended both kinds of institution.)[13] Court documents for one lawsuit, brought by former students, included a 1968 letter to Catholic Church superiors from a priest at St. Francis Mission on the Rosebud Sioux Reservation. After a chatty opening in which the priest reports that he has been "kinda busy" and that "all goes along quietly out here," he mentions, almost as an aside, that a certain Brother Chapman has been "fooling around with little girls—he had them down the basement of our building in the dark, where we found a pair of panties torn." Subsequent reports show that "Chappy" continued to abuse children for years, briefly became "a new man," then relapsed into more "difficulty with little girls."[14]

Any effect this abuse may have had on the children, physical or emotional, did not seem to come up. During the years I reported on former students' sexual-assault allegations—approximately 2011–15—I viewed original documents, read testimony, and conducted interviews. I never saw any indication that staff believed they had a duty of care toward the students who were in their charge. Quite the opposite: a contemporary Catholic

Church lawyer told me in 2011 that the plaintiffs who had filed the lawsuits were "trying to grab the brass ring" and "thinking that's your ticket out of squalor."[15] The South Dakota courts eventually threw out the suits after the state legislature passed a bill called HB 1104 in 2010.[16] The statute prohibited child-sexual-abuse claims against institutions by anyone over age forty. Since the schools had closed in the 1970s, most former students were in their fifties or older at that point. Their cases were neatly swept away.

Native former students in the Northwest and Alaska did reach a settlement with the Jesuits in 2011,[17] and additional ex-students who had been in Montana schools did in 2014.[18] The latter settlement was with the Diocese of Helena and the Ursuline Sisters of the Western Province. It included an offer of counseling by the Church. One plaintiff I interviewed regarded it as far too little, far too late, and even outlandish. "It's absurd," scoffed the plaintiff, whom the lawsuit listed as John Doe to protect his privacy. "So, they're going to get the rapists and abusers together and put them in charge?"[19]

Trust was another victim of the assaults. "We lost trust in the priests and nuns," said the John Doe plaintiff. "When we tried to tell family members, they didn't believe us. How could they imagine religious people did such things? So we lost trust in our families. We victims wander the earth alone, bearing heavy burdens, with no place to put them down."[20] The lawsuits typically result in little money for individual plaintiffs, once any financial settlement is divided up and parceled out. Plaintiffs I asked about this said that they had not sued for the money but found that it was the only way they could create change. At least, John Doe said, lawsuits like the one he participated in meant a lower chance of children being abused in the future.[21]

Children ran away continually from the schools, so barred windows, locked classrooms and dormitories, and barbed-wire fences were common at the facilities. At Saint Paul's Indian Mission on the Yankton Sioux Reservation in South Dakota, I was able to view the derelict buildings as well as photographs from decades past. The church had been surrounded by barbed wire during the boarding-school era, lest congregants make a run for it. Still, students managed to get out. "I was always trying to escape," said one woman about another school. "We all did. We weren't trying to get home because we didn't know where that was. We were completely disoriented. We just took off and took our chances in the world, hitchhiking down the road. Then they'd find us and bring us back."

Punishments meted out by the schools for running away and other supposed offenses were extreme. Interviews I did revealed that staff beat children with boards, sticks, and hoses; they threw them down stairs and locked them outdoors in winter; the teachers and others pulled children's hair out by handfuls, shaved their heads, and withheld food.[22] Tribal members on several reservations described so-called belt lines, in which children were lined up and made to whip others as they crawled by. One man said that no matter how painful his memories were of being hit, those of hitting other boys and seeing them beg for mercy were far worse.[23] "They took away our sense of belonging to anyone, our opportunities to develop relationships," said one woman. "But they could never take away the truth, that what they were doing was wrong."[24]

This cataclysm, which took place over a century, roiled individual lives and devastated communities as succeeding generations were swept into a bizarre, sadistic world that lasted into the 1970s. "Isolated groups of vulnerable children, plus religious people in charge, equals abuse. It's just a fact. I have not found a residential institution for Indian children where it didn't happen, no matter the location or the denomination," said investigator Ken Bear Chief, who is Gros Ventre, Nez Perce, and Nooksak. He worked for Tamaki Law Firm in Yakima, Washington, which brought several of the successful sexual-abuse lawsuits.[25]

During the mid-twentieth century, the schools began to be closed down or turned over to the tribes. The process paralleled other increases in tribal self-determination in those years. President Nixon was particularly helpful. In his 1970 Special Message to Congress, he denounced the so-called termination policy of the 1950s and 1960s, which had destroyed certain tribes legally and economically in order to force their members to assimilate. Nixon also advocated for protection of sacred sites and the tribal takeover of programs that served their members in health, economic development, education, and other areas.[26] In 1978, the American Indian Religious Freedom Act reversed constraints and outright bans on Native religious observances.[27]

WHILE THE BOARDING SCHOOLS WERE fading away, other ways to separate Indian children from their families were coming into focus: adoption and foster care. In 1969 and 1974, Association on American Indian Affairs surveys showed that as many as 35 percent of Indian youngsters had been removed from their homes, with almost all of them placed in non-Native foster homes, adoptive homes, or group settings.[28] Owing to the professionalization of social work over the course of the twentieth century, child-welfare workers began to replace the clergy, police, and soldiers who once showed up to take tribal youngsters. The federal Indian Adoption Project and the prestigious Child Welfare League of America were key groups behind this policy. Later, the Adoption Resource Exchange of North America took over the program.

Some states had extreme disparities in the placement of Native children. Recognizing the crisis, the Association on American Indian Affairs collected research and testimony from experts nationwide and published it in 1977.[29] In Minnesota, the statistics revealed, Native children were placed in foster care or adoption at a rate five times that of non-Native children. In Wisconsin, it was seventeen times higher. In Washington State, placements in foster care were ten times higher, and the adoption rate was nineteen

Throughout Indian country these days, young Natives participate avidly in their heritage cultures. Bridgette Mongeon of Zuni Pueblo, New Mexico, rehearses with the virtuosic Zuni dance group Soaring Eagle; the musicians are Howard Lesarlley, left, and Arlen Quetawki Jr. This troupe may be profoundly traditional, but it also has a YouTube channel, 505soaringeagle. (Joseph Zummo)

times greater. Child-welfare workers often tricked, bullied, or physically forced Native parents to relinquish their children, with no regard for due process.[30] In an essay in the book, South Dakota's Democratic congressman, James Abourezk, accused the federal government of allowing state agencies "to strike at the heart of the Indian community by literally stealing Indian children."[31]

"People may know about the boarding-school era and how bad it was," said White Hawk. "But few know that the subsequent adoption era even existed."[32] Those she invited to the conference I reported on in Saint Paul were determined to change that. They wanted to share what had happened and to understand better the legal, social, and personal devastation it had wrought. "A few small studies of adult adoptees have been done, and we're just learning how to talk about what happened," White Hawk told the group. "We need think tanks and conferences and scientific research to explore what occurred and how it affected us." That understanding will inform current Indian child-welfare cases, as when courts consider returning a child to his or her family or terminating parental rights. "When experts take the stand to testify in a child-welfare hearing," White Hawk said, "they need academic backup to explain the relationship between suicide and being disconnected from your culture, let's say. The courts want PhD-level research to back up what we tell them."[33]

"Lost bird" is a term often used to refer to the children. It recalls one of the earliest Indian adoptees: a baby girl who survived the 1890 Wounded Knee massacre in the shelter of her mother's frozen corpse. She was subsequently claimed as a trophy by an army officer. He took her home as a kind of living curio and named her Lost Bird. Newspaper coverage of the massacre and its aftermath made Lost Bird a celebrity. However, her fame did not save her from a fate that was a harbinger of what was to come for too many Native adoptees.[34]

In her new home, Lost Bird experienced intolerance and isolation, and her adoptive father apparently abused her sexually. When she rebelled as a teenager, she was shipped back to her birth family, where she no longer fit in. After a stint in Buffalo Bill's Wild West Show, two disastrous marriages, one of which left her with syphilis, and the loss of three children, Lost Bird was felled by influenza in 1920. "Throughout her life of prejudice, exploitation, poverty, misunderstanding, and disease, she never gave up hope that one day she would find out where she really belonged," wrote Renée Sansom Flood in her biography, *Lost Bird of Wounded Knee: Spirit of the Lakota.*[35]

At repatriation events White Hawk has organized, modern-day adoptees recount their dramatic life journeys, sometimes for the first time. "The stories vary from the most abusive to the most beautiful, but that's not the point," White Hawk said. "Even in loving families, Native adoptees live without a sense of who they are. Love doesn't provide identity."[36]

"I'm an angry Indian," Roger St. John, of the Sisseton Wahpeton Oyate, in North and South Dakota, told the conference in Saint Paul. "I'm more than glad to tell you I'm pissed off. I was the youngest of sixteen children, grabbed at age four, along with three older brothers—no paperwork, nothing. The other kids in my family escaped because they took off." Soon, St. John and his siblings were in New York City. The year was 1966, and it was Thanksgiving. "We were in the newspaper, along with lots of good talk about the holiday and adoption. We were brought up without our culture, which took a terrible toll on our lives. I grew up angry and miserable. If I ever got hurt, it wounded me to my soul, because I felt no one was there for me," said St. John, a forty-nine-year-old truck driver with dark hair pulled back in a ponytail.

When St. John turned eighteen, or aged out of the adoption system, his parents turned him out—a fate I heard from several adoptees. Suddenly at loose ends, some adoptees joined the armed forces, as St. John did. Others ended up on the street or in prison. As an adult, St. John found his birth mother and reconnected with his adoptive parents. "They were so young," he said of the latter, "in their twenties, when a priest convinced them to adopt four Sioux boys from South Dakota. It was too much—for all of us."

Almost any personal or family setback, from minor to serious, could precipitate an Indian family losing a child. When I interviewed adoptees from several reservations, two said they were separated from their families after hospital stays as young children, one for a rash, the other after contracting tuberculosis. A third was seized at the home of his babysitter; he recalled her being punched and knocked over in the process. A fourth said that he was taken after his father died, though his mother did not want to give him up. A fifth described being snatched, along with siblings, because his grandfather was a medicine man who would not abandon his traditional ways.

I sat with one extended family on a South Dakota reservation and listened to stories about several siblings, who were then middle-aged and older adults. It was late afternoon, and the sun slanted in through the living room windows, sinking in the western sky as they methodically recounted how every child had been removed from the family, temporarily or permanently. Their experience bridged the boarding-school and adoption eras. The older ones had been sent to residential schools. The youngest was an adoptee, who had tracked down his birth family through a series of lucky connections. As with St. John's family, no home studies or comparable investigations had apparently been done to support his removal. Nor did the families appear to have been offered help for any perceived problems. "I have questions, but there are no records," the adoptee said. "I lost my culture and my relatives. There should have been something to protect me as a child. Why did the state do what it did?" His sister-in-law answered, "Because they could." In a separate interview, another tribal member explained, "We Indians had no way to stop white people from taking our kids. We had no rights."

Then, and even now, Native families do not receive the assistance they need to get back on their feet. "Non-Native families experiencing adversity may get a wide range of aid," said Danialle Rose, of the Cheyenne River Sioux Tribe. She is a clinical social worker who runs the Medicine Voice Healing Center in Hot Springs, South Dakota. "Native families don't know to ask for help and, in my observation, aren't told."[37]

In 1978, Congress tried to check the flood of Native children from their families by passing the Indian Child Welfare Act, or ICWA. The law was intended to protect Native children, preserve their families, and promote the stability of tribes.[38] ICWA allows federally recognized tribes to intervene when agencies want to remove children who are, or are eligible to become, members under the tribe's rules; it also allows child-welfare cases to be transferred to tribal court. ICWA requires agencies to make active efforts to ascertain whether youngsters are Native, to provide services to Native families so they can avoid losing their children, and to reunify families when their offspring have been taken. Revelations about the large number of Native children who had been separated from their families were central to getting the law passed. However, the numbers remain extreme today. According to the US Department of Health and Human Services, in 2013 American Indian and Alaska Native children had the highest rate of representation in foster care, increasing over recent years even as other groups saw declines.[39]

Indian child-welfare expert Frank LaMere is a member of the Winnebago Tribe of Nebraska, and director of Four Directions Community Center, in Sioux City, Iowa. He is involved in state and national policy matters and advocates for individual families. "I sit in on many meetings to determine the fate of Native families—along with judges, lawyers, social workers, and others involved—and I observe that they do not apply objective standards," LaMere said. "If one standard were applied to all, Native children would go home more often than not. Time after time in these meetings, the Native parent has solved the issue—typically alcohol or drugs—that caused the children to be taken away. The parent proudly announces, 'I've been sober for twenty-two months,' or what have you. We all congratulate them on their new wellness. After that conversation dies down, a social worker inevitably says, 'Well, yes, but . . .' and raises a long-resolved issue, from literally twenty years ago, or something new."

LaMere recalled that at one meeting he attended, a social worker announced that she had found dirty dishes in the sink during her last visit to the mother's home. "She said the mother therefore shouldn't get her kids back. I became unglued. I stressed that the mother didn't lose her children over dirty dishes, and they couldn't be kept from her for this reason. I deal with this kind of thing every single week."[40]

"Native families have to prove their worth in order to keep their children, or to become legal guardians of a relative's children," said Danialle Rose. "In contrast, Caucasian families are worthy until proven unworthy. This is an important distinction, and I don't think it's understood or even talked about."[41]

Terry Yellow Fat called it the criminalization of poverty. He was a child-welfare official of the Standing Rock Sioux Tribe, in South and North Dakota, when I spoke to him in 2012. He pointed out that approved Native foster homes sat empty, while tribal children were overwhelmingly placed in non-Native facilities. Yellow Fat and other South Dakota tribal officials noted another alarming trend. In the state, the "other" category for Native children in care—those who died, ran away, or were transferred to correctional or mental-health facilities—had grown from 6.9 to 32.8 percent per year over a recent decade. "The emotional and cultural damage to our children is enormous," said Yellow Fat. "I had one case earlier this year in which a young child said, 'I'll kill myself if I can't go home.' That child is back with us and is doing well, but others stay in the system until they age out at eighteen. At that point, they're lost, they don't fit in anywhere, and many end up on the streets, on drugs."

"Vicious" was how Yellow Fat described state welfare workers. "Their attitude is, 'They're just Indians.' Why? Why? We're human. So many tribal members have come forward to say they lost their children, sometimes years ago, and don't know where they are. *Wakan injan*—our children are sacred. We must take care of them."[42]

"We can't be afraid to use words like genocide," Anita Fineday told the repatriation conference in Saint Paul. She is from the White Earth Band of Ojibwe and a director of Indian child-welfare programs at Casey Family Programs. "The endgame, the official federal policy, was that the tribes wouldn't exist. A lot of federal laws don't make sense, laws resulting in the checkerboarding of reservations and so on, but they were passed anyway because no one thought the tribes would continue to exist."

The financial incentives for removing Native children are high. The billions in federal dollars disbursed annually on behalf of all fostered and adopted children—Native and non-Native—are parceled out among state agencies, foster and adoptive parents, group homes, research projects, law firms, and other entities. They, in turn, make purchases, hire employees and independent contractors, pay taxes, and engage in other economic activity that has local and regional impact. The multibillion-dollar private adoption industry is another beneficiary of the increased availability of children. Bottom line, adoption and other child-welfare services are worth some $14 billion annually for all population groups in this country.[43]

When Native children are disproportionately taken, the greater numbers mean more money for all concerned. In reporting on ICWA issues in 2011, National Public Radio asked former South Dakota governor William Janklow, now deceased, how important the federal child-care funds were to his state. His answer was unequivocal. "Incredibly important," he responded. "Look, we're a poor state. We're not a high-income state. We're like North Dakota without oil. We're like Nebraska without Omaha and Lincoln. We don't have factories opening here, hiring people at high-wage jobs."[44]

"Our children feed the system," said LaMere. "They will continue to do so, because the funding is set up that way. Those who work for the system won't speak up. Beyond that, many social workers and courts nationwide feel they know better than we do about what's good for our children. It remains for Native people to speak up. We must keep blowing the whistle on the child-welfare system to local, state, and national lawmakers. Only then will we have a chance to keep our families intact." According to LaMere, nothing will change "until someone feels uncomfortable. That includes us. It is hard to confront those who control the systems that control our lives, but we must. Our children and their futures are in jeopardy. We have a long way to go, but we will prevail."[45]

According to Ken Bear Chief, the end result of taking Native children from their families is unresolved personal and community-wide grief. On reservations, he observes much loss-related dysfunction, including alcoholism, divorce, and spousal abuse. This is often referred to as historical trauma, because the pain is passed down by means of damaged identities and relationships that can be perpetuated when the survivors form their own families. Danialle Rose described the difficulty Native children can have when they return home. "They're mistrustful in public situations," she said. "Before they were placed in foster care or a residential setting, they went to powwows but now have forgotten how to dance, for example. If returning children were taken when they were at school, they may be afraid to go there again. Even children who have never been removed from their families may be fearful when they see an unknown vehicle because they know about the possibility of being taken away."

Still, Rose said, she had also observed Native adults who had had a very difficult time in adoptive and foster settings yet had managed to move on to full, productive lives. "It was a rough road for them, especially during their teen and early adult years, but some had done it nevertheless," she said. "They were strong, and they had extensive community support."[46]

The pain cannot be cured with quick-fix programs, according to Terry Cross. He has examined locations in Canada where the suicide rate was highest and found that they included places where the culture had been most disrupted. Confronted with the question of whether to start with a suicide-prevention or other individual-aid program or to begin with the community as a whole, with self-governance help, for example, he decided the latter was the essential first step. Balance had to be restored in the community; then they could move on to working on the symptoms of imbalance, such as suicide and other individual issues.

Linear thinking—see a problem, apply a simple solution—is ineffective, Cross told his audience at the repatriation conference. "Mainstream society's services are so fractured. Medical doctors get the body, psychologists get the mind, judges get the social context, and clergy get the spirit. But, in fact, we are all whole people, and real solutions have to address that." Cross described the indigenous sweat lodge ceremony as a way of caring for the whole person while reconstituting the traditions and the community. The ceremony involves groups of participants, teachers, stories, and protocols for how to conduct oneself, he noted. "You sweat, and you experience aromatic herbs, which heal the body. You participate in prayers and songs, which are in the realm of spirit, and when you come out, you have moments of clarity that are aspects of mind," Cross said.

Running counter to these improvements is the vigor with which some states and adoption agencies continue to pursue Native children and families. In 2013, the American Civil Liberties Union filed a federal class-action lawsuit on behalf of the Oglala and Rosebud Sioux Tribes and individual tribal members.[47] The complaint sought a ruling that would compel courts in Pennington County, which encompasses Rapid City on the western side of South Dakota, to provide prompt and meaningful hearings when Indian children in the county are removed from their homes.

The lawsuit followed a sixteen-month ACLU investigation that found that Pennington County's courts routinely prevented Native parents facing custody hearings from being represented by lawyers, from seeing the affidavits of those making abuse or neglect claims against them, from cross-examining their accusers, and from introducing evidence on their own behalf.[48] According to the ACLU, the state triumphed against Indian parents in 100 percent of cases. As an example, the hearing for tribal plaintiff Madonna Pappan, her husband, and their two children lasted about sixty seconds. During the hearing, the court did not permit the Pappans to see the complaint that state officials had lodged against them. At the end of the Pappans' lightning-fast court appearance, the judge entered an order asserting that taking their children was "the least restrictive alternative available."[49]

The federal judge hearing the ACLU's case ruled on behalf of the Native plaintiffs in December 2016, saying that violating their rights was the defendants' only consistent policy. While the ACLU victory—which the state is appealing—may alleviate some of the aforementioned problems, it is not specifically about individual issues, according to ACLU senior staff attorney Stephen Pevar. Instead, the lawsuit is about systemic change and constitutional rights. The Supreme Court has long held that when the government takes anything from you, even your driver's license or your furniture, you get a full accounting, contends Pevar. "If it's true in those cases, it's certainly true when government takes your children," he said.[50]

In 2017, after a two-year comment period, the Bureau of Indian Affairs clarified ICWA regulations—including those protecting the Native family unit, a tribe's right to determine its own membership, and Native parents' right to counsel—and made them more easily enforceable. To counter this, powerful adoption-industry groups and conservative organizations have brought a spate of lawsuits challenging ICWA.[51] Most suits claim that the law interferes with states' rights to make child-welfare decisions and/or that the law amounts to racial discrimination against Native children. So far, federal courts have dismissed or rejected the suits. In 2017, an Arizona district court dismissed a suit by ICWA opponents and warned them that lawsuits should be "based on actual facts before the court, not on hypothetical concerns"; the court said any effort to amend the suit would be "futile."[52] Also in 2017, the Supreme Court refused to hear the appeal of a foster family that wanted to prevent the transfer of a Native foster child staying with them to her own relatives.[53]

These lawsuits are usually accompanied by energetic public-relations campaigns. Fevered press coverage presents Native families and homelands as no place to raise a child, regardless of the facts of any particular case. A coalition of prominent Native organizations is pushing back with information and legal assistance for tribes and parents who are trying to keep Native families together. The group calls itself the ICWA Defense Project. Participants include the National Congress of American Indians, National Indian Child Welfare Association, Native American Rights Fund, and ICWA Appellate Project at Michigan State University College of Law.[54]

"FOREVER IS A LONG, LONG time / So I will forever remember you." The refrain floated over a November 2013 grieving ceremony on the Standing Rock Sioux Reservation. About seventy-five people had gathered for a meal and remembrance in a meeting room of the tribe's hotel in Mobridge, South Dakota. The singer of the song said she had composed her plaint for relatives lost to suicide—a son, a nephew, a niece, and cousins, in deaths stretching back to the 1970s. Tribal member Veronica Iron Thunder, who survived her own suicide attempts, sang a traditional Lakota song intended to restore damaged spirits. In a slide show, the beautiful, smiling faces of those lost to suicide slid across the screen, radiating hope. Almost all were in their teens and twenties.

According to a Centers for Disease Control and Prevention report in 2016, the suicide rate for Natives aged fifteen to twenty-four was not only the highest in the nation, it had climbed steadily over the fifteen years between 1999 and 2014.[55] The phenomenon has been marked not just by high rates of actual deaths but by clusters of copycat suicides and attempts. During one visit I made to Standing Rock, I was sitting in on a district council discussion when word arrived that a child in a nearby village had killed himself. The councilors fell silent, and one explained quietly to me that they were braced for the news that more children would do the same. "It can feel like wartime," said Diane Garreau, a child-welfare official on the Cheyenne River Sioux Reservation, just south of Standing Rock, in South Dakota. "I'll see one of our youngsters one day, then find out a couple of days later she's gone." The tragedies ripple through reservations, which are essentially small towns. "People are overwhelmed," said Garreau. "Sometimes they'll say, 'I just can't go to another funeral.'"[56]

Native youth carry heavy burdens. They may experience not just separation from their families, but also extreme poverty, hunger, and health disparities. Diabetes rates are high in tribal communities, and untreated mental illnesses such as depression are common. There may be few jobs, even part-time or after-school ones. Bullying and peer pressure pile on more trauma during the vulnerable teen years. Community-wide grief stems from the loss of land, language, and more, a study reported in 2011.[57] Said Garreau, "Our kids hurt so much, they have to shut down the pain. Many have decided they won't live that long anyway, which in their minds excuses self-destructive behavior, like drinking—or suicide."

When suicide is common, it can become an acceptable solution as burdens build up, according to Alex Crosby, a medical epidemiologist with the CDC's injury-prevention center: "If people run into trouble—a relationship problem, a legal problem—this compounds the underlying risk factors, and one of the options is suicide."

"It crosses your mind," said Jake Martus, who is Alaska Native. "I've never acted on suicidal thoughts, but they've been there my entire life. It's sad, it's shocking, but in our communities it's also somehow normal." Martus, who is a patient advocate at a Native medical center, said suicide is so frequent among his people, he wondered, "Is it in our blood?" He recalled that behind his dad's suicide were overwhelming memories of sexual abuse by his village's Catholic priest. The term "historical trauma" did not make sense to Martus. "It was genocide," he said. "They set us up to kill ourselves. The point of all the policies was 'take them out.'"[58]

In some communities, suicide is so common that children— boys in particular—dare each other to try it. They may not be depressed, but simply responding to a challenge. Part of the difficulty is boys misunderstanding the warrior tradition that informs Native male identity, according to Alvin Rafelito, who is Ramah Navajo and a former director of his community's health and human services department. "We have a prayer that describes a warrior as someone who goes the distance spiritually for his people. Nowadays, that ideal has been reduced to fighting and violence. In teaching kids to be modern warriors, we have to convey the term's full, traditional meaning."[59]

For many men, their activities as providers have also shifted dramatically as they hold down jobs rather than hunt and fish, said Yup'ik storyteller and elder mentor Keggulluk (pronounced *kuth-look*). That, in turn, means critical life lessons are hard to come by. He recalled that his grandfather once told him, "Those who don't listen die young."[60] In the unforgiving North of old, a hunter stayed alive from moment to moment by listening to elders, fellow hunters, the natural world, and his own instincts. He was sensitive to subtle clues that made the difference between a successful hunt and losing his life under the ice or in an avalanche.

The practical side of the attentiveness was matched by a metaphysical component that Keggulluk called spiritual listening:

"This is a huge part of what's missing nowadays for our young people. The onslaught of outside information fights with what's running in their veins. The contrast between life here on the tundra and elsewhere is staggering. When our young people go away to school, they find new models for success and learn things that are not relevant at home. This can cause raging conflict."

The federal government funds tribal suicide-prevention programs, and tribes have declared states of emergency and set up crisis-intervention teams. Throughout Indian country, even very young children are included in prevention activities. "On Pine Ridge, our kindergarteners can tell you about how Daddy hung himself. They go to wakes and funerals. Suicide has become normal to them," according to Yvonne "Tiny" DeCory, who directed the Sweet Grass Project, a tribal suicide-prevention program, when I met her on the Pine Ridge Indian Reservation in South Dakota in 2013.[61] The only choice is to face the crisis square on, with frank words and compassion. "We start talking to them about this in preschool," DeCory said. "We have to end the silence and walk out of the darkness together."

Hayes Lewis was cocreator of the Zuni Life Skills Development curriculum,[62] one of the first suicide-prevention school- and community-based programs designed specifically for Native Americans.[63] The lesson series includes coping skills like stress management, as well as role-playing for dealing with suicide threats. It was created in the late 1980s in response to then-rising youth-suicide rates at Zuni Pueblo, New Mexico. After the curriculum was put into place in 1991, youth suicide stopped almost immediately, according to Lewis's collaborator, Stanford University education professor Teresa LaFromboise. Fifteen years later, the Pueblo's schools shelved the program, which had apparently achieved its goal. Suicides crept back, and the shocked community asked Lewis to resume the post of school superintendent and reestablish the curriculum.

When I interviewed Lewis at the Pueblo in 2012, he had been doing just that over the past two academic years. When the Zuni school system ended its program, its officials did not realize "how fragile the peace was" and how much vigilance was required to maintain it, according to Lewis. He added that many activities ("a school camping trip, a traditional dance group") could qualify as suicide prevention.

Former Zuni Pueblo superintendent of schools Hayes Lewis talks about cocreating the Zuni Life Skills Development curriculum, a suicide-prevention program designed for Native Americans. (Joseph Zummo)

When Diane Garreau's sister, Julie, asked Cheyenne River kids what would make things easier for them, the response was overwhelmingly, "a safe place to have fun." Julie Garreau and other adults created the Cheyenne River Youth Project, a busy after-school facility where children listen to elder storytellers, play basketball, and tend a two-acre organic garden. They get healthy meals and homework help. They study in a library, go online in an internet café, stage fashion shows, and organize local beautification projects. "Everything we do—from serious to seemingly frivolous—is about letting our kids know we care," said Julie Garreau. Social scientists agree that the key is weaving the child into the community and supporting cultural connections.[64]

In Alaska, it was a moose that made the difference. Keggulluk[65] was setting up a camp in northern Alaska with the help of an at-risk teen. The youngster had been abusing alcohol and gas-huffing, that is, inhaling gasoline fumes, which causes hallucinations and brain damage and can be fatal. The teen was on track to become one of the many Alaska Natives who kill themselves each year, a rate at least three times the national average. "It's a grueling, nonstop battle to save our youth," said Keggulluk, who is also known as Earl Polk.

Area tribes had put together a suicide-prevention camp. For several days, the kids would live in the wilderness and benefit from its lessons. On a cool, clear September morning, Keggulluk and the at-risk teen began putting up tents and hauling wood and water to prepare for the arrival of fifteen more campers. The plan was for several days of songs, dances, traditional games, storytelling, and outdoor activities like hunting and fishing. Suddenly, an enraged bull moose appeared and charged Keggulluk. The youngster grabbed a hunting rifle and took aim. "Don't miss!" Keggulluk shouted. The teen fired.

When the smoke had cleared and the moose was on the ground, the youngster said, "I thought you were going to lecture me on gas-huffing." "I will," promised Keggulluk, "but we had to take care of this other thing first."

For the teen, the shock of simultaneously killing his first moose, saving a man's life, and provisioning his community in the manner of his ancestors put him on the road to recovery, said Keggulluk. "It was a spiritual moment, an honorable moment. As the young man took care of the dying animal in our way, pouring water from his own mouth into the moose's, the animal breathed his last breath, and the young man felt it go through him. It was a blessing."

The youngsters referred to the camp may have abused alcohol or drugs, experienced domestic violence or neglect, suffered from fetal alcohol effects, or been a bullying perpetrator or victim. "We aren't told why a youth is referred to us, though it often comes out in the safe space the camp gives them," said another organizer, Evon Peter, who is Neetsaii Gwich'in and Koyukon and is now a vice chancellor at the University of Alaska Fairbanks.[66] I asked Peter why the children needed to be in traditional camps, engaging in heritage activities, with just Natives present. "These interactions are about being ourselves in unguarded moments, not as we've been told to be by outsiders," he responded. "It's not so much what we adults say as how we are that's important—how we interact, how we solve problems. That is the real lesson."

Alvin Rafelito was hopeful. He was standing in a Ramah Navajo community garden, surrounded by ripening heirloom crops—bushy, low-growing Navajo corn plants, yellow squashes, scarlet tomatoes and chilies. He observed that Native people and their traditions endure, despite centuries of depredations and violence. "Look at our history," Rafelito said. "It's been survival of the fittest. We're the smartest and the toughest anyone can be. Our message to our kids should be, 'We're okay.'"

6.

The Arc from Past to Future

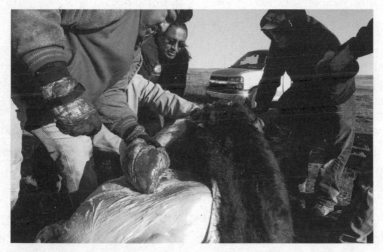

Standing Rock Sioux tribal members field-dress a buffalo. (Stephanie Woodard)

A FIRE GLOWS OUTSIDE A SWEAT LODGE. Sparks fly up toward the Milky Way streaming overhead in the night sky, while inside the tarp-covered dome, Western Shoshones sing and pray in the language of their ancestors. Around them is the ancient landscape they have occupied for many tens of thousands of years; since time began, they tell me. It is a scene repeated in many forms across Indian country, as tribal people participate in age-old ceremonial and daily practices. Some of these lifeways have survived intact in the face of the many challenges, incursions, and losses we have looked at in the preceding chapters. Others are being reclaimed, with Native people seeking out knowledge that was marginalized over the centuries as their communally occupied lands were broken up and sold off, their economies and foodways destroyed, their languages and cultures pummeled out of their children in punitive boarding schools, their spiritualities recast as "devil worship."

Today, original languages, traditional medicine, restorative justice, herds of buffalo, flocks of rugged Navajo Churro sheep, canoe journeys, heritage crafts, and heirloom-foods gardening and gathering are thriving in indigenous communities. The activities connect first peoples' deep past—a past that seems unimaginably distant to newcomers to this land—with the future. These actions and many others underpin the resilience I have observed in visits to widely separated places, from the Southwest to the Northeast, from the plains across to the Northwest and Alaska. While surviving violence and privation—much of it recent, and indeed much of it ongoing—Native communities manage to move forward with optimism. Native America is an ancient and beautiful place, with enduring connections among people and the land.

Native Americans invariably focus on their youth, who are their future. The affirmation of continuity through the generations includes not just age-old activities but decidedly modern ones as well. These encompass Cheyenne River Sioux kids working with an international contingent of graffiti artists to beautify their reservation; authors and artists creating Native-themed comics, graphic novels, and science fiction;[1] Native chefs and farmers finding receptive audiences;[2] and Myron Dewey's stunning aerial drone videos of shocking police violence during the Standing Rock pipeline resistance.

The affirmations include world-champion hoop dancer Nakotah LaRance freestyling along a Santa Fe sidewalk in 2015. Gliding, popping, and waving in hip-hop style while spinning the hoops of a traditional Native dance form, LaRance was lyrical and dazzling, laser-focused and relaxed. The twenty-six-year-old from Ohkay Owingeh Pueblo wore an oversized print shirt, jeans, and sunglasses. His costume was a statement in offhand cool. Nakotah's father, Steve LaRance, called his son's creation "hip-hop hoop."[3] The heritage version is a healing ceremony that restores physical and emotional balance. So does the modern hip-hop adaptation, Steve LaRance said to me in an interview in 2016: "Just look at audiences and how happy they are seeing it. The dance has done that."

Further examples include exhibitions of contemporary Native art at Red Cloud Indian School's Heritage Center, on Pine Ridge Indian Reservation. As then-curator Peter Strong told me while I was viewing a show there, both traditional and modern Native art are defined by vital connections among artist, community, culture, and homeland.[4] Dominating the Heritage Center's gallery that day was a stunning red-and-silver jingle-dance dress by Oglala artist and poet Layli Long Soldier. She made the piece, called *Dis/con/nect*, from metal mesh and coiled cutouts of Coca-Cola cans and placed it in front of three text-covered banners. The form of the work referred to traditional jingle dancing, a healing form for which the dancer's regalia is ornamented with clinking metal cones. Long Soldier's piece later appeared at other museums. It was utterly contemporary, yet with a traditional resonance that was distinctively indigenous and arising from a particular culture in a particular place.

I have learned during my reporting trips to Indian country that many non-reservation residents, even those who live very close to Indian communities, have never visited there, met their residents, or experienced a modicum of their culture. In this chapter, I will take you to a few of the places and events to which I was taken by Native people I was interviewing. The buffalo hunt, the gardens, the dancing, and other activities you will read about in the following pages are the things that indigenous people felt I, and other outsiders, should experience in order to understand their cultures and their issues.

IT WAS A BRIGHT FALL day at Standing Rock, several years before the reservation would become famous for its resistance to the Dakota Access Pipeline crossing its water supply. A small group of Sioux tribal members were sawing the head off a freshly killed buffalo. Rolling hills were the pale gold of fall prairie grasses, and the early-morning sky was a brilliant cloudless blue. Children, from first-graders through teens, watched the grown-ups work. Two little girls with braided hair and pink parkas were delighted when they got to touch the buffalo's heart, pulled warm from the body. "Is it beating?" one asked, as other children crowded in for a closer look.

Joyful occasions like this offer Native children profound lessons they cannot learn within the four walls of a classroom. "This is the natural classroom," said tribal official, now chairman, Mike

Faith. "It's so important for our children to learn about these animals right here on the prairie—what we use each part for and how today they still keep the people and the prairie healthy."[5] Faith pointed to a cloven hoofprint. I could see grass seeds in the depression in the soil. "As buffalo graze and walk along, their hooves press fallen seeds into the ground, reseeding the prairie," he explained. "They also eat a lot of woody plants, so they clean the prairie and leave a healthy mix of grasses and other plants." The buffalo's varied diet concentrates in its body the thinly spread resources of the prairie and makes its meat especially nutritious, added tribal member Aubrey Skye, then a diabetes program staff member who helped organize the day's event. The animal, Skye said, is both a physical and a spiritual bond between a healthy people and a healthy environment.[6]

"We brought the children because we want them to be part of culturally related activities like this," said elementary-school teacher Kimberly White Bull.[7] After observing from the sidelines for a half hour or so, the kids started pitching in, pulling hard on the buffalo's hide so the adults could use skinning knives to cut the wire-tough fascia that binds the skin to the meat beneath. The children tugged the rib cage open to make it easier for the grown-ups to remove the animal's innards. Everyone worked quickly, sharing the heavy labor. The carcass weighed one thousand to eleven hundred pounds, Faith estimated, and to remove the hide it had to be rocked from side to side and, at one point, tipped up to a sitting position. "Everyone get behind and push!" someone shouted. If one person tired, another stepped in. Praise and humor flowed. "That's old-school!" said one young man, as he admired an elder's knife skills.

The kids asked, "Is this a vein?" "How do I cut the stomach open?" "What's all that green stuff in it?" As the animal was skinned and broken down, everyone got to try some of the raw liver. It was sweet, metallic-tasting, and custardy-crunchy—just so you know. It was considered a delicacy, and the old-time hunters would eat it on the spot before packing up the field-dressed animal for the return to camp. After I chewed and swallowed my chunk of raw liver, someone asked if I would like seconds. "Oh, thank you, but I wouldn't want to be greedy!" I quickly demurred.

Earlier that morning, in preparation for the taking of the buffalo, Faith drove close to a herd cantering around the top of a rise north of the tribe's capital in Fort Yates, North Dakota. Eventually, the group of eighty or so animals came to a stop. The bulky bulls faced us squarely, broad foreheads slightly lowered, while the more diminutive cows and calves milled around behind them. A cool breeze ruffled the animals' dark brown fur, which had begun to thicken for the winter. "They like to be on high ground, so they can keep an eye on us," said Faith. With him was Ken McLaughlin, one of the tribe's designated buffalo shooters. According to Faith, they always use their best marksmen in such a situation: "We'd never want to have an animal run off, wounded."

At the bottom of the hill were about forty tribal members, including Skye, additional staff of the Standing Rock Sioux Diabetes Program, and a dozen children each from the tribe's elementary school and a Boys and Girls Club chapter. The tribe's Game and Fish Department had given permission for one buffalo to be killed today. The diabetes program would distribute the lean, grass-fed meat to schools and tribal members to help control the illness, which affected some 12 percent of the approximately nine thousand tribal members.[8] Like other tribes, Standing Rock has among the highest rates of diabetes in the country.[9] Anyone who requires dialysis receives *wasna* prepared by the diabetes program; the traditional food is made from finely shredded dried buffalo meat and berries. Eating it does not send blood sugar soaring, according to Skye.

As we watched the herd, Faith and McLaughlin conferred quietly. They wanted a young bull. "How about that one, with one horn up, one sideways?" asked Faith, and McLaughlin agreed. As if guessing the men's intention, the bull turned away and ducked back into the herd, taking refuge among the cows and calves. It then swerved and trotted back out. McLaughlin took aim and, with one rifle shot, felled it. The other buffalo scattered across the hilltop and quickly regrouped about one hundred yards away. They stood shoulder to shoulder, heads up, eyes alert, surveying us carefully—and in perfect unison, wheeled and galloped away.

Tribal members arrived with a pickup and trailer. John Buckley, head of the tribal diabetes program, made an offering of tobacco, stuffing some in the fallen bull's nostrils before it was loaded onto the trailer and hauled to the main group at the bottom of the hill.

The healthful lifestyle being promoted on Standing Rock through many tribal projects, including gardening, wild-plant gathering, and buffalo programs, descends from two historical Sioux economies. The Lakota/Dakota buffalo tradition is well-known. When that ended with the massive federally encouraged continent-wide buffalo slaughters of the late 1800s, the Standing Rock Sioux and other tribes confined to reservations along the Missouri River and its tributaries replaced it with a less-well-known agriculture-based economy. This economy would be called sustainable today, since it fit perfectly with existing, constantly renewing resources. In fertile, tree-sheltered riparian areas, tribal members raised livestock, fished, hunted deer and other game, and gathered wild food and medicine plants. They used fallen timber and the driftwood that the river tossed onto its banks for heating, cooking, and building.

They also planted household gardens. However, their definition of gardening was broader than the typical European one, according to the late Sioux elder Philip Lane, who lived in a Missouri-side village called White Swan on the Yankton Sioux Reservation in the early years of the twentieth century. "The Sioux idea of gardening encompassed caring for plants where they naturally arose, not just where they were seeded in prepared ground. As a result, we had an abundance of food," Lane told me.[10] He gave an example of an *in situ* gardening technique that was as much a philosophical statement as a way to plant, accomplishing both harvesting and reseeding, both taking and giving, with one continuous gesture. "On the brows of the hills above White Swan, we grew wild turnips," Lane said. "Toward the end of June, we'd take an ash digging stick, push it into the soil alongside the root, and pry it up. We'd then take the top with its purple flowers, put it into the depression formed by removing the root, and step on it with the heavy untanned soles of our moccasins. We thereby reseeded the plant. We maintained that growth because we were thinking of the children. We didn't want to take the turnips without ensuring that there would be more for the future."

That way of life continued until the 1950s and the coming of the Pick-Sloan Project, when the US Army Corps of Engineers built giant dams along the Missouri in order to generate electricity and control flooding downstream. On reservations in Nebraska and North and South Dakota, the closing of the dams' gates created lakes that inundated valuable riparian farmland, swept away thriving villages, and, often without warning, forced families onto the windswept prairie. Once self-sufficient, tribal members were suddenly homeless, destitute, and dependent on high-starch, high-fat foods that the federal government supplied, which are termed "commodity foods." The low-nutrient commercially processed food that was increasingly available during this era took its toll as well. By the 1960s, diabetes appeared for the first time at Standing Rock, Aubrey Skye said.

The CDC says that maintaining a healthy weight is a major way to defend against diabetes.[11] That is traditional, too, according to Skye, who ran a multiyear CDC gardening program at Standing Rock. "When I give presentations to our people, I show them a photo of a large group of nineteenth-century Sioux chiefs," Skye said when I interviewed him in 2011. "I ask, 'What do they have that we don't?' After the audience hems and haws for a while, I say, 'Cheekbones.' Some of us have gained too much weight and have big, full fry-bread faces. If we want to be healthy, we have to eat right, get more of our food through energetic pursuits like hunting, gardening, and gathering, and get our cheekbones back."[12]

Returning to old-time nutrition sources, including the buffalo, is about restoring spiritual as well as physical health, said diabetes program head John Buckley, who recounts the assistance the buffalo gave humans when they first emerged on earth from an underground cave. "One of those buffalo who was still underground asked the Creator for permission to follow us up here and help us, and that's why we have been related to them ever since." At the beginning of this very buffalo harvest, Buckley reminded me, the group had prayed to the Creator for help in carrying out their tasks in a good way: "For us, everything has a spiritual grounding."[13]

Back at the buffalo pasture, the young bull's carcass had been cut up, and the biggest hunks of meat were on their way in the back of a pickup to a nearby meatpacking plant, where the meat would be processed into cuts that could then be given to tribal members. The buffalo's head would become a sun-dance altar, the liver had already been eaten, and other organs had been parceled out, including the stomach, which an elder said she would make into tripe soup. "Now we know where we're going for dinner tonight," Skye joked.

Just the hide remained. "A good hide for a vision," Buckley said. He and a fellow tribal member folded it lengthwise and, staggering under its weight, carried it to the back of Buckley's pickup truck. Tribal members dispersed, returning home, to school, or to work. As I left, I looked back over my shoulder. All that was left on the prairie was the blessing.

SEATED ON A COUCH IN their house in Manokotak, in Alaska's southwestern Bristol Bay region, Yup'ik elders Mike and Anecia Toyukak paged through a notebook containing early-grade math lessons. The couple were accomplished community leaders; it was 2014, and he was lead plaintiff in the *Toyukak v. Treadwell* voting-rights lawsuit, which had expanded Native ballot access, and she was a retired teacher.

They were also part of a team of elders, educators, and curriculum writers that had worked on a Yup'ik-based mathematics project, Math in a Cultural Context, for more than thirty years. The curriculum the team produced for schools supported Yup'ik culture and values. Importantly, the lessons were child-centered, with students working collaboratively rather than competitively or in isolation. Guided, rather than directed, by a teacher, the children were encouraged to work harmoniously and at their own pace toward a common goal. These principles allowed students of different abilities to learn together.

In a 2005 article in the *Journal of American Indian Education*, one of the mathematics team members, Evelyn Yanez, a retired Yup'ik teacher and a University of Alaska Fairbanks adjunct professor, wrote that a central cultural precept of Yup'iks is to not force people to do things. She gave the example of a subsistence activity involving water travel. In such a situation, if a person were made to do something before he or she was ready, drowning might result, Yanez wrote: "It's the same with teaching. You don't force kids to learn."[14] The Math in a Cultural Context lessons were reinforced when students saw their parents and grandparents using similar approaches to design clothes, boots, snowshoes, kayaks, fish-drying racks, and other objects.

Sassa Peterson, a Yup'ik educator, described traditional Yup'ik life as "rich in mathematics."[15] In the Yup'ik view, the human body is the measure of the world, whether the item to be gauged is small, like one geometrical element of a hat pattern, or large, like an expanse of ocean that must be navigated at night. "Here's how we measure," Anecia Toyukak said, as I watched her jump up from the couch to demonstrate units that were determined by the distance between the first and second knuckle of her forefinger, by her open and closed hand, and by one or both outstretched arms.

Math in a Cultural Context lessons imparted measuring skills, which led children to understand numbers, proportionality, geometry, algebra, data collection, graphing, probability, and more. According to Peterson, the modules successfully covered in the earliest grades what is generally considered higher mathematics. "Both Evelyn and I have said we wish the curriculum had been available when we were young teachers," Peterson told me.

In the first module, Patterns and Parkas, the youngest students learn geometry by folding an irregular item to create a symmetrical form, such as a square or circle. In a practical setting, this lesson might be applied to make the uneven shape of a hide into the large rectangles needed to make a parka, or to create the small forms used in clothing border patterns. The module also laid the groundwork for understanding symmetry, a basic element of Yup'ik thought. "You cannot have the whole without the half," said Yanez. In the Star Navigation module, fourth, fifth, and sixth graders use cultural knowledge about angles and the stars to determine location, direction, and distance. In Salmon Fishing, sixth and seventh graders integrate probability and environmental science as they study salmon species and their life cycles.

The US Department of Education's Alaska Native Education Program and the National Science Foundation have supported Math in a Cultural Context. Schools across Alaska have taught the curriculum. Research into the experience of students of various ethnicities—Yup'ik, other tribes, and non-Native—indicated that those who used the system improved their test scores and outperformed peers.[16] The curriculum has been called "a small step in reversing power relations and what constitutes legitimate school knowledge."[17]

The project also has an international component. In addition to working with partners in Alaska, the group has explored the relationship of culture and mathematics with Sami people in Sweden and Norway, Koryaks from Russia's Kamchatka region, Yapese in Micronesia, and Inuit in Greenland. The work is ongoing, as researchers and elders continue to meet and delve into the subtleties of the mathematics embedded in Yup'ik daily activities.[18]

IN NEW MEXICO, THE REMAINS of ancestral Pueblo gardens are scattered over thousands of acres from north of Santa Fe to the Albuquerque region to the south. This giant complex of cobble-bordered, gravel-mulched garden beds is an engineering feat that rivals the aqueducts of ancient Rome, according to archaeologist Kurt Anschuetz, program director of Rio del Oso Anthropological Services.[19] However, while the aqueducts are impossible to miss, the Pueblo fieldworks are barely visible modifications of the landscape that offer lessons about sustainable land use and the power of subtlety.

They also offer data that may be used for the adjudication of Pueblos' land and water claims. Many New Mexico communities are engaged in long-standing disputes over water, a precious resource in the arid West. "We have aboriginal water rights, but increasingly the courts want more detailed information. The old gardens will be useful in providing it," said the late Herman Agoyo, former governor and then tribal councilman.[20] "Farming has been neglected in terms of establishing water and land rights."

Rediscovered techniques from the old gardens also have practical applications in today's fields, Agoyo told me. Farmers have

Is it or isn't it? Archaeologist Kurt Anschuetz, left, and Tesuque Pueblo councilman and permaculture expert Louie Hena examine a rock to determine if it is an ancestral farming tool. (Stephanie Woodard)

reintroduced ancient ideas, and the gardens have been used as teaching tools in gardening courses run by the Traditional Native American Farmers Association, headquartered in nearby Santa Fe. "The gardens have contributed to our education about the activities of our ancestors and to our understanding that ecology is about interconnectedness," said Agoyo. "It's inspiring to see that our forebears were so knowledgeable. What they were doing with the land and environment shaped our lives today and all of the connections throughout the universe."

Meanwhile, at Tesuque, it appeared that demolition was in the cards for ancestral garden beds around the pueblo. New Mexico's utility company was planning to march a power line over a hilltop that tribal official Louie Hena suspected was dotted with old gardens.[21] The utility had done an archaeological study, as required under federal historic-preservation law before such a project. It had found no evidence of old plots. However, Hena, a traditional gardening and permaculture expert, knew that most archaeologists could not identify the little-understood fields. He called in Anschuetz, an expert on them, to see if the archaeologist would agree that portions of Tesuque's ancient farming heritage were in harm's way.

When I first called the utility company for a comment on the power project and its potential effect on the gardens, a spokesperson responded that state and federal agencies had approved the line; later, he said that the company would "mitigate" damage to any historic and cultural items that were present. As we learned in the discussion of sacred sites in Chapter 3, mitigation can take various forms under the law, few of them satisfying to Native communities. Mitigation might involve digging up the endangered items, putting them in a box, and storing them on a museum shelf. It can even mean simply photographing the artifacts or the place before the bulldozers arrive.

I arranged to meet Kurt Anschuetz. In addition to working for the Rio del Oso Anthropological Services, Anschuetz directed the Rio Grande Foundation for Communities and Cultural Landscapes, a Santa Fe nonprofit that helped groups preserve traditional lifeways. We decided to meet at a popular Santa Fe breakfast spot before heading to Tesuque. I asked how I would recognize him. "I look like an archaeologist," he responded. He was right. Serious and professorial, with rugged clothes and boots suitable for tramping around the desert, he stood out from the crowd.

As we drove north to Tesuque, Anschuetz told me he first met Hena at a 1994 environmental conference at Taos Pueblo. The two men discovered their mutual fascination with the early agriculture of northern New Mexico and undertook a cross-cultural collaboration. Combining the analytical tools of the scholar with the practical knowledge of the Indian farmer, they have copublished papers and given presentations to groups including Native communities, gardening students, and lawyers. For them, knowledge of the material world—whether archaeological, for Anschuetz, or agricultural, for Hena—is at the service of the cultural and spiritual.

The story the two men tell starts around the year 1250, when the ancestors of today's Pueblo people moved south from the Four Corners area, where Colorado, Utah, New Mexico, and Arizona now meet. As the ancestral Puebloans built new villages, they used agricultural techniques they had already perfected, including terracing and ways of capturing and diverting water. In their new home, they added a novel technique: gravel-covered, rock-bordered fields. They eventually constructed about ten thousand acres' worth of the rectilinear plots in the valleys of the Rio Grande and its tributaries. They installed most of these fields between the years 1300 and 1500. Scattering a mix of technologies across the land was insurance against environmental challenges, such as long-term drought or localized storms, and human demands, such as population growth. The new grid gardens were a sophisticated, successful approach that drew together developments in construction and siting, plant breeding, planting, and cultivating.

The garden beds are mostly about nine feet by twelve feet and bordered by cobbles that are about seven inches high and ten inches long, laid end to end. The farmers covered the topsoil within each rectangle with gravel mulch, which helped trap rainfall, melt snow, and prevent evaporation. The layer of small stones also encouraged moisture to soak deep into the ground, where it seeped downslope, watering the roots of crops in one hillside field after another. It was essentially an underground irrigation system. Little evaporated or ran off, a boon in this region of meager precipitation.

In the gardens, the farmers grew cotton for clothes, as well as foodstuffs including corn, beans, squash, sunflowers, and perennial herbs. They also bred specialized domesticated plants, such as corn with an especially long mesocotyl (the first shoot that breaks the surface after germination); this variety can be planted at depths of up to sixteen inches to take advantage of underground moisture. In and around the beds, they managed other, undomesticated plants (not literally "wild" plants, since they were cared for, not merely discovered). The huge array of affiliated crops included purslane, lamb's quarters, amaranth, panic grass, little barley, devil's claw, tobacco, and yucca. The gardens provided everything from food and medicine to fiber and soap.

Prickly pear cactus, which naturally seeds itself in cracks in rocks, sprang up between the cobbles, providing edible pads and flowers as well as a low, spiky fence that kept out small predators. Remnants of these prickly pear populations can still be seen in some plots. At the end of the growing season, the farmers left a cover of stubble. This sheltered birds and small animals and enticed browsing deer, which they hunted for meat. In this way, the gardens provided food year-round. The stubble also added organic material to the soil as it decayed.

The plots were under cultivation until the mid-1700s, when confinement to reservations meant Pueblo people could not range over the land the way they once did. Nevertheless, many of the disused grid gardens I saw in the Santa Fe region were still doing what they were designed to do—hold moisture and topsoil and promote growth—though no farmer had turned up to maintain them in nearly three hundred years. Clusters of grid gardens range from a few isolated plots to hundreds of contiguous ones. Often, you can spot the gardens because they have grass growing vigorously in them, according to Anschuetz. In aerial photographs, the groupings look like nets cast over hills bordering the rivers. Because of their hilltop locations, they have caught the eye of pilots as far back as Charles Lindbergh, who photographed them in the 1920s. In fact, their patterns can be easier to see from the air than on the ground, a local pilot told me.

Initially, I could not pick out the gardens when I hiked into the hills above the Rio Chama with Clayton Brascoupé, head of the Traditional Native American Farmers Association. We headed for the fields of Poshuouinge ("Village above the muddy water" in Tewa, a language of the Northern Pueblos); the remains of the thirteenth- to eighteenth-century pueblo is set in the Santa Fe National Forest, south of Abiquiú, New Mexico. It was my first visit to the area and, frankly, it looked to me like an undifferentiated expanse of rocks, sand, and the occasional shrubby tree. Then, as Brascoupé indicated garden after garden, their faint rectangular outlines swam into focus. He pointed out stone-lined watercourses connecting gardens, what appeared to be collecting pools, "slicks" where the farmers sharpened their tools on boulders, depressions that may have been sheltered plant nurseries, and petroglyphs.

By siting gardens on hills and mesa tops, the ancestral farmers did not irrigate in the usual fashion, with water diverted from streams, as was done for fields in lower elevations. Manipulating rain and snow became critical on the hilltops. Analyses of the hilltop fields by Steven Dominguez Sundjordet, an archaeologist with a specialty in hydrology, showed how the farmers got water to higher elevations without conventional irrigation or pumps. Digging into the gardens with a mason's trowel, and then using sieves with graduated mesh sizes to separate rock from soil, Sundjordet gathered data. Upon analyzing the numbers, he discovered that the fields operated with diamond-cutter accuracy.[22]

The farmers used optimum stone sizes for their gravel mulch, which cut evaporation and runoff, increased water absorption, and checked erosion. "Fifty millimeters is the upper limit for the diameter of stones that can be used effectively," Sundjordet explained as we drove around back roads to find examples of the fields. In the gardens he studied, he found that most stones' diameters were between two and fifty millimeters. Further, he told me, the entire layer should be at least three centimeters thick. At a site dubbed La Mesita, the rock coverings of north-facing plots averaged just that; in south-facing beds, where plants faced additional hours of desiccating sunlight, the thickness was plumped up to an average of five centimeters.

Snowmelt was as important as rain in a region where the winter months are among the wetter ones. "I was out in the middle of a snowstorm when I realized how effectively the gravel mulch melts snow, building up moisture for spring planting," Sundjordet recounted. "The rocks hold heat, so the garden beds were patches of bare gravel that day, even as the snow was piling up around them." The cobble borders also helped collect winter precipita-tion. As a rule, Sundjordet said, hydrologists find that the most efficient snow fences, including low ones like these, have gaps no larger than twenty-five centimeters, with all the openings adding up to 40 to 60 percent of surface area. The barriers at La Mesita met these exact requirements, he said.

Sundjordet checked topographical maps to see where the structures were placed on the landscape. Again, the farmers were spot on, responding to the terrain with precision: The cobblestone borders were at ideal angles to the prevailing winds and at opti-mum spots to gather snow. The distance between cobble rows was precisely calibrated so that the snow would fill one plot with a drift before hitting the next row of stones and forming another billow. The dimensions of the beds deviated from the nine-by-twelve-foot norm in spots where changes in a hill's incline caused wind speed to increase or decrease, thereby altering the lengths of the drifts.

"For me, book learning was just part of doing this work," Sundjordet said. "The other part was getting out there, seeing the rain falling or the snow blowing. The old-time farmers were walk-ing the land, observing spring growth, looking at plants respond-ing to different conditions, watching how everything interacted. And many generations of meticulous observers preceded them. The farmer we're familiar with nowadays—the farmer of agribusiness—is a technician. He follows instructions. The expertise resides not in him, but in a company like John Deere or Monsanto."

As modern people, we may have a hard time believing that a human being can perceive so accurately without instruments. However, we have to consider that the ever-proliferating number of instruments and techniques we rely on means that our ability to detect and measure without them has atrophied over the centuries. The old-timers did not labor under that burden. The ancestral farmers even figured out that you had to deliver air as well as water to the plants' roots, according to Anschuetz and Hena. The two found that some old Pueblo irrigation ditches spilled water through openings that were partially blocked with rocks, creating turbulence. This aerated the water so that it was oxygen-rich when it got to the plants. "The symbology of that facet of the planting is so incredible," commented Tessie Naranjo, a sociologist from Santa Clara Pueblo. "We have a supernatural being called the water serpent. You see him in decorations on our pots. He is the aerator of the ground and makes it breathe so the crops can come up."[23]

Today, roads, buildings, and other facilities have obliterated many old grid gardens; I saw cattle lumbering through some. All-terrain vehicles cause havoc, ripping up the ecologically fragile desert surface and enabling their owners to bounce through once-inaccessible places. The thousands of acres of remaining fields sit on land with an unrelated patchwork of ownership— individuals, Indian reservations, and local, state, and federal governments, among others. Some of these entities are determined to protect the gardens. Others may not know they exist.

The ancestral Puebloans' gardens are mainly nuanced—but not always. La Bajada Mesa is a 500-foot escarpment south of Santa Fe that overlooks a mountain valley. Whoever built the garden plots on its rim enjoyed some of the most dramatic scenery in the region. It was also an exquisitely practical place to plant, said Anschuetz: "At the very edge of the escarpment, the slope of the mesa top flattens out, so it receives the slowest-moving water, delivered continuously to the plants."

"The instant apprehension of the beautiful and the practical describes the Pueblo mind," said Naranjo. "I have looked at many of the old sites, and at every one, I marveled at the choice of location. At Hopi, I talked to a woman who remembered her grandfather placing dried flowers within walls he was building to make passersby happy and to make their children beautiful. I love the idea of being continuously in search of beauty. The old agriculturalists were doing that."

At Cochiti Pueblo, south of Santa Fe, I was treated to a contemporary example of this notion: water passing through unlined irrigation ditches had given rise to a grove of trees near the cultivated fields. In the thicket, elders had placed a bench, where they periodically rested in the surprisingly cool, damp air and admired the scene framed by the boughs. The fronds of tasseled corn rustled over bright chilies, birds cheeped, and distant mountains limned the boundary between earth and sky. "It's beauty and function all rolled into one," commented Naranjo.

Back at Tesuque: Anschuetz and I arrived at the pueblo, picked up tribal official Hena, and headed out to see the community's endangered hilltop gardens. With Anschuetz at the wheel of his pickup, we bumped along the uneven bottom of an arroyo, tilting over hillocks and skirting boulders as we made our way into the surrounding hills. From the front passenger seat, Hena scanned the sixty-foot walls on either side of us. Lean and intense, the Pueblo farmer was looking for the spot where he had seen what might be the remains of old gardens.

As we lurched along, Hena and Anschuetz provided context for what they might find. "My ancestors treated the land as a sponge, encouraging water to soak into the ground," Hena explained. In contrast, he said, modern irrigation systems flush water over the earth's surface in concrete-lined canals. "It looks efficient, but a lot is lost to evaporation that ends up as rain somewhere else," added Anschuetz. Hena said, "You aren't feeding the roots of beneficial plants or recharging wells along the way. When the Bureau of Indian Affairs did Tesuque the supposed favor of lining our irrigation ditches with concrete, the wild plum trees along the channels died, and we lost a food source."

"I think this is the place," Hena told Anschuetz, who stopped the pickup. Hena climbed out and sprinted up the nearly vertical walls. As he walked along the top of the cliff, Anschuetz and I followed along in the bottom of the canyon. Hena found what he was looking for, and Anschuetz and I climbed up to join him. Juniper and piñon trees dotted the hilltop. Across the Rio Grande Valley, the crags of the Sangre de Cristo Mountains hulked on the eastern horizon, and cumulus clouds floated in a clear blue sky.

"Okay, let's see what you see," Hena challenged Anschuetz, who suddenly crouched by one of several low four-foot-wide mounds of broken stones. "Fire-cracked rock," Anschuetz explained for my benefit. "Here are the distinctive right-angle breaks and the orange markings of iron oxidized by heat. These may have been pits for roasting corn. Now, because of erosion, they look like mounds." For several hours, the two men worked their way over the hilltop, finding more fire pits, garden beds, terraced gardens, a *metate* or flat stone for grinding corn into meal, and a flake of rock knocked off a larger chunk when one of Hena's ancestors fashioned it into a tool.

Each discovery provoked a spirited debate. "Louie will challenge me every step of the way now," joked Anschuetz. As an archaeologist, Anschuetz looked for evidence of human interaction with the artifacts. Those included conchoidal fractures on the edges of tools ("like the breaks when a BB goes through glass," he said) and alignments of rocks that could not have been caused by geological processes. In addition to looking at rocks, both men sought living proof of the old farming activities. They noted a bit of land that was greener than its surroundings and tried to discern whether this meant it was an agricultural bed that was still collecting topsoil and water. Or they noticed a row of trees thriving in what seemed to be cobble-rimmed enclosures, perhaps because of better growing conditions there.

At one point, Anschuetz pointed out patches of rabbitbrush on the slope leading down to the Rio Grande Valley. "It's a diagnostic," he told me. "Rabbitbrush grows in places that are also good for corn, so this area may have been agricultural. I may be able to find clear evidence of old fields here. And look over there. See that nice open area with dense grass? It may have had old planting beds."

Hena picked up a stone and said it looked like an old hand hoe. He tested its heft, then used it to make a furrow in the soil. "Much better than a modern hoe," he said. "I've done a lot of fieldwork, and these rock tools are good. I found an old double-handed shovel near here. I use it now, and it goes down easy."

"I don't see a working edge," riposted Anschuetz, as he turned the palm-sized rock over in his hands. He defended his position: "I take a conservative approach. This rock may have been used as a tool. I can see how beautifully it works when Louie uses it, and one of his ancestors may also have found this to be true. Nevertheless,

I need to see clear indications of use on the surface. When Louie points out places that would be good to plant or tools that feel right in the hand, I listen. Then I look for what lets me define them as such and nearby pottery sherds that date them. Archaeologists base their version of the story on the most redundant, unquestionable material evidence."

As a result of this approach, Anschuetz said, archaeology offers just part of the whole picture: "If it's not material, we can't see it. We may miss things, like fields that were bordered by brush or worked with wooden tools. But that doesn't mean they're not there." When I joked about Hena and Anschuetz "duking it out" over the artifacts, Hena struck a boxing pose and danced around the hilltop while both men laughed. I could see that they did not merely agree to disagree. More than that, their collaboration synthesized divergent views of the ancient Puebloans and the ways they interacted with plants and the landscape. "Multiple lenses on the past mean a greater understanding for all," said Anschuetz.

After the two men finished discussing an artifact, Hena deftly fitted it back into the cavity created when he removed it—patting the dirt around the chunk of stone as tenderly as if he were transplanting a seedling. Finally, Anschuetz conceded the larger point: "We're getting close to where I could say that these are old fields and that identifying them as such would hold up in court."

Over the course of our afternoon on the Tesuque hilltop, clouds had gathered and thunder had begun rumbling. Lightning bolts crackled across the darkening sky and plunged into the Sangre de Cristo Mountains across the Rio Grande Valley. Silhouetted against the storm and speaking urgently, Hena explained how important the ancestral landscape was to his people. The sky was the vault of their cathedral, he said, and the earth was their altar: "Wouldn't you call this place sacred?"

Postscript: Ultimately, the utility company sent the power line by a different route, sparing the old Tesuque gardens for future generations.

IN NORTHEASTERN NEBRASKA, PLANS FOR a museum are already connecting times gone by with a hopeful future. "This museum is not about the past," said Omaha tribal member and historian Dennis Hastings, an anthropologist, activist, and author.[24] In design elements both major and minor, a museum planned by the Omahas for their reservation will seek to reattach tribal members to their land, their traditional clan structure, their history, and their cosmology. "It will ensure that our children become better human beings," Hastings said. The museum will do this by building on the past, literally: atop a bluff that is sacred to the tribe, the site overlooks the Missouri River and offers extensive views of the community's ancestral territory to the east.

Hastings said that he and fellow members of the impoverished Omaha Tribe are survivors of federal assimilationist policies, including the boarding schools used to tear children from their ancestral cultures. He saw the building as a way to heal the wounds caused by those policies and to make certain today's Omaha youngsters grow up knowing who they are and where they belong. The plans for the building, called New Moon Moving, in memory of a famed Omaha medicine woman of that name, have already won three major architectural awards, even though funds have not yet been found to build it. In the meantime, to put its ideas into circulation in the community, Hastings and his collaborators have created child-centered products, including culturally relevant curriculum materials and comic books.

The building is designed to reaffirm Omaha culture from the first moment the visitor comes in contact with it. "Each child who enters through the east door of the museum will find his or her clan inscribed on the walls of the rotunda in exactly the orientation the clan would have occupied in an historic camp circle," said the architect, Vincent Snyder, a University of Texas at Austin professor and former associate of renowned architects Frank Gehry and Michael Graves. "A child would be able to say, for example, 'I belong to this clan, and I'm located here in relation to the other Omaha clans.'"[25]

Brought up in Nebraska, Snyder went into the project with fond childhood memories of attending powwows and participating in boxing matches on the Omaha Reservation. Before setting pen to paper, he did extensive research under Hastings's guidance on the tribe's intellectual, spiritual, and material life. They discussed innumerable related issues with elders. "The elders expressed very complex ideas in elegant, economical language," Snyder recalled. "I tried to bring this thinking and kind of expression to the project, which needed to be unquestionably Omaha."

As a result, subtle Omaha ideas came together in the building. The structure's plans glorify such concepts as the primacy of the circle, the importance of duality, the relationship of the tribe's earth and sky clans, the theoretical horizon where these come together and where the Omaha people were born, mythic figures, sacred numbers, and the cardinal directions and their relationship to the seasons. These concepts are manifested physically in the building. For example, a window is positioned to catch the light on the last day of winter and carry it inside in a symbolic regeneration that welcomes the first day of spring. In the rotunda, the clan names circling the room will be inscribed in a way that conjures up the graceful, nodding grasses of the surrounding prairie. The font to be used for the names was designed with the geometric forms of the traditional Omaha tipi—its lines, curves, and proportions. Blue-green and white slate will clad the outer walls in a version of the sacred "hailstone" pattern used in plains tipi coverings.

Hastings said that tribal members did not want the museum to be a "foursquare" building. "We wanted to 'tribalize' everything about the structure. If archaeologists dig it up many years from now, the building will teach them something about the people who made it." The 45,000-square-foot, energy-efficient, low-maintenance structure will offer varied ways for tribal members to interact with it. The plans show community gathering places, exhibition spaces, tribal offices, classrooms, a library for the many scholars who make requests to do research on the tribe, and a restaurant that will serve Omaha specialties. As a cultural-tourism attraction, the museum can be an economic engine, bringing in money via events, memberships, and fundraising. The Omaha language will be used at every opportunity in the building. Since few speakers of the traditional language are left on the Omaha Reservation, maintaining the language and the unique cultural concepts it supports is hugely important. The museum will also inspire professional development for Omaha youngsters; when they train in anthropology, museum management, and related careers, they can return to work there.

One tribal elder called New Moon Moving a positive project for which Omahas have been waiting a long time. The germ of the idea emerged during indigenous people's 1969–71 takeover of Alcatraz Island, off San Francisco. Hastings was there and sat on committees that hoped to construct a museum on the island. They were not able to create one before the eighteen-month occupation ended (the National Park Service has since created its own museum, with information on the Native occupation included). But when Hastings returned home to the Omaha Reservation, he told himself, "We'll do it here, and it'll serve as a model for other Native communities, so they can say, 'We can do this too.'"

When the museum is built, important artifacts will be repatriated and shown there. Hastings has spent decades discovering the whereabouts of items that landed in what he called "protective custody" at various museums. Among these is a cottonwood pole that is the tribe's most vital entity. It was once at the Peabody Museum of Archaeology and Ethnology, the Harvard-affiliated institution in Cambridge, Massachusetts. Now the pole is closer to home, in a University of Nebraska archive, in preparation for its eventual return to the reservation. Called Umon'hon'ti (translated as "Venerable Man" or "Real Omaha"), the pole originated in a burning bush that was not consumed by the fire that raged around it. Umon'hon'ti accompanied the Omaha on their journey for centuries, as both a living being and a physical object, according to Hastings and Robin Ridington in their book, *Blessing for a Long Time: The Sacred Pole of the Omaha Tribe.*[26]

When the museum is completed, it will display Umon'hon'ti and nearly fourteen hundred other pieces that need to return home, said Hastings. As an expression of the living culture of the tribe, the items and the structure that houses them will tie a proud past to the future. "When we're gone, our kids will take over the museum, because everything about it will be about them and will be to their liking," he said.

I MET NAKOTAH LARANCE AFTER his appearance with the Brooklyn Ballet in December 2016. The dance company incorporated him into its annual *Brooklyn Nutcracker,* shown at the Brooklyn Museum. He was a hit, as might be expected of a Cirque du Soleil star and eight-time World Hoop Dance champion. LaRance's solo variation that night, with its innovative mix of heritage Native hoop dance and hip-hop moves, was done to

Yomba Shoshone medicine man and traditional chief Johnny Bob leads a sundown ceremony and round dance to bless the upcoming fall pine-nut harvest in Nevada. (Joseph Zummo)

the accompaniment of an electronics-plus-powwow-drum track by the Native band A Tribe Called Red. The audience cheered at several points, including the moment when he swirled the hoops into the form of a globe and lifted it overhead. The gesture was a wonderful expression of the world focus of the show, with its contemporary New York City references and a multiethnic troupe offering an innovative version of the classic. The globe imagery was especially vivid in the context of the recent election of a climate-change denier to the presidency and the unease that produced. The Brooklyn audience clearly appreciated the reassurance that LaRance provided that night.

After his variation, LaRance joined four African American hip-hop dancers. Together, they danced against projected photographs of the Brooklyn Bridge and other city scenes. Each performer had a specialty—glide, flex, or pop-and-lock—and a propensity to tickle the audience with takeoffs on the ballet idiom. Sometimes the jokes were broad, as when they pranced on the tips of their shoes; at other times, they were subtle and knowing, as they squeezed and stretched the Tchaikovsky musical phrasing. At the end of the variation, the five dancers oozed their way offstage in a sinuous conga line.

When I got a chance to talk to LaRance after the show, he told me he also coached the kids who twirled the red-and-white-striped hoops in the *Nutcracker*'s more traditional Candy Cane section. "They're my hoop-dance cousins," he quipped. "I showed them a few moves, and they caught on quickly." It was LaRance's first ballet appearance, but the performance featured a mix of tradition and community that felt familiar to him.

The Brooklyn performances over, LaRance was heading to the airport and thence home to Ohkay Owingeh Pueblo in New Mexico. There he would participate in his community's annual Christmas dances. The age-old round would complete the arc from past to future, from dark to light; community members would dance and together ensure that the earth would twirl past the quiet cold of the winter solstice and head for the ebullient growth of spring.

Acknowledgments

It took many villages and so many people to bring this book to you. During the approximately twenty years that I have been involved in Indian country articles—for a couple of years as an editor, then as a reporter—those quoted in this text took time out of their busy lives to answer my questions, explain details I may have missed, and refer me to additional interviewees and material. I sincerely hope that anyone I mistakenly omit here will forgive me. Lapses of this sort and other errors are mine alone. I owe profound gratitude to Robert Lasner and Elizabeth Clementson of IG Publishing; to my agent, Kirsten Neuhaus, and her colleagues at Foundry Literary + Media; and to my husband, Peter Zummo, and my daughter-in-law, Julia Zummo, for their confidence in this project. Special thanks go to Peter's and my son, Joseph Zummo, both for his support and for photographing much of my work in Indian country. A small selection of those photographs can be seen in this book.

I am indebted for some of my early Indian-country articles to residents of the Ihanktonwan Dakota, or Yankton Sioux, homeland in South Dakota. They include rights advocate Faith Spotted Eagle and her family and the late Tessa Lehto, editor of the tribal newspaper. Also on the Yankton Sioux Reservation, Izzie Zephier, his family, and his wife, Janet DeLoughery Zephier, saw me through my coverage of the federal government's decision to allow a factory hog farm to force its way onto the land, a story about a tribal constitutional crisis, reporting in 2008 on the Keystone Pipeline, and a year of writing about the notoriously violent boarding schools Native people were forced to attend until the 1970s, among other articles.

On the Sisseton Wahpeton Oyate's reservation, which spans North and South Dakota, Mary-Catherine Renville, Mary Jane Wanna, their relatives, and additional tribal members shared their recollections of one of the most horrific of the boarding schools, the local, Catholic-run Tekakwitha. While writing the articles that resulted, I met investigator and paralegal Ken Bear Chief, who is Gros Ventre, Nez Perce, and Nooksak; his tireless work helped reveal severe crimes against Native children there and elsewhere and bring the perpetrators to justice.

The numerous determined and energetic people I interviewed over the years include Four Directions Community Center director and fighter for the rights of Native children and families Frank LaMere, of Nebraska's Winnebago Tribe, and Bristol Bay Native Corporation head April Ferguson and her colleagues, including Grace Mulipola, who helped me cover the 2014 federal election in Alaska. In South Dakota, I relied on Crow Creek Sioux Reservation tribal chairman Brandon Sazue and voting-rights advocate Donita Loudner; Oglala Nation's former vice chairman Tom Poor Bear and tribal members Kevin Killer, a state legislator, and Jesse Short Bull, a filmmaker and photographer; and Cheyenne River Sioux Reservation tribal member Julie Garreau, head of the lively and creative Cheyenne River Youth Project.

Up the highway on the Standing Rock Sioux Reservation, in

South and North Dakota, I visited the Porcupine District, where I met local council members and economic-development planners Darrel Iron Shield, Mary Louise Defender-Wilson, Dennis Paint, and others. This occurred years before Standing Rock became world-famous for its stand for environmental justice. Also in Porcupine, organic gardener Aubrey Skye was the subject of several stories, as he developed many scores of gardens around Standing Rock with the support of the tribal and CDC's diabetes programs. I had the great fun of meeting CDC scientists and Ojibwe artist Patrick Rolo at Comic Con in New York City, where their cheerful exhibit of books and other Rolo-illustrated classroom materials attracted convention attendees costumed as superheroes and other pop-culture figures.

My guides through the vibrant modern and ancient gardens of the Pueblos of New Mexico included Cochiti Pueblo elder farmers Gabe Trujillo and Joe Benado; Santa Clara Pueblo scholar Tessie Naranjo; Clayton Apikan Brascoupé, a Mohawk living at Tesuque Pueblo who runs the Traditional Native American Farmers Association; Tesuque tribal official and heritage agriculture expert Louie Hena; the late Ohkay Owingeh Pueblo official Herman Agoyo; and archaeologists Kurt Anschuetz and Steven Dominguez Sundjordet. In recent years, Ohkay Owingeh dancer Nakotah LaRance and Zuni dance groups Soaring Eagle and Anshe:kwe have offered their choreographic perspective on the age-old Pueblo tradition in the modern day.

Most of the voting-rights battles I reported on were waged by a Rosebud Sioux couple, O.J. and Barb Semans, their South Dakota rancher partner, Bret Healy, and their legal director, Greg Lembrich, an attorney and New Jersey town official. Under the aegis of the nonprofit Four Directions, the quartet are bringing Native voters into the polling place and thereby into the political conversation. The group has filed federal voting-rights lawsuits in states where the Native population—though small on the national scale—makes up a large minority group that can become an influential swing vote.

In just a few years, I have seen greater ballot-box access improve Native people's lives, as they have elected indigenous officials, protected land and water, and more. Four Directions collaborators I have been privileged to meet include Northern Cheyenne spiritual teacher Mark Wandering Medicine, Gros Ventre tribal member and former Fort Belknap Indian Community chairman William "Snuffy" Main, Blackfeet tribal member and Carlyle Group lobbyist Tom Rodgers, and Indian People's Action official Michaelynn Hawk, who is Crow.

Western Shoshone people introduced me to their vast and magical landscape, which is centered on, but extends much beyond, the state of Nevada. They include Battle Mountain Band councilman Joseph Holley, Shoshone-Paiute Tribes chairman Ted Howard, traditional chief Raymond Yowell, and medicine men Reggie Sope and Johnny Bob, as well as their families and fellow tribal members. Paul Huet and Lucy Hill of Klondex Mines Ltd. also went out of their way to help in this regard.

Retired Interior Department administrative judge Sally Willett, a Cherokee tribal member, and Quinault tribal member Terry Beckwith, both of ICC Indian Enterprises, and Cris Stainbrook, the Oglala president of the Indian Land Tenure Foundation, decoded for me the myriad federal regulations hemming in tribal land use and economics. Lance Morgan, attorney, business leader, and Winnebago Tribe of Nebraska member, was unerring on a wide range of business and economic issues. Retired US senator Byron Dorgan, his former aide Erin Bailey, and others from the Center for Native American Youth assisted mightily during a year of reporting on Indian child suicide, an alarmingly common occurrence nationwide. On the Navajo reservation, brothers Patrick and Frank Adakai, their cousin Roberta Tovar, and additional relatives showed me the enormous burdens imposed on tribal members as they strive for prosperity; Leona Gopher described similar issues on the Blackfeet reservation.

Researchers Jean Schroedel and Roger Chin of Claremont Graduate University, and Marlee Kanosh, a Paiute Tribe of Utah member who lost her brother, Corey, to a police shooting, provided invaluable help in understanding the high rate of police killings of Natives. Puyallup tribal council member James Rideout lost a niece to a police shooting. He and his relatives warmly welcomed me and photographer Joseph Zummo to Puyallup and helped us investigate the tragedy.

I am particularly grateful to those who took the time to read and comment on chapters prior to publication and thank each and every one. Most are mentioned or quoted in the text; I would like to add a special mention for editor and playwright Traci Parks; my nephew, mycologist Peter Oviatt, and his wife, writer and editor Jamie McPartland. Early in my years in Indian country, Oglala attorney Brett Lee Shelton of the Native American Rights Fund and Robert Bertsche, an attorney with Prince Lobel Tye, helped by commenting on drafts of my investigative stories. Later, as I reported on the Native struggle for equal rights, attorneys Laughlin McDonald, director emeritus of the ACLU's

Voting Rights Project, Greg Lembrich, and Colorado attorney Maya Kane steered me through the maze of federal election law. Attorneys Peter d'Errico, retired from the University of Massachusetts Amherst, and Rollie Wilson, of Fredericks Peebles & Morgan, provided additional guidance on federal Indian law and on Western Shoshone matters, in particular.

Bolts of insight came at unexpected times. Here are a few among many: While I was writing about a harvest festival on the Navajo reservation for *Saveur* magazine, tribal members Valencia Herder and Roberto Nutlouis criticized the Bureau of Indian Affairs for encouraging big-box stores to set up on or near Indian reservations; the two young advocates said that the stores' cheap goods undercut local barter economies and the age-old indigenous trade in traditionally produced items, from organic vegetables to household goods. In nearby Winslow, Arizona, I ordered a lamb dish at the Turquoise Room restaurant. After the meal, chef John Sharpe quizzed me about what exactly I had tasted. I responded that the tender cut seemed to be seasoned from within, with none of the usual gaminess of lamb. Turned out I was right! Sharpe told me that the shepherdess from whom he purchased his lamb, Navajo tribal member Colleen Biakeddy, kept her flock on the move among stands of herbs, flowers, and grasses; the traditional grazing method was not only better for the landscape, it produced exceptional meat that was naturally seasoned.

On a very somber note, Melvin Houston, of the Santee Sioux Reservation, sent me a video of his 2011 trip to the Minnesota Historical Society. Curators there pulled out drawer after drawer to show him and other visiting Dakotas exquisite regalia, bows and arrows, household goods, children's toys, and more created by their ancestors. Made of wood, stone, feathers, hide, bone, and other natural materials, the articles depicted a fine-tuned relationship to the world that predated their makers' deadly 1863 exile to a prison camp in South Dakota. To the horror of the 2011 Dakota visitors, one drawer held a noose used to hang one of their ancestors in 1862 in what remains the largest mass hanging in US history.

My debt to my editors at various publications is enormous. They included the newspapers *Native Sun News* and *Indian Country Today*. The latter became the large and very successful online news site *Indian Country Media Network*. I found inspiring Native and non-Native editors, including Chris Napolitano, Ken Polisse, David Melmer, Lucinda Rowlands, Leeanne Root, Bob Roe, Tim Giago, Ernestine Chasing Hawk, and others. The Native American Journalists Association, of which I am an associate (non-Native) member, has awarded me honors over the years, including its top annual prize, the Richard LaCourse Award for Investigative Reporting.

In These Times, with its editors Joel Bleifuss, Jessica Stites, and John Collins, and its associated Leonard C. Goodman Foundation, was especially supportive, as was *100Reporters,* edited by Diana Schemo. Arianna Huffington gave me a *Huffington Post* blog at a time when I needed a place to get news stories up fast. Additional support came from the George Polk Center for Investigative Reporting, under the direction of John Darnton, the Fund for Investigative Journalism, run by Sandy Bergo, and the University of Southern California's Annenberg School of Journalism, among other foundations and nonprofits. Discriminating thinkers, including journalists Louise Farr, Leslie Wayne, and Susan Crandell, and choreographer Marilyn Klaus, a Cherokee descendant, have been continual sources of encouragement and advice.

Ahead of a Western Shoshone festival, a tipi is
ready for its covering and the arrival of guests.
(Joseph Zummo)

Notes

Thoughts on nomenclature: In this book, I use the name of a tribe, or nation, when I am referring specifically to it, or to the affiliation of a member. For general references to multiple tribes and/or their members, I use widely acceptable terms, such as Native, Native American, American Indian, Alaska Native, and indigenous. I use the word Indian in a legal context; the word is used in statutes of the United States to designate federally recognized tribes, enrolled members, and reservations, as well as all Indian property taken as a whole, as in "Indian country."

INTRODUCTION

1. For more on this, see the US Department of Defense in conjunction with President Obama's National Native American Heritage Month proclamation and the article, Walter T. Ham IV, "Soldiers, Civilians Salute Native Americans' Contributions," US Department of Defense website, November 14, 2014.

2. Daniel McCool et al., *Native Vote: American Indians, the Voting Rights Act, and the Right to Vote* (Cambridge, Great Britain: Cambridge University Press, 2007); and Laughlin McDonald, *American Indians and the Fight for Equal Voting Rights* (Norman, Oklahoma: University of Oklahoma Press, 2010).

3. See Chapter 1, "Destitute by Design," for a detailed look at this phenomenon.

4. M. Y. H. Brave Heart, "Wakiksuyapi: Carrying the Historical Trauma of the Lakota," Tulane Studies in Social Welfare (2000); and M. Y. H. Brave Heart & L. DeBruyn, "The American Holocaust: Historical Unresolved Grief," National Center for American Indian and Alaska Native Mental Health Research 8, no. 2 (1998).

5. See Chapter 1, "Destitute by Design," for more.

6. District court case *Hopi Tribe et al. v. Trump et al.,* filed in 2017.

7. Nauman Talli, "Tribes Promise 'War' over Gold Mining in Sacred Black Hills," *Native Sun News Today*, December 11, 2017.

8. For more on Salyers's death and its aftermath, see Chapter 4.

9. The connection between culture and emotional health is considered a given by most tribal people; among the many peer-reviewed scientific studies corroborating the concept are Henson et al., "Identifying Protective Factors to Promote Health in American Indian and Alaska Native Adolescents: A Literature Review," *Journal of Primary Prevention* 38, no. 1–2 (April 2017); and Garroutte et al., "Spirituality and Attempted Suicide among American Indians," *Social Science & Medicine* 56, no. 7 (April 2003).

10. Warren Schultz, "The Story of Rosanne's Guitar," *Garden Design*, (November 1997).

1: DESTITUTE BY DESIGN

1. *Western Refining Southwest Inc. and Western Refining Pipeline, LLC, v. Acting Navajo Regional Director, Bureau of Indian Affairs,* 63 IBIA 41 (2016). For more, see Stephanie Woodard, "How the US Government Is Helping Corporations Plunder Native Land," *In These Times*, (September 2016).

2. US Department of the Interior, *2015 Status Report: Land Buy-Back Program for Tribal Nations* (November 2015).

3. US Department of Energy and US Department of the Interior, *Report to Congress: Energy Policy Act of 2005, Section 1813, Indian Land Rights-of-Way Study* (May 2007).

4. See Chapter 1, note 3.

5. The information and statements that Terry Beckwith provided in this chapter came from many interviews and email communications during 2016 and 2017.

6. Navajo Nation Division of Economic Development, "Fast Facts," on the division's website, http://www.navajobusiness.com, accessed October 2017.

7. Arizona Department of Health Services, "Prevention Services"; figure based on the US Census Bureau's *2011–2015 5-Year American Community Survey* (2017).

8. US Census Bureau, *Small Area Income and Poverty Estimates: 2015 All Ages in Poverty*, interactive map https://www.census.gov, accessed October 2017.

9. Narayana Kocherlakota, "Persistent Poverty on Indian Reservations: New Perspectives and Responses," *Ninth District Notes*, Federal Reserve Bank of Minneapolis (June 2015).

10. Eric C. Henson et al., *The State of the Native Nations: Conditions under US Policies of Self-Determination*, the Harvard Project on American Indian Economic Development (New York: Oxford University Press, 2008).

11. The district court case *Western Refining Southwest, Inc., et al. v. 3.7820 Acres of Land in McKinley County, New Mexico, et al.*, filed in 2014 and stayed in 2016 pending the resolution of a related matter.

12. Brian Sawers, "Tribal Land Corporations: Using Incorporation to Combat Fractionation," *Nebraska Law Review* 88, no. 2 (February 2009).

13. Emails and interviews on this and related subjects with Nedra Darling, director of public affairs for the Bureau of Indian Affairs, took place during June 2016.

14. Email communications in July 2016 from Gary Hansen, then vice president of corporate communications for Western Refining, and in November 2017 from Brendan Smith, senior communications specialist at Andeavor Logistics, which purchased Western Refining that year in a deal valued at $1.7 billion.

15. *Leonie Gopher v. Rocky Mountain Regional Director, Bureau of Indian Affairs*, 60 IBIA 189 and 60 IBIA 315 (2015); material in this section also includes material from interviews with Leona Gopher.

16. General Allotment Act of 1887, ch. 119, 24 Stat. 388, as amended, 25 U. S. C. § 331 et seq., 49th Cong., 2nd sess., Feb. 8, 1887.

17. David Grann, *Killers of the Flower Moon: The Osage Murders and the Birth of the FBI* (New York: Doubleday, 2017) is an exploration of this period.

18. Several interviews with Lance Morgan took place mainly in 2011 and 2016; see also innumerable articles and books describing the Native American development of corn. One book is Jack Weatherford, *Indian Givers: How the Indians of the Americas Transformed the World* (New York: Fawcett Columbine, 1988); another is Charles C. Mann, *1491: New Revelations of the Americas Before Columbus* (New York: Knopf, 2005).

19. Interview with Cris Stainbrook in March 2016; follow-up emails in April, October, and November 2016 and November 2017.

20. Theodore Roosevelt, "First Annual Message," accessed via The American Presidency Project, hosted on the internet by the University of California, Santa Barbara, October 2017.

21. *Congressional Record: Proceedings and Debates of the Forty-Eighth Congress, 2nd Sess.* (Washington, DC: Government Printing Office, 1885).

22. US Office of Indian Affairs, *Annual Reports of the Department of the Interior for the Fiscal Year Ended June 20, 1897: Report of the Commissioner of Indian Affairs* (Washington, DC: Government Printing Office, 1897).

23. Donald Wharton et al., *Examination of the United States 7th, 8th and 9th Periodic Reports of June 2013: Joint Submission of Two Alternative Reports Regarding the Violations of Indigenous Children's Right to Culture and Continuing Legacy of the Boarding School Policies*, submitted to the United Nations Committee on the Elimination of Racial Discrimination (CERD), 85th sess. (2014).

24. Indian Land Tenure Foundation, "Land Tenure Issues," on the group's website, https://iltf.org, accessed 2017.

25. "The Great Chief: Red Cloud Meets His White Brethren at Cooper Institute," *New York Times, June 17, 1870*.

26. Fort Laramie Treaty, 1868, accessed via The Avalon Project of Yale Law School, October 2017.

27. This statement came from interviews with Walter Littlemoon in July, August, and September 2011 and on related subjects in the following years.

28. Mann, *1491*. Mann looks at controversies over population numbers, which may have been higher than 100 million for the entire New World or, as other scholars have claimed, a small fraction of that. The long-running disagreement arises partly from lack of direct evidence, Mann writes, but also from the politics of colonization. That is, it is easier for non-Natives to accept the seizure of lands that were empty or nearly so.

29. Indian Land Tenure Foundation, "Land Tenure History," on the group's website, https://iltf.org, accessed 2017.

30. Indian Reorganization Act, 48 Stat. 984, 25 USC. § 461 et seq.; 73rd Cong., 2nd sess., June 18, 1934.

31. House Concurrent Resolution 108, a 1953 formal statement by Congress calling for termination; Stainbrook, interview.

32. "Klamath Tribes History," on the tribal website, http://klamathtribes.org/history, accessed October 2017.

33. "Brief History," on the tribal website, http://www.menominee-nsn.gov, accessed October 2017; see also the website of Menominee Tribal Enterprises, http://wwwmtewood.com.

34. American Indian Policy Review Commission, *Final Report, Submitted to Congress May 17, 1977*, vol. 1 (Washington, DC: Government Printing Office, 1977).

35. Vine Deloria Jr., *Custer Died for Your Sins: An Indian Manifesto* (New York: Macmillan, 1969).

36. Richard Nixon, "Special Message to the Congress on Indian Affairs" (July 8, 1970), accessed via The American Presidency Project in 2017.

37. US Department of Agriculture, *2012 Census of Agriculture, American Indian Reservations*, vol. 2, Subject Series, part 5 (National Agricultural Statistics Service, 2014).

38. Interview and email communications with Carroll Webster and additional tribal officials in November and December 2016.

39. Valerie Volcovici, "Trump Advisors Aim to Privatize Oil-Rich Indian Reservations," Reuters, December 5, 2016.

40. "Rep. Markwayne Mullin Refutes Speculation of 'Privatizing' Tribal Land," *Indianz.com*, December 7, 2016.

41. Robert J. Miller, "Indian Entrepreneurship," in *Unlocking the Wealth of Indian Nations*, edited by Terry L. Anderson (Lanham, Maryland: Lexington Books, 2016).

42. Innumerable books and articles have analyzed these sites; for descriptions, see the World Heritage List on UNESCO's website, https://whc.unesco.org.

43. Interview with Curley Youpee, director, Fort Peck Tribes Cultural Resources Department, in April 2008.

44. Lindsay Jones and Richard D. Shiels, eds., *The Newark Earthworks: Enduring Monuments, Contested Meanings* (Charlottesville, Virginia: University of Virginia Press, 2016).

45. Miller, "Indian Entrepreneurship."

46. Frank Pommersheim, *Broken Landscape: Indians, Indian Tribes, and the Constitution* (New York: Oxford University Press, 2009).

47. Martin Case, "Treaty Signers: Making the American Myth," (lecture, Minnesota Humanities Center, St. Paul, Minnesota, broadcast on Minnesota Native News, May 5, 2015); additionally, emails clarifying various issues during 2016.

48. Journals of the Continental Congress, Rufus King and William Samuel Johnson, annotators, "An Ordinance for Ascertaining the Mode of Disposing of Lands in the Western Territory" (Philadelphia: John Dunlap, 1785).

49. Matthew L.M. Fletcher, "The Iron Cold of the Marshall Trilogy," Faculty Publications, Michigan State University College of Law (82 N.D. L. Rev. 627, 2006); see also the Supreme Court cases *Johnson v. McIntosh*,

decided in 1823, *Cherokee Nation v. Georgia*, decided in 1831, and *Worcester v. Georgia*, decided in 1832.

50. *The Supreme Court case United States v. Sioux Nation of Indians*, decided in 1980; see also Fletcher, "The Iron Cold of the Marshall Trilogy."

51. Walter R. Echo-Hawk, *In the Courts of the Conqueror: The 10 Worst Indian Law Cases Ever Decided* (Golden, Colorado: Fulcrum Publishing, 2010).

52. Lance Morgan, "The Rise of Tribes and the Fall of Federal Indian Law," *Arizona State Law Journal*, 2017; this section was amplified by interviews and email communication with Morgan in 2011 and 2016.

53. "Bureau of Indian Affairs Opens Consultation on Big Economic Proposal," *Indianz.com*, February 7, 2017.

54. Morgan, "The Rise of Tribes and the Fall of Federal Indian Law."

55. Ibid.

56. The Supreme Court case *Nevada et al. v. Hicks et al.*, decided in 2001.

57. Interviews with tribal attorney Mary Wynne during 2001 and 2002.

58. Numerous interviews between 2001 and 2011 with tribal member and leading rights advocate Faith Spotted Eagle and Tessa Lehto, editor of the Yankton Sioux Tribe's *Sioux Messenger* for several years.

59. Interviews with attorneys for the Yankton Sioux Tribe: Mary Wynne, in 2001, and Charles Abourezk, in 2011.

60. "2010–11 Term Supreme Court Cases," National Indian Law Library of the Native American Rights Fund, https://www.narf.org/nill, accessed October 2017.

61. Interviews with tribal members and officials in 2011 and again in 2013 when the sign was erected; see also Mary Annette Pember, "'How Could Anyone Have So Much Hate?' New Kind of Range War in So. Dakota," *Indian Country Media Network*, September 16, 2013.

62. Miller, "Indian Entrepreneurship."

63. Numerous interviews with Frank LaMere and Mark Vasina in 2011 and 2012; interview with a Whiteclay shopkeeper in February 2012.

64. Stephanie Woodard, "Gold Mines in Hell," *100Reporters.com*, February 21, 2012; in a 2012 interview, Nick Tilson, head of the Thunder Valley Community Development Corporation, in the northern part of Pine Ridge, told me that Whiteclay and other border towns have a "parasite-host" relationship with their neighboring reservations.

65. Nebraska Supreme Court case *Stuart Kozal et al. v. Nebraska Liquor Control Commission et al.*, decided in 2017.

66. Stephen L. Pevar, *The Rights of Indians and Tribes,* 4th ed. (New York: Oxford University Press, 2012).

67. Steven Peterson, *2010 Economic Impact Report: The Five Tribes of Idaho,* report prepared for the Coeur d'Alene tribe and others (2010).

68. Information Insights, *The Economic Impact of Alaska Native Organizations on Interior Alaska,* report prepared for Doyon Limited et al. (Fairbanks, Alaska, 2008).

69. Phone interview with and email from Dr. Malia Villegas, director of the Policy Research Center of the National Congress of American Indians, in June 2013; see also Mark Fogarty, "The Growing Economic Might of Indian Country," *Indian Country Media Network,* March 15, 2013.

70. President Barack Obama signed the Claims Resolution Act in December 2010; see also the district court case *Cobell v. Kempthorne,* filed in 2008; and see Indian Trust Settlement, http://www.cobellsettlement.com.

71. Timothy Egan, "Indians Win Major Round in Fight over Trust Accounts," *New York Times,* February 23, 1999.

72. Alan Balaban, *Site Visit Report of the Special Master to the Office of Appraisal Services in Gallup, New Mexico and the Bureau of Indian Affairs Navajo Realty Office in Window Rock, Arizona,* made part of the *Cobell* case record by Judge Royce C. Lamberth in 2003.

73. See Chapter 1, note 70.

74. Stainbrook, interview.

75. For a helpful explanation of fractionation, see US Department of the Interior, *2015 Status Report: Land Buy-Back Program for Tribal Nations.*

76. Jacob W. Russ and Thomas Stratmann, "Creeping Normalcy: Fractionation of Indian Land Ownership," *CESifo Working Paper Series* no. 4607 (January 31, 2014); material in this section was amplified by an interview with Thomas Stratmann.

77. US Department of the Interior, *2015 Status Report: Land Buy-Back Program for Tribal Nations.*

78. Kristin T. Ruppel, *Unearthing Indian Land: Living with the Legacies of Allotment* (Tucson, Arizona: University of Arizona Press, 2008).

79. Stainbrook, interview.

80. Stainbrook, email.

81. Rob Capriccioso, "Bill and Hillary Clinton's Global Initiative Ups Support of Tribes," *Indian Country Media Network,* June 24, 2013.

—

2: ON THE VOTING-RIGHTS FRONTLINE

1. Daniel McCool et al., *Native Vote: American Indians, the Voting Rights Act, and the Right to Vote* (Cambridge, England: Cambridge University Press, 2007). See also Jean Schroedel et al., "Vote Dilution and Suppression in Indian Country," *Studies in American Political Development* 29, no. 1 (April 2015); additionally, interviews with McCool in 2014 and Schroedel in 2014, 2015, 2016, and 2017. For more information and background, see Stephanie Woodard, "The Missing Native Vote," *In These Times*, June 2014.

2. This information and other statements throughout this chapter from O. J. and Barb Semans, Four Directions consultant Bret Healy, and the group's legal director, Greg Lembrich, came from interviews that took place from 2010 through 2017; for a discussion of voting ahead of Election Day nationwide, see Diana Kasdan, *Early Voting: What Works*, a research report from The Brennan Center for Justice at New York University School of Law, 2013.

3. This problem was discussed at length by voting-rights advocates and federal, state, and county officials during the September 2010 meeting in Fall River; in addition, Chris Nelson, then South Dakota's secretary of state and head elections official, testified about it during 2012 hearings for a lawsuit Oglala Sioux voters subsequently filed.

4. Multiple interviews and emails with candidates, including then state senator Larry Lucas (D-Dist. 26), who was running for reelection, and state and party officials. See also the National Republican Congressional Committee's breathless description of the fry bread fests and another purported imbroglio involving bowls of chili and the high-level law-enforcement officials in the state to whom the GOP appealed for help: "Democrat Dirty Laundry: Embattled Herseth-Sandlin Caught Trying to Buy Votes, Desperate South Dakota Democrat Caught in the Crosshairs of Food-for-Votes Investigation," nrcc.org, October 10, 2010.

5. The district court case *Brooks v. Gant*, decided in 2012.

6. The district court case *Poor Bear v. The County of Jackson*, decided in 2017.

7. The district court case *Wandering Medicine et al. v. McCulloch et al.*, filed in 2012 in Montana and appealed to the Ninth Circuit Court of Appeals, which issued a decision in 2014

8. The district court case *Sanchez v. Cegavske*, settled in 2016, including an emergency court order for provision of on-reservation early in-person voting.

9. McCool et al., *Native Vote.*

10. For more detail on different states' rules, see Chapter 2, note 2 for the report of the Brennan Center.

11. The district court cases *Navajo Nation v. San Juan County,* decided in 2015; *Navajo Nation v. San Juan County,* decided in 2016; and *Navajo Nation, a federally recognized Indian tribe, et al. v. San Juan County,* decided in 2017.

12. The district court case *US v. San Juan County,* decided in 1985.

13. Information and statements from Maya Kane in this chapter came from multiple interviews during 2015, 2016, and 2017.

14. Jean R. Schroedel, *An Evaluation of Factors Affecting Indian Voting in Three Montana Counties,* expert witness report in *Wandering Medicine v. McCulloch* (2014)

15. *Navajo Nation Human Rights Commission et al. v. San Juan County et al.,* No. 2:2016-cv-0154 (D. Utah 2016).

16. For more, see *Navajo Nation Human Rights Commission v. San Juan County, et al.,* on the Lawyers' Committee for Civil Rights Under Law website, https://lawyerscommittee.org, accessed November 2017.

17. The Supreme Court case *Yick Wo v. Hopkins,* decided in 1886.

18. The district court case *Ramah Navajo Chapter et al. v. Jewell,* filed in 1990.

19. US Department of Justice, "Attorney General Loretta E. Lynch and Secretary of the Interior Sally Jewell Announce Settlements of Tribal Trust Accounting and Management Lawsuits," Office of Public Affairs, September 26, 2016.

20. Healy, interview.

21. *Trans-Pecos Pipeline, LLC,* 155 FERC ¶ 61,140 (2016) (May 2016 Order).

22. Posted to the Big Bend Conservation Alliance Facebook page on September 21 and 22, 2016.

23. Kevin K. Washburn, "Trump Proposes Hundreds of Millions in Cuts to Federal Appropriations for Indian Country," *Indian Country Media Network,* May 25, 2017.

24. The district court case *Veasey v. Abbott,* filed in Texas in 2014; originally decided in favor of minority vote access, a decision that was overturned on appeal in 2018.

25. Mark Trahant, "#NATIVEVOTE16—Indian Country Wins with More Representation in the States," https://trahantreports.com, July 2016.

26. See Chapter 2, note 1.

27. Frank L. Baum, "The Sitting Bull Editorial," *Aberdeen Saturday Pioneer*, December 20, 1890.

28. See Chapter 2, note 1.

29. Ibid.

30. William Janklow, "Official Opinion No. 77-73, Voting Rights Act of 1965, as amended by Public Law 94-73: bilingual elections," August 23, 1977, accessed in 2011 and 2018 on the website of the South Dakota attorney general, https://atg.sd.gov.

31. Laughlin McDonald, *American Indians and the Fight for Equal Voting Rights* (Norman, Oklahoma: University of Oklahoma Press, 2010).

32. The Supreme Court case Shelby County, Ala. v. Holder, decided in 2013.

33. See Chapter 2, note 16 for more on the distance issue.

34. South Dakota Advisory Committee to the United States Commission on Civil Rights, *Native Americans in South Dakota: An Erosion of Confidence in the Justice System*, March 2000.

35. United States Commission on Civil Rights, *Discrimination Against Native Americans in Border Towns: A Briefing Before the United States Commission on Civil Rights Held in Washington, D.C.*, 2007.

36. The district court case *Daschle v. Thune*, decided in 2004.

37. Aura Bogado, "From Arizona to Montana, Native Voters Struggle for Democracy," *Colorlines*, January 28, 2013.

38. Information about activities surrounding the 2014 election on Pine Ridge came from interviews on the reservation with Donna Semans.

39. Interview with county auditor (head elections official) for Fall River County, South Dakota, in October 2014.

40. Interview with sheriff of county overlapping much of Pine Ridge in October 2014.

41. Email from the office of the US Attorney for South Dakota; the telephone call was also confirmed during the in-person interview in the polling-place with county auditor Ganje.

42. O. J. Semans, interview.

43. Donna Semans, interview.

44. Interviews with county officials from 2010 to 2017.

45. See Chapter 2, note 6 for the lawsuit.

46. Jonathan Ellis, "Voting Rights Lawsuit Enters Costly Phase: Despite

Adverse Ruling and Other Hurdles, Jackson County Continues Costly Court Fight," *Argus Leader,* August 15, 2015.

47. Cory Allen Heidelberger, "Jackson County Spending $1.5M to Resist Setting Up $20K Voting Centers for Indians," *Dakota Free Press,* August 16, 2015.

48. "So What's the Connection Between Sioux Falls Democratic Mayor Huether and a Voting Rights Lawsuit in Jackson County?" *South DaCola,* August 18, 2015.

49. Interview with Jeff Barth in September 2015.

50. McDonald, *American Indians and the Fight for Equal Voting Rights.*

51. Interview with Laughlin McDonald in September 2013.

52. *Sanchez v. Cegavske.*

53. Interview with Bobby Sanchez in October 2016.

54. Interview with Vinton Hawlcy in October 2016.

55. The district court case Brakebill v. Jaeger, filed in 2016, amended complaint filed in 2017, judge's order issued in 2018 with significant victories for voters seeking access to the ballot box.

56. Interview and emails with Matthew Campbell, Native American Rights Fund attorney, in December 2015 and January 2016.

57. The district court cases *Nick v. Bethel, Alaska,* decided in 2010, and *Toyukak v. Treadwell,* decided in 2014; see also articles by Native American Rights Fund attorney Natalie Landreth and others, posted on the organization's website in the section titled "Our Work," www.narf.org/our-work/.

58. Interviews and emails with James Tucker over several months in 2014; the documents included the plaintiff's motion for summary judgment in *Toyukak v. Treadwell,* filed on April 4, 2014.

59. Numerous press accounts included Richard Mauer, "Alaska Elections Worker Ignored Mangled Yup'ik Translation, Court Hears," *Alaska Dispatch News,* June 26, 2014, updated September 28, 2016.

60. Interview with Grace Mulipola, Bristol Bay Native Corporation.

61. Interviews with Greg Lembrich and South Dakota state senator Troy Heinert (D-Dist. 26) in November 2014.

62. Interviews and emails with Native Youth Leadership Alliance communications director Jesse Short Bull, as well as with state senator Kevin Killer (D-Dist. 27), in November 2014.

63. Stephanie Woodard, "In a Rare Move, the Justice Department Drafts a Bill of Its Own—to Ensure Native Voting Rights," *Rural America In These Times,* June 1, 2015.

64. Interviews with Mark Wandering Medicine about voting and other rights issues spanned the years 2012 through 2016.

65. Webster's conclusions, as described in Schroedel's expert report, see Chapter 2, note 14.

66. Interviews and emails with Bryan Watt, then Montana Democratic Party communications director, in March 2014.

67. Interview with Pratt Wiley, Democratic National Committee national director of voter expansion, in March 2014.

68. Interviews and emails with Tom Rodgers in March and April 2014, along with additional interviews on related matters in 2012 and 2013.

69. Interviews with Greg Lembrich, O. J. Semans, Bret Healy and Daniel McCool; see also Chapter 2, note 1.

70. The district court lawsuit Large v. Fremont County, Wyo., decided in 2010.

71. For more on this, see the US Department of Defense in conjunction with President Obama's National Native American Heritage Month proclamation and in an article, Walter T. Ham IV, "Soldiers, Civilians Salute Native Americans' Contributions," Americans' Contributions," US Department of Defense website, November 14, 2014.

3: GODS AND MONSTERS

1. The email was part of the administrative record of an Interior Board of Land Appeals (IBLA) claim, *Waterton Global Mining Company, LLC.*, IBLA 2015-23, which I received from attorney Rollie Wilson, of the law firm Fredericks Peebles & Morgan LLP, who was handling the case for the Battle Mountain Band.

2. According to the website of the Bureau of Land Management, https://www.blm.gov, accessed October 2017.

3. I interviewed Joseph Holley, chairman and later tribal council member of the Battle Mountain Band of the Te-Moak Tribe of Western Shoshone Indians, and Ted Howard, cultural resources director and later chairman of the Shoshone-Paiute Tribes, on the subject of Tosawihi during 2015, 2016, and 2017; I also visited the area in 2016 and 2017. The information Holley and Howard imparted appears throughout this chapter. Related interviews were with Raymond Yowell, South Fork Band of the Te-Moak Tribe of Western Shoshone Indians; Colleen Burton and Kathleen Holley, Battle Mountain Band; Reggie Sope and Murray Sope, Shoshone-Paiute Tribes; and others as identified here.

4. Amy Goodman of *Democracy Now!* reported on the September 3, 2016, incident at Standing Rock. She broadcast a video of the event the following day; it can be seen at https://www.democracynow.org, accessed October 2017.

5. Inteviews about this larger context were with many tribal members over nearly twenty years, including Tessie Naranjo, Santa Clara Pueblo; Izzy Zephier and Faith Spotted Eagle, Yankton Sioux Tribe; Tim Mentz, Kenny Painte, Dennis Painte, and Aubrey Skye, Standing Rock Sioux Tribe; James Rideout and Chester Earl, Puyallup Tribe; Brett Lee Shelton, Oglala Sioux Tribe; Justin Willie, Navajo Nation; and Barbara Wilson, Haida Nation.

6. Te-Moak Tribe of Western Shoshone website, "Battle Mountain Band Colony," http://www.temoaktribe.com/battlemountain.shtml, accessed October 2017.

7. The Wilderness Society, *No Exit: Fixing the BLM's Indiscriinate Energy Leasing*, June 18, 2016.

8. Email from Greg Deimel in November 2017.

9. Bureau of Land Management, "Wild Horse and Burro Program: Myths and Facts," https://www.blm.gov, accessed October 2017.

10. The text of the letter and its signatories, as well as a list of major media outlets covering the effort, has been archived at http://thenaturalhistorymuseum.org, accessed October 2017.

11. See Chapter 3, note 1.

12. See Chapter 3, note 1; see also Bureau of Land Management, *Hollister Underground Mine Project Record of Decision, Plan of Operations Amendment Approval, and Approval of Issuance of Right-of-Way Grants*, Elko District, Tuscarora Field Office, Elko, Nevada, March 31, 2014.

13. Press release, Waterton Global Resource Management, promulgated in May 2014. In November 2014, according to the Bureau of Land Management, Waterton changed the name of the local subsidiary working at the mine to Carlin Resources LLC. In 2017, Waterton sold the mine to Klondex Mines Ltd.

14. Bureau of Land Management press spokesperson Jeff Krauss via email in September 2015; spokesperson Greg Deimel reiterated this view in November 2017, emailing to say the work was "permitted in a sound manner."

15. Ted Howard and Joseph Holley, interviews.

16. Interview and emails with Robert G. Elston, a professor of anthropology at the University of Nevada, Reno, in October 2016.

17. Agenda, Dispute Resolution for the Hollister Mine, Conference call, November 16, 2015.

18. See Chapter 1, in particular references to information from Frank Pommersheim and Martin Case.

19. For a facsimile of the treaty, see "Sioux Treaty of 1868" on the website of the US National Archives and Records administration, https://www.archives.gov, accessed October 2017.

20. Interviews with Izzy Zephier, Yankton Sioux Tribe, and Mark Wandering Medicine, Northern Cheyenne. See also David Rooks, "'World's Largest Biker Bar' Puts Sin City at Base of Bear Butte," *Indian Country Media Network*, June 23, 2016, and "Sturgis Rally Threatens Native American Sacred Site," *Indian Country Media Network*, September 9, 2011.

21. The Supreme Court case *United States v. Sioux Nation of Indians*, decided in 1980.

22. Interview with Raymond Yowell in March 2017.

23. Interviews with Ted Howard and with Native American Rights Fund attorney Brett Lee Shelton in 2015.

24. National Park Service Cultural Resources, "Traditional Cultural Properties: What You Do and How We Think," *CRM* 16 (1993).

25. Section 1 of the National Historic Preservation Act, Pub. L. No. 89-665, as amended by Pub. L. No. 96-515, protects US historic sites and created the Advisory Council on Historic Preservation, the National Register of Historic Places, and tribal and state historic preservation offices; the act describes preservation as a federal partnership with tribes, states, and other entities.

26. "Programmatic Agreement among the Department of the Interior, Bureau of Land Management Tuscarora Field Office, the Nevada State Historic Preservation Office, Advisory Council on Historic Preservation and Rodeo Creek Gold, Inc. Regarding the Hollister Underground Mine Project," signed in April and May 2013; assumed by the Waterton Global Mining Company, LLC, on March 11, 2014. In response to a public records request, the Nevada State Historic Preservation Office provided many additional documents showing the steps involved in the mining approval process as it applied to Tosawihi.

27. In 1996, President Clinton affirmed the federal commitment to tribal sovereignty and the need to consult tribes on issues and actions that affected them in his "Executive Order 13007: Indian Sacred Sites." Four years later, Clinton upheld the commitment with "Executive Order 13175:

Consultation and Coordination with Indian Tribal Governments"; in 2009, President Obama's "Presidential Memorandum on Tribal Consultation" reconfirmed Clinton's stance.

28. Native American Graves Protection and Repatriation Act (NAGPRA), Pub. L. 101-601, 25 USC. 3001 et seq., 104 Stat. 3048.

29. National Park Service Cultural Resources, "Traditional Cultural Properties: What You Do and How We Think"; information updated during interviews with Kurt Anschuetz and other archaeologists in 2001 and with Ted Howard from 2015 through 2017.

30. Interview with Paul Loether in September 2015.

31. The Nevada State Historic Preservation Office has posted the Nevada State listing for the National Register of Historic Places, effective date February 1, 2016, on its website, http://www.shpo.nv.gov.

32. Information on the sewing and basketmaking tools came from an interview with Western Shoshone basketmaker Leah Brady in September 2016.

33. Interview with Western Shoshone craftsman and stone knife maker Seth Jones in February 2017.

34. The district court case *Battle Mountain Band of the Te-Moak Tribe of Western Shoshone Indians v. United States Bureau of Land Management et al.*, with order denying plaintiff's request for restraining order filed in 2016.

35. Information and statements appearing throughout this chapter from Rollie Wilson, of the law firm Fredericks Peebles & Morgan LLP, were gathered during interviews and via emails in 2015 and 2016.

36. Interview with Tanya Reynolds in September 2016.

37. Email from spokesperson Greg Deimel in November 2017.

38. *National Geographic* and numerous other magazines, newspapers, and blogs published photographs, videos, and satellite imagery of ISIS demolishing the Gates of Nineveh in April 2016, as well as of ISIS fighters smashing museum exhibits, tombs, shrines, and other places and artifacts at around that time.

39. The many outlets that reported the Taliban dynamiting the Buddhas of Bamiyan in Afghanistan in 2001 included the BBC, the *Guardian*, the *Washington Post*, and the *New York Times*.

40. The Mining Law of 1872 is officially known as the Act of May 10, 1872 (R.S. §2319 et seq.; 30 USC. 22 et seq.).

41. Bureau of Land Management, "Programs Overview," https://www.blm.gov, accessed October 2017.

42. Bureau of Land Management Abandoned Mine Lands Program, with National Park Service, US Forest Service, Office of Surface Mining, and the Environmental Protection Agency, *Dangers at Abandoned Mines: AML Safety Brochure*, BLM/WO/GI-13/009+3720, P-416, September 2014.

43. Information on the EPA's 2011 Toxics Release Inventory accessed and analyzed by Progressive Leadership Alliance of Nevada.

44. Center for Western Priorities, *The Mining Burden: States Would Shoulder Significant Costs of Cleaning Up Abandoned Mines If They Take Over American Lands*, December 2, 2015.

45. Interview and emails with Gene Hattori, curator of anthropology at the Nevada State Museum, in Reno, in September 2016.

46. Elston, interview and emails.

47. Ibid.

48. William Hildebrandt et al., "Prehistory of Nevada's Northern Tier: Archaeological Investigations along the Ruby Pipeline," American Museum of Natural History Anthropological Papers, no. 101, March 11, 2016.

49. Hattori, interview and emails.

50. Shelton, interview.

51. Edward Winslow et al., *A Relation or Journal of the Beginning and Proceedings of the English Plantation Settled at Plimoth in New England, by Certain English Adventurers Both Merchants and Others* (London: John Bellamie, 1622), transcribed from facsimiles by Caleb Johnson for http://www.mayflowerhistory.com.

52. Jeffrey L. Hantman et al., "The Enlightened Archaeologist: Recent Excavations in Virginia Offer New Insight into Jefferson's Study of an Indian Mound," *Archaeology* 46, no. 3 (1993).

53. David Hurst Thomas, with a foreword by Vine Deloria Jr., *Skull Wars: Kennewick Man, Archaeology, and the Battle for Native American Identity*, (New York: Basic Books, 2001).

54. Ashley Dunn, "A Heritage Reclaimed; From Old Artifacts, American Indians Shape a New Museum," *New York Times,* October 9, 1994; see also the National Museum of the American Indian's website at http://www.nmai.si.edu.

55. The Peabody Museum of Archaeology and Ethnology; the museum's description of its collections, accessed on its website, https://www.peabody.harvard.edu.

56. For an account of what is today considered a great tragedy, see David

La Vere, *Looting Spiro Mounds: An American King Tut's Tomb* (Norman, Oklahoma: University of Oklahoma Press, 2007).

57. Interview with Marcella LeBeau in October 2012.

58. M. Rasmussen, et al., "The Ancestry and Affiliations of Kennewick Man," *Nature* 523 (July 2015); see also Richard Walker, "Kennewick Man Returns Home: After 20 Years, Kennewick Man, or the Ancient One, Is Reburied," *Indian Country Media Network*, February 21, 2017.

59. American Indian Religious Freedom Act, S.J. Res. 102, August 11, 1978, Pub. L. 95-341, 92 Stat. 469, codified in part 42 USC. § 1996.

60. Interviews with Jonathan Holley and Kiana Vance in October 2016 and August 2017.

61. Interviews with Kathleen Holley in September 2016 and August 2017.

62. Interview with Noah Morris, EMT with the Standing Rock Medic & Healer Council in November 2016; see also the district court case *Dundon et al. v. Kirshmeier et al.*, filed on November 28, 2016; and also a November 20, 2016, press release from the Standing Rock Medic & Healer Council, "Standing Rock: Critical Injuries after Police Attack with Water Cannons, Rubber Bullets in Freezing Temps."

63. HB 1203, 65th Legislative Assembly of North Dakota: "A Bill for an Act to create and enact section 32-03.2-02.2 of the North Dakota Century Code, relating to the liability exemption of a motor vehicle driver; and to amend and reenact section 39-10-33 of the North Dakota Century Code, relating to pedestrians on roadways."

64. On December 4, 2016, the US Department of the Army, Office of the Assistant Secretary, Civil Works, sent a memo to the commander of the US Army Corps of Engineers: "Proposed Dakota Access Pipeline Crossing at Lake Oahe, North Dakota." The document rescinded permission for the easement allowing the pipeline to cross the Missouri River just upstream of the Standing Rock Sioux Tribe's water supply intake; the memo also directed that an environmental impact statement be prepared. The memo was made part of the tribe's lawsuit against the corps: *Standing Rock Sioux Tribe (plaintiff) and Cheyenne River Sioux Tribe (plaintiff-intervenor) v. US Army Corps of Engineers (defendant) and Dakota Access, LLC. (defendant-intervenor)*; Case 1:16-cv-01534-JEB, filed July 27, 2016. In February 2017, the Trump administration granted the easement, the pipeline was finished, and oil began flowing through it. At publication time, the lawsuit was still before the courts.

65. Interview with Wendsler Nosie in November 2016.

66. Interview with Ramona Bennett in June 2016; see also Trova Heffernan, *Where the Salmon Run: The Life and Legacy of Billy Frank Jr.* (Seattle, Washington: University of Washington Press, reprint edition, 2013).

67. Interviews with Frank LaMere, Winnebago Tribe of Nebraska and director of Four Directions Community Center in Sioux City, and Mark Vasina, director of the documentary *The Battle for Whiteclay* (2008), http://www.battleforwhiteclay.org;; see also John A. Maisch, director, *Sober Indian / Dangerous Indian: A Story of Empowerment through Sobriety*," (2014), http://www.soberindian.com.

68. Interview with Judith LeBlanc; see also Stephanie Woodard, "The Never-Ending Indian Wars: Spotlight Returns to Standing Rock," part of a special report, "Standing Rock on the Move," *Yes! Magazine*, January 24, 2017.

69. Interview with Frankie Orona in December 2016.

70. LeBlanc, interview; see also Woodard, "The Never-Ending Indian Wars."

71. Andy Rosen, "18 Arrested in Gas Pipeline Protest in Western Massachusetts," *Boston Globe*, May 2, 2017.

72. LeBlanc, interview.

73. Mark Trahant, "The Real Standing Rock Victory Is This: 'Inevitable' Is Not What It Used to Be," *Yes! Magazine*, December 4, 2016.

74. Elizabeth Miller, "'As Close as the US Gets to Egypt's Pyramids': How Chaco Canyon Is Endangered by Drilling," *Guardian*, November 8, 2017.

75. "USDA Final Report Pursuant to Executive Order 13783 on Promoting Energy Independence and Economic Growth," published in the *Federal Register* on November 1, 2017.

76. Environmental Protection Agency, *An Assessment of Potential Mining Impacts on Salmon Ecosystems of Bristol Bay, Alaska*, EPA 910-R-14-001ES, January 2014.

77. Drew Griffin et al., "EPA Head Met with a Mining CEO—and Then Pushed Forward a Controversial Mining Project," CNN, October 24, 2017.

78. Interviews with Alannah Hurley in November 2016 and October 2017; see also Stephanie Woodard, "Warnings from First Americans: Insidious Changes Are Underway That Will Affect Us All," *Rural America In These Times*, October 5, 2017.

79. Interview with Bonnie Gestring, November 2016.

80. Ibid.

81. Tour of the area and review of environmental analyses while in the Fort Belknap Indian Community.

82. Interview with William Main.

83. Earthworks announced the campaign in a November 2017 press release entitled, "Groups Ask DEQ to Halt Unlawful Mining by Former Leader of Bankrupt Mining Company."

84. Alaska Bristol Bay Mining Ban, Ballot Measure 4 (2014). Election results archived by the state of Alaska at http://www.elections.alaska.gov, accessed November 2017.

85. Interview with Kimberly Williams in November 2016.

86. Alannah Hurley, 2016 interview.

87. Interview with Carina Miller in November 2016.

88. Aaron Payment, in a transcript for the *Tribal Council Listening Session*, in Phoenix, Arizona, on October 11, 2016; prepared for the US Department of the Interior.

89. Interview with Stella Kay in November 2016.

90. Michigan Department of Attorney General and Michigan Department of Environmental Quality, *Michigan Petroleum Pipeline Task Force Report*, Lansing, Michigan, July 2015.

91. Aaron Payment, transcript.

92. Information archived by the Pipeline and Hazardous Materials Safety Administration, https://www.phmsa.dot.gov, accessed January 2016.

93. Personal communication with Ryan Duffy.

94. Michigan Department of Attorney General and Michigan Department of Environmental Quality, *Michigan Petroleum Pipeline Task Force Report*.

95. Interview and emails with Rollie Wilson in December 2016.

96. Interview with Dylan Jennings in January 2017.

97. Interview with Mark Maryboy in December 2016.

98. Utah Diné Bikéyah has archived a timeline of the Bears Ears proposal on its website, http://www.dinehbikeyah.org.

99. "EPA Update on Gold King Mine Response: San Juan River Data," an undated memo on the Environmental Protection Agency's website, https://www.epa.gov, which provides links to the 2015 data.

100. Doug Brugge, Timothy Benally, and Esther Yazzie-Lewis, eds., with a foreword by Stewart L. Udall, *The Navajo People and Uranium Mining* (Albuquerque: University of New Mexico Press, 2006) is a devastating account, with first-person testimony, of the Navajo people's experience in the mines. They dug uranium from the earth with picks and shovels but no safety

gear or information about the danger of what they were doing, and no regard for the health and safety of their families living nearby.

101. Maryboy, interview.

102. Interview with Lydia Johnson in August 2017.

103. Interview with Paul Huet in May 2017.

104. Interview with Marleine Knight in August 2017.

4: ROUGH JUSTICE

1. This description of Corey Kanosh's death comes from interviews and email communications in August and November 2016 with his sister, Marlee Kanosh, who runs the Facebook page, Native Lives Taken by Police. The description also comes from the December 14, 2012, announcement of the results of the police investigation of Kanosh's death by the Office of the Millard County [Utah] Attorney and from recordings of the incident and the investigation posted online and accessed in August 2016. Kanosh's passing was covered at the time by media outlets including Fox 13 in Salt Lake City and *Indian Country Media Network*; see Christina Rose, "Natives Call for Attention to Police Killing of Paiute Corey Kanosh," *Indian Country Media Network*, January 13, 2015.

2. This information derives from interviews and email communications during the summer of 2016 with Drew Dalton, attorney for Jeanetta Riley's husband, and with April Linscott, attorney for Riley's children; from the April 2016 complaint Linscott filed on the children's behalf, *Dana Maddox et al. v. The City of Sandpoint et al.*; from the Sandpoint Police Department report on the incident, obtained via a public records request; and from dash-cam video posted online; see Myriah Towner, "Shocking Moment Two Cops Shot Dead Pregnant Mother-of-Three Who Was Threatening to Kill Herself with a Knife," *Daily Mail*, April 4, 2015.

3. Material on this incident and its aftermath, described throughout this chapter, comes from numerous interviews ranging from January 2016 to January 2018, as well as from visits to Seattle and Tacoma, Washington, visits to the scene of the death and to the Puyallup Reservation in Tacoma. The interviews were with several relatives of the dead woman, including her mother, Lisa Earl, her uncle James Rideout, her cousin Chester Earl, fellow tribal members including council member Tim Reynon, and her Tacoma neighbor Gary Harrison. Much material also comes from the Tacoma Police Department's report on the incident, obtained via a public records request, from a February 2016 interview with Tacoma Police Department

spokesperson Loretta Cool, and from email communications in succeeding months with Cool and another spokesperson, Shelbie Boyd.

4. The Justice Department memo on this subject, dated March 31, 2017, calls for "local control and responsibility" for police departments and redefines what extensive reviews had found to be widespread, long-standing problems as instead the "misdeeds of individual bad actors." The promulgation of the memo was widely reported, including by Mark Berman, "Sessions Wants a Review of Consent Decrees, Which Have Been Used for Decades to Force Reforms," *Washington Post,* April 4, 2017.

5. Christopher Hartney and Linh Vuong, *Created Equal: Racial and Ethnic Disparities in the US Criminal Justice System,* National Council on Crime and Delinquency, March 2009.

6. US Sentencing Commission, *Quick Facts: Native Americans in the Federal Offender Population,* https://www.ussc.gov, August 2017; see also US Sentencing Commission, *Quick Facts: Offenders in the US Bureau of Prisons,* June 2017.

7. Kevin K. Washburn, "American Indians, Crime, and the Law," *Michigan Law Review* 104, no. 4 (2006).

8. Numerous interviews with Mark Wandering Medicine took place from 2013 through 2016.

9. US Department of Justice, Offices of the United States Attorneys, "Jurisdictional Summary," https://www.justice.gov, accessed November 2017.

10. Pevar, *The Rights of Indians and Tribes.*

11. Interview with Matthew Rappold in January 2018. For more on issues like these, see Frank Pommersheim, "Is There a Little (or Not So Little) Constitutional Crisis Developing in Indian Law? A Brief Essay," *University of Pennsylvania Journal of Constitutional Law* 5, no. 2 (2003).

12. Major Crimes Act, ch. 341, § 9, 23 Stat. 362, 385 (1885), as amended 18 US § 1153 (2000). For a discussion of the imposition of an alien, adversarial justice system on tribes and the contemporary return by some to traditional justice, often called peacemaking, see Juliana E. Okulski, "Complex Adaptive Peacemaking: How Systems Theory Reveals Advantages of Traditional Tribal Dispute Resolution Methods," *American Indian Law Journal* 5, no. 1 (2017). See also the Indigenous Peacemaking Initiative materials on the Native American Rights Fund website, https://www.narf.org, accessed November 2017. See also Vine Deloria Jr. and Clifford M. Lytle, *American Indians, American Justice* (Austin, Texas: University of Texas Press, 1983).

13. Under the Sixth Amendment, we Americans have a right to

counsel—unless the person in the dock is a tribal member facing a charge in tribal court. In such courts, an individual is not necessarily represented by a lawyer; if convicted, he or she has a record that can result in an "upward departure," or increased sentence, in a subsequent federal proceeding. The US Supreme Court found this acceptable in *United States v. Bryant*, decided in 2016.

14. The Supreme Court cases *United States v. Wheeler*, decided in 1978, and *United States v. Lara*, decided in 2004. In 2017, the Ninth Circuit Court of Appeals, which covers the nine westernmost states, also denied a double-jeopardy claim. A Northern Cheyenne woman had been convicted in tribal court and had served time for charges arising from a 2014 matter. In 2016, the federal government indicted her in connection with the same events. In refusing her appeal, the Ninth Circuit judges said legal precedent showed that "successive prosecutions for the same offense are not barred by the Double Jeopardy Clause if brought by separate sovereigns," and that tribes "count as separate sovereigns under the Double Jeopardy Clause." See district court case *United States v. Bearcomesout*, decided in 2016, then appealed to the Ninth Circuit Court of Appeals, which issued a decision in 2017.

15. For additional reporting and analysis on these and other Indian-country legal matters, see the exceptional and comprehensive blog Turtle Talk at https://turtletalk.wordpress.com.

16. Carole Goldberg and Duane Champagne, *Final Report: Law Enforcement and Criminal Justice Under Public Law 280*, a publication of the Native Nations Law and Policy Center, November 1, 2007. See also *Public Law 83-280 (18 USC. § 1162, 28 USC. § 1360)*, a report of the Tribal Court Clearinghouse, a project of the Tribal Law and Policy Institute, http://www.tribal-institute.org, accessed November 2017. See also Ada Pecos Melton and Jerry Gardner, *Public Law 280: Issues and Concerns for Victims of Crime in Indian Country*, a report from American Indian Development Associates, http://www.aidainc.net, accessed November 2017.

17. Washburn, "American Indians, Crime, and the Law."

18. See *World Prison Brief*, an online database hosted by the Institute for Criminal Policy Research, London, http://www.prisonstudies.org, accessed November 2017; for similar figures, see the American Civil Liberties Union's "The Prison Crisis," accessed on its site *aclu.org* in January 2018; see also The Sentencing Project, "Criminal Justice Facts" and *Trends in U.S. Corrections*, The Sentencing Project, http://www.sentencingproject.org, accessed November 2017.

19. Interviews and email communications with Matthew Rappold in March and April 2017 and in January 2018.

20. Interviews and email communications with Vaughn Vargas in June 2017.

21. Funding from the John D. and Catherine T. MacArthur Foundation supports the police department's efforts. Statistics and other information are posted under "Pennington County, SD" on the foundation's website http://www.safetyandjusticechallenge.org, accessed January 2018.

22. B.J. Jones and Christopher Ironroad, "Addressing Sentencing Disparities for Tribal Citizens in the Dakotas: A Tribal Sovereignty Approach," *North Dakota Law Review* 89, no. 1 (2013). Information amplified in an interview with Jones in July 2017.

23. Jones and Ironroad, "Addressing Sentencing Disparities for Tribal Citizens in the Dakotas."

24. US Sentencing Commission, Ad Hoc Advisory Group on Native American Sentencing Issues, *Final Report of the Native American Advisory Group*, November 4, 2003.

25. US Sentencing Commission, Tribal Issues Advisory Group, *Report of the Tribal Issues Advisory Group*, May 16, 2016.

26. Washburn, "American Indians, Crime, and the Law"; Jones and Ironroad, "Addressing Sentencing Disparities for Tribal Citizens in the Dakotas.

27. Washburn, "American Indians, Crime, and the Law."

28. Charles Wohlforth, "Disbelieved Fairbanks Four Alibis Show How Anti-Native Bias Taints Justice," *Alaska Dispatch News*, March 26, 2016, updated July 1, 2016.

29. Email communications with Garfield Feather were in 2011 and 2017; the judge was Myron H. Bright, who was with the Eighth Circuit Court of Appeals until his death in December 2016.

30. Interview with O. J. Semans in May 2017.

31. *Fatal Force* is the *Washington Post* database, while *The Counted* is the tally kept by the *Guardian*. Database errors were noted and conveyed to me by the families of Jacqueline Salyers and Daniel Covarrubias, as well as by Claremont Graduate University researchers Jean Schroedel and Roger Chin.

32. Mike Males, "Who Are Police Killing?" Center for Juvenile and Criminal Justice, August 26, 2014; interview with Mike Males in July 2016, along with multiple email communications with him between June and August 2016.

33. Jean Schroedel and Roger Chin, "Whose Lives Matter: The Media's Failure to Cover Police Use of Lethal Force Against Native Americans," *Race and Justice* (October 2017). Additional information came from statistics and analysis in the study, as well as from discussions of police practices and training methods during numerous interviews with Roger Chin between December 2015 and October 2017.

34. Males, interview.

35. Dean Williams and Joe Hanlon, *Alaska Department of Corrections: An Administrative Review*, commissioned by Alaska governor Bill Walker August 10, 2015, submitted November 13, 2015; the document included investigations of the deaths of Alaska Natives Larry Kobuk, Joseph Murphy, and Gilbert Joseph, among others.

36. Interview with Federal Bureau of Investigation spokesperson Kyle Loven in July 2016.

37. Media reports on these deaths included Sarah Sunshine Manning, "Manning: Sarah Lee Circle Bear Died While in Police Custody; Family Seeks Justice," *Indian Country Media Network*, July 28, 2015; Sheena Louise Roetman, "Here Is What We Know About the Death of Choctaw Medicine Man Rexdale W. Henry," *Indian Country Media Network*, July 28, 2015; Tabitha Soden, "Eureka Man Found Hanged at Humboldt County Jail," *Times-Standard*, June 27, 2015; and Ernestine Chasing Hawk, "Eagle Butte Man Dies after CRST Police Officers Beat Him," *Native Sun News*, September 23, 2015. Supporters of the family of Phillip High Bear, of Eagle Butte, have posted extensive video online of the protest rally on his behalf.

38. US Commission on Civil Rights reports include: *Native Americans in South Dakota: An Erosion of Confidence in the Justice System* (South Dakota Advisory Committee, 2000); *Equal Educational Opportunity for Native American Students in Montana Public Schools* (Montana Advisory Committee, July 2001); *A Quiet Crisis: Federal Funding and Unmet Needs in Indian Country* (2003); *Broken Promises: Evaluating the Native American Health Care System* (2004); *The Farmington Report: Civil Rights for Native Americans 30 Years Later* (New Mexico Advisory Committee, 2005); *Discrimination Against Native Americans in Border Towns: A Briefing Before the United States Commission on Civil Rights Held in Washington, D.C.*, the transcript of a November 9, 2007, meeting; and *The US Commission on Civil Rights Concerned with Dakota Access Pipeline*, a November 2016 statement about "excessive use of force by police, the civil and sovereign rights of Native Americans, and environmental justice."

39. Interview with Malee Craft in September 2016 about several topics, including a meeting announced by USCCR as "Bordertown Discrimination in Montana: A Briefing Meeting by the Montana State Advisory Committee to the US Commission on Civil Rights"; see also Clara Caulfield, "Civil Rights Commission Hosts Hearing on Bordertown Discrimination in Montana," *Native Sun News*, September 14, 2016.

40. Interview with Darleen Tareeq in September 2016.

41. Information and commentary from Bonnie Duran throughout this chapter comes from an interview with her in June 2016.

42. Tabulation made by Jessica Stites, executive editor of *In These Times* magazine, in preparation for publication of Stephanie Woodard, "The Police Killings No One Is Talking About," *In These Times*, October 17, 2016.

43. Schroedel and Chin, "Whose Lives Matter."

44. Interview with Jim Trainum in June 2016.

45. Interview with Melissa Russano in June 2016.

46. Suicide Prevention Resource Center, *Suicide Among Racial/Ethnic Populations in the US: American Indians/Alaska Natives* (Waltham, MA: Education Development Center, Inc., 2013).

47. National Congress of American Indians, *FY 2016 Indian Country Budget Request: Promoting Self-Determination, Modernizing the Trust Relationship* (Washington D.C., January 2015).

48. Suicide Prevention Resource Center, *Suicide Among Racial/Ethnic Populations in the U.S.: American Indians/Alaska Natives*.

49. This information comes from numerous discussions with Chin about police training and related matters.

50. Multiple interviews with trainers and observation of training at the Washington State Criminal Justice Training Commission facility in Burien, Washington, in June 2016.

51. Information on the Puyallup Tribe and the response to Jacqueline Salyers's death comes from visits, public records requests, and numerous interviews with many individuals, as described in Chapter 4, note 3, above.

52. Nancy Krieger et al., "Police Killings and Police Deaths Are Public Health Data and Can Be Counted," *PLOS/Medicine* 12, no. 12 (December 2015).

53. For more on the march, see Brynn Grimley and Natalie DeFord, "Hundreds Gather to March in Protest of Tacoma Police Shooting," *News Tribune*, March 16, 2016.

54. The report, *The Maze of Injustice: The Failure to Protect Indigenous Women*

from Sexual Violence in the USA," can be found on the Amnesty International website, http://www.amnestyusa.org.

55. Brittney Bennett, "Law Was Meant to Let American Indians Prosecute Violence; Is It Working?" *USA Today*, March 25, 2017.

56. Information on the number and types of deaths at Pine Ridge was obtained in interviews during May 2012 with then tribal vice chairman Tom Poor Bear, with law-and-order committee chair James "Toby" Big Boy, and with a relative of one of those found dead at Pine Ridge.

57. Craft, interview.

58. Signed by Special Agent in Charge Douglas Domin of the Minneapolis Division, the 2000 report lists information associated with each death, along with the FBI investigation's "finding" related to the event. This information was supported by an interview with another special agent in the FBI's Minneapolis office, which covers several states including South and North Dakota; he could not say why these particular fifty-seven cases had been chosen for the report.

59. Poor Bear, interview.

60. Information about Chase Iron Eyes and his involvement in Native Lives Matter comes from an interview in September 2016.

61. Iron Eyes, interview.

62. Ibid.

63. Interviews with Troy Amlee and J. R. Bobick in September 2016.

64. Interviews with Marlee Kanosh in late 2016.

65. The fatalities were reported by Marlee Kanosh for the Facebook page Native Lives Taken by Police, as well as in Stephanie Woodard, "A Deadly Month: Police Shootings of Natives Spike in October," *Indian Country Media Network*, November 16, 2016; the article and this section include information from interviews and email communications with Kanosh in November 2016.

66. Kanosh, interview.

67. The Supreme Court case *Salazar-Limon v. City of Houston*, decided in 2017.

5: TAKE THE CHILDREN

1. Information about the First Nations Repatriation Institute speeches and activities comes from my attendance at the meeting in 2011 and from interviews then and in succeeding years with conference organizer Sandra White Hawk and meeting attendees, including Roger St. John. The George

Polk Program for Investigative Reporting funded my articles on this issue; a portion of the writing appears in Trace A. DeMeyer and Patricia Cotter-Busbee, eds., *Two Worlds: Lost Children of the Indian Adoption Project* (Greenfield, Massachusetts: Blue Hand Books, 2012).

2. Andrea Smith, *Indigenous Peoples and Boarding Schools: A Comparative Study*, prepared for the Secretariat of the United Nations Permanent Forum on Indigenous Issues (New York, February 2008). "Let All That Is Indian within You Die!" Native American Rights Fund *Legal Review* 38, no. 3 (summer/fall 2013). Other valuable sources of information on the boarding schools' methods over the years and their effect on the pupils include Maria Yellow Horse Brave Heart and Lemyra M. DeBruyn, "The American Indian Holocaust: Healing Historical Unresolved Grief," *American Indian and Alaska Native Mental Health Research* 8, no. 2 (February 1998); and the books Margaret Archuleta et al., *Away from Home: American Indian Boarding School Experiences* (Phoenix, Arizona: Heard Museum, 2000); Walter Littlemoon with Jane Ridgway, *They Called Me Uncivilized: The Memoir of an Everyday Lakota Man from Wounded Knee* (New York, Bloomington: iUniverse Press, 2009), which Randy Vasquez made into the documentary film *The Thick Dark Fog* (2012); Karl Markus Kreis, ed., and Corinna Daily-Starna, trans., *Lakotas, Black Robes, and Holy Women: German Reports from the Indian Missions in South Dakota, 1886–1900* (Lincoln, London: University of Nebraska Press, 2007); Tim Giago (Nanwica Kciji), *Children Left Behind: The Dark Legacy of Indian Mission Boarding Schools* (Santa Fe, New Mexico: Clear Light Publishing, 2006); Irene Mahoney, O.S.U., *Lady Blackrobes: Missionaries in the Heart of Indian Country* (Golden, Colorado: Fulcrum Publishing, 2006); Marilyn Irvin Holt, *Indian Orphanages* (Lawrence, Kansas: University Press of Kansas, 2001); and David Wallace Adams, *Education for Extinction: American Indians and the Boarding School Experience, 1875–1928* (Lawrence, Kansas: University Press of Kansas, 1995).

3. Smith, *Indigenous Peoples and Boarding Schools*.

4. Ibid.

5. *Legal Review*, "Let All That Is Indian within You Die!"

6. Dane Coolidge, "'Kid Catching' on the Navajo Reservation: 1930," in Steven Unger, ed., *The Destruction of American Indian Families* (New York: Association of American Indian Affairs, 1977).

7. For an example, see *Congressional Record: Proceedings and Debates*, December 28, 1922.

8. *Legal Review*, "Let All That Is Indian within You Die!" as well as additional information from the sources in Chapter 5, Note 2.

9. Theodore Roosevelt, "First Annual Message," accessed via The American Presidency Project in October 2017.

10. Numerous personal communications on several reservations during 2011 and succeeding years, along with information from "Let All That Is Indian within You Die!"

11. Conversation with Roderica Rouse in 2012 took place on the Yankton Sioux Reservation, in South Dakota.

12. *Legal Review*, "Let All That Is Indian within You Die!" See also William Yardley, "Catholic Order Reaches $166 Million Settlement with Sexual Abuse Victims," *New York Times*, March 25, 2011.

13. Conversations in 2012 with various tribal members, who asked for anonymity, on Sisseton Wahpeton Oyate's South and North Dakota reservation.

14. The letters and reports were given to me in 2011 by an attorney from the law firm Manly, Stewart & Finaldi; the firm and that of Gregory A. Yates brought scores of claims of childhood sexual abuse on behalf of Native clients.

15. Interview in 2012 with attorney Steven Smith of Chamberlain, South Dakota, who represented a Catholic Church school and spoke to the legislature in support of HB 1104.

16. The legislature's HB 1104 became SDCL [South Dakota Codified Law] 26-10-25.

17. Yardley, "Catholic Order Reaches $166 Million Settlement with Sexual Abuse Victims."

18. Interview in 2015 with John Doe, who asked that his real identity not be provided to the public; the district court lawsuit was *John Does 1–16 et al. v. Ursuline Sisters of the Western Province* et al.

19. Doe, interview; material from the related lawsuit.

20. Doe, interview.

21. Doe, interview; material from the related lawsuit.

22. This information came from interviews, mainly during 2011, with Walter Littlemoon on the Pine Ridge Indian Reservation in South Dakota; with Izzy Zephier, Roderica Rouse, Sherwyn Zephier, and others on the Yankton Sioux Reservation; Charles Baxter of the Omaha Reservation, in Nebraska and Iowa; members of the extended Wanna family and numerous others on the Sisseton Wahpeton Reservation; attendees at the First Nations Repatriation Institute conference in Minneapolis–Saint Paul; and in 2004 with Justin Willie in the Arizona portion of the Navajo Reservation.

23. Baxter, interview.

24. Anonymous interview in 2011 on the Sisseton Wahpeton Reservation.

25. Interviews and emails with Ken Bear Chief from 2011 through 2014.

26. Richard Nixon, "Special Message to the Congress on Indian Affairs," July 8, 1970, accessed via The American Presidency Project in October, 2017.

27. American Indian Religious Freedom Act, Public Law No. 95-341, 92 Stat. 469; August 11, 1978, codified at 42 USC. § 1996.

28. For a description of the surveys, see William Byler, "The Destruction of American Indian Families" in Unger, ed., *The Destruction of American Indian Families*.

29. Byler in *The Destruction of American Indian Families*.

30. Ibid.

31. James Abourezk, "The Role of the Federal Government: A Congressional View" in Unger, ed., *The Destruction of American Indian Families*.

32. Interview in 2011 with Sandra White Hawk.

33. Sandra White Hawk's speech to the 2011 First Nations Repatriation Institute conference.

34. Renée Sansom Flood, *Lost Bird of Wounded Knee: Spirit of the Lakota* (New York: Scribner, 1995).

35. Flood, *Lost Bird of Wounded Knee*.

36. White Hawk, speech.

37. Interviews with Danialle Rose in 2011, 2012, and 2018. She now runs the Medicine Voice Healing Center. When I first spoke to her, she worked on the Crow Creek Sioux Reservation in South Dakota as an in-home family therapist.

38. Indian Child Welfare Act, Pub. L. 95-608, 92 Stat. 3069 (1978), codified at 25 USC. §§ 1901-1963.

39. US Department of Health and Human Services, Administration for Children, Youth and Families, Office of Data, Analysis, Research, and Evaluation, *Recent Demographic Trends in Foster Care*, September 2013. For an analysis of the current situation and the Supreme Court's involvement, see Matthew L. M. Fletcher, "The Next Justice's Impact on the Indian Child Welfare Act," Law360.com, August 23, 2016.

40. Numerous interviews with Frank LaMere from 2010 through 2014.

41. Rose, interview.

42. Interview with Terry Yellow Fat in 2012.

43. IbisWorld, *Adoption & Child Welfare Services in the US Market Research*, January 2017.

44. Laura Sullivan, "Native Foster Care: Lost Children, Shattered Families," *All Things Considered*, NPR, October 25, 2011.

45. LaMere, interviews.

46. Rose, interviews.

47. The district court case *Oglala Sioux Tribe v. Van Hunnik (Fleming)*, filed in 2013; the lawsuit is ongoing.

48. Stephen Pevar, "In South Dakota, Officials Defied a Federal Judge and Took Indian Kids Away from Their Parents in Rigged Proceedings," American Civil Liberties Union, posted on the organization's website, https://www.aclu.org, February.

49. Interviews with ACLU senior staff attorney Stephen Pevar in 2013.

50. Stephen Pevar, interviews. See also the extensive reporting on this issue by Cherokee journalist and author Suzette Brewer, archived on *Indian Country Media Network*.

51. Kate Fort, "ICWA Defense Project Memorandum," February 18, 2017, https://turtletalk.wordpress.com.

52. The district court case *A.D. et al. v. Kevin Washburn*, judge's order on behalf of tribes' ability to intervene filed in 2016.

53. Fort, "ICWA Defense Project Memorandum."

54. "ICWA Appellate Project," https://turtletalk.wordpress.com.

55. Sally C. Curtin et al., *Suicide Rates for Females and Males by Race and Ethnicity: United States, 1999 and 2014*, NCHS Health E-Stat., National Center for Health Statistics, April 2016.

56. Interviews with Diane Garreau in 2011 and 2012.

57. Diane Garreau, interviews; also, M. Y. Heart et al., "Historical Trauma among Indigenous Peoples of the Americas: Concepts, Research, and Clinical Considerations," *Journal of Psychoactive Drugs* 43, no. 4 (October–December 2011).

58. Interview with Jake Martus in 2011.

59. Interview with Alvin Rafelito in 2012.

60. Interview with Keggulluk in 2013.

61. Interview with Yvonne "Tiny" DeCory in 2013.

62. T.D. LaFromboise and H.A. Lewis, "The Zuni Life Skills Development Program: A School/Community-Based Suicide Prevention Intervention," *Suicide and Life-Threatening Behavior* 38, no. 3 (June 2008).

63. For additional research and academic papers on the ways culture can counterbalance suicide risk factors among Native children, see D. Henry

et al., "Patterns of Protective Factors in an Intervention for the Prevention of Suicide and Alcohol Abuse with Yup'ik Alaska Native Youth," *American Journal of Drug and Alcohol Abuse* 38, no. 5 (September 2012); J. Mackin et al., "The Power of Protection: A Population-Based Comparison of Native and Non-Native Youth Suicide Attempters," *American Indian and Alaska Native Mental Health Research* 19, no. 2 (2012); N.V. Mohatt et al., "Assessment of Awareness of Connectedness as a Culturally-based Protective Factor for Alaska Native Youth," *Cultural Diversity & Ethnic Minority Psychology* 17, no. 4 (October 2011).

64. Numerous interviews with Julie Garreau from 2010 to 2017.

65. Interview with Keggulluk in 2012.

66. Interview with Evon Peter in 2012.

6: THE ARC FROM PAST TO FUTURE

1. Michael A. Sheyahshe, *Native Americans in Comic Books: A Critical Study* (Jefferson, North Carolina, and London: McFarland & Company, Inc., 2008); Hope Nicholson, ed., *Moonshot: The Indigenous Comics Collection*, vol. 1 (Toronto, Canada: Alternate History Comics Inc., 2015); and Grace L. Dillon, ed., *Walking the Clouds: An Anthology of Indigenous Science Fiction* (Tucson, Arizona: University of Arizona Press, 2012).

2. Look for the work of chef Sean Sherman, who is Oglala Lakota; White Mountain Apache chef Nephi Craig; and chef and cookbook writer Lois Ellen Frank, who is Kiowa and Sephardic; among many.

3. Interview with Steve LaRance in 2016.

4. Interview with Peter Strong in the Heritage Center's gallery in 2012.

5. Interview with Mike Faith in the Standing Rock buffalo field in 2011.

6. Interview with Aubrey Skye in 2011; additional interviews with Skye from 2004, when I met him at Slow Food's Terra Madre conference in Turin, Italy, to 2017 supported this point.

7. Interviews with Kimberly White Bull and other participants mentioned in the text took place during the field-dressing of the buffalo.

8. Interviews with Standing Rock Sioux Diabetes Program head John Buckley in 2011.

9. Ibid.

10. Interview with Philip Lane in 2002.

11. Centers for Disease Control and Prevention, *The Health Effects of Overweight and Obesity*, https://www.cdc.gov, accessed early 2018.

12. Skye, 2011 interview.

13. Buckley, interviews.

14. Jerry Lipka, Joan Parker Webster, and Evelyn Yanez, "Introduction: Factors That Affect Alaska Native Students' Mathematical Performance," *Journal of American Indian Education* 44, no. 3 (2005).

15. Interview with Sassa Peterson in 2015.

16. Interviews with Jerry Lipka in 2015, and additional information from him in 2018. Lipka is principal investigator for Math in a Cultural Context; he has retired from the University of Alaska Fairbanks, where he taught for many years, including in the Cross-Cultural Education Development Program in Alaska's Bristol Bay region.

17. Lipka, interview.

18. Ibid.

19. Numerous interviews with Kurt Anschuetz from 2001 to 2011. For more on his many published papers, see Kurt F. Anschuetz and Kurt E. Dongoske, "Hadiya:Wa: Hearing What Traditional Pueblo Cultural Advisors Talk About," Collaborative and Community Archaeology Symposium, Annual Meeting of the Society for American Archaeology, Vancouver, Canada, April 2, 2017. See also Damian Garcia and Kurt F. Anschuetz, "Movement as an Acoma Way of Life: An Archaeology of the Pueblo's Pathways and Impressions," Pueblo Movement and the Archaeology of Becoming, Meeting of the Society for American Archaeology, Vancouver, Canada, March 30, 2017.

20. Interview with Herman Agoyo at Ohkay Owingeh Pueblo in 2001; subsequent interviews with him in succeeding years. For more on the Pueblo gardens, see also V. B. Price and Baker H. Morrow, eds., *Canyon Gardens: The Ancient Pueblo Landscapes of the American Southwest* (Albuquerque, New Mexico: University of New Mexico Press, 2006).

21. Interview with Louie Hena at Tesuque Pueblo prior to going out to look for the old gardens.

22. Interviews with Steven Dominguez Sundjordet in 2002 and succeeding years, including 2018. For more, see Steven Sundjordet, "Let Them Plant Their Own: Implications of Interactive Crop-Loss Processes During Drought in Hopi Maize Fields," *Journal of Ethnobiology*, Volume 37, number 2, 2017; Steven Dominguez, "Optimal Gardening Strategies: Maximizing the Input and Retention of Water in Prehistoric Gridded Fields in North Central New Mexico," *World Archaeology* 34, no. 1 (2002; published

online February 15, 2012); Steven Dominguez and Kenneth E. Kolm, "Beyond Water Harvesting: A Soil Hydrology Perspective on Traditional Southwestern Agricultural Technology," *American Antiquity* 70, no. 4, (October 2005).

23. Interviews with Tessie Naranjo in 2001 and succeeding years. She has taught and published widely, is a past chair of the Native American Graves Protection and Repatriation Review Committee, and has coordinated and participated in scholarly projects.

24. Interviews with Dennis Hastings in 2011 and succeeding years; additional information from his collaborators at the Omaha Tribal Historical Research Project, Richard Chilton and Margery Coffey, in 2011 and 2018.

25. Interviews with Vincent Snyder in 2011; Snyder also forwarded photographs and drawings of the museum in order to clarify its design.

26. Robin Ridington and Dennis Hastings (In'aska), *Blessing for a Long Time: The Sacred Pole of the Omaha Tribe* (Lincoln, Nebraska: University of Nebraska Press, 2000).

The author in the Badlands, north of Pine Ridge Indian Reservation, in South Dakota. (Joseph Zummo)

For nearly two decades, **Stephanie Woodard** has reported on Indian country for publications including Native-owned *Indian Country Media Network* and *In These Times*, where she is a contributing writer for its Rural America website, along with *Yes!*, billmoyers.com, *Huffington Post*, *Preservation*, and *Saveur*. In hundreds of widely cited articles, she has covered Native American voting rights, sacred sites, food, gardening, health, child welfare, economic development, and other subjects. The numerous awards she has received include the Richard LaCourse Award for Investigative Reporting, the top annual prize of the Native American Journalists Association, where she is an associate (non-Native) member. The Fund for Investigative Journalism and George Polk Center for Investigative Reporting are among the major journalism organizations that have supported her work.

After several days of photographing people and events on Pine Ridge Indian Reservation, in South Dakota, Joseph Zummo explores the Badlands, north of the reservation.
(Stephanie Woodard)